CW00617815

Deaf Characters
in Literature

Deaf Characters
in Literature

By

Paul Dakin

Cambridge
Scholars
Publishing

Deaf Characters in Literature

By Paul Dakin

This book first published 2023

Cambridge Scholars Publishing

Lady Stephenson Library, Newcastle upon Tyne, NE6 2PA, UK

British Library Cataloguing in Publication Data
A catalogue record for this book is available from the British Library

Copyright © 2023 by Paul Dakin

ISBN (10): 1-5275-3950-4
ISBN (13): 978-1-5275-3950-1

This book is dedicated to my wife Jean,
who has shown me what it means to be deaf.

TABLE OF CONTENTS

LIST OF ILLUSTRATIONS

Figure 2-1: Image of the fingerspelling alphabet chart from *The History of The Life and Adventures of Mr. Duncan Campbell*, 1720. With the permission of the British Deaf History Society.

Figure 5-1: A sculpture by Thomas Woolner of a brother and sister, entitled "Constance and Arthur", on show at the International Exhibition, South Kensington, London, 1862. Photograph by William England. London Stereoscopic Company/Hulton Archive via Getty Images.

Figure 6-1: Image advertising the film *Sign Gene*. With the permission of Pluin.

FOREWORD

As with the publication of many books, *Deaf Characters in Literature* has been a long time in the making. It develops a rich and lucid consideration of how hard of hearing people, and those completely deaf to sounds of spoken language, are represented in British and American imaginative writings of the past three centuries. The book explores the changing expression, pitch, and resonance of portrayals of deaf people in novels, plays, poetry, and comics directed at adult audiences, and it also discusses deaf roles and characters in films.

Paul Dakin has long been interested in understanding why hearing authors write deaf characters into their works. A general practitioner who worked for most of his career in a busy practice in north London that served many deaf people, Paul dates the stirrings of his interest in deaf cultures to the waning of his wife's hearing, which began some forty years ago. He and his family turned to a signing patient of the practice to teach them British Sign Language, after which the practice gained a reputation for the care it provided to the health and communicative needs of deaf people. This was the medical and experiential context that engendered an interest in the history of deafness and brought Paul to study for the MA in Literature and Medicine at King's College London, in 2006. As part of his many forays into literary studies at this time, he researched an outstanding master's thesis, which dangled before his examiners many of the ideas and findings he has developed and elaborated in *Deaf Characters in Literature*.

His monograph shows that the deaf characters of imaginative literature typically occupy very minor roles that convey little about the lived reality of being deaf. In contrast to the much fuller characterisations of hearing protagonists, deaf characters often function merely as props. And although the stockpile of literary tropes which writers have employed has changed over time, many of the earliest images, dramatic devices and metaphors have proved remarkably persistent, such as figurations of the deaf as isolated and alienated, which continue to feature in more recent media and genres.

As a prelude to discussing these issues, Paul furnishes expositions and plot summaries for readers like myself who are not familiar with many of the works examined. While taking account of theories of deafness and disability studies without becoming in thrall to them, he shows how enmeshed deaf people have been in cultural stereotypes, which find expression in stock characters who appear morally deficient and cognitively impaired. Deaf listening practices may be caricatured for comic and narrative purposes and the rich multisensory soundscapes they construct–which go beyond an auditory deficit model of communication–can be misunderstood or ignored by authors. And even when deaf people are represented in a positive light, their characterisation can read as over sentimentalised, hollow correctives, rather than as positive depictions in their own right. These negative images are not necessarily intentionally meant but originate in societal views of people with many different types of sensory impairment, which are unconsciously absorbed and expressed in imaginative images that have influenced, and in turn been influenced by, the mission and methods of deaf education over the past two centuries.

This book has opened my ears to the depth and extent of the marginalisation of non-hearing people as human subjects in literature. Yet it senses, too, a gathering interest in deaf experience and a tendency on the part of recent hearing, non-hearing and signing authors, to develop more rounded and positive images of deaf people. *Deaf Characters in Literature* has certainly been worth the wait. It is an important contribution to sensory history, to d/Deaf cultures, and to their flourishing.

Brian Hurwitz
Emeritus Professor of Medicine and the Arts, Department of English and Centre for the Humanities and Health, King's College London

PREFACE

Forty years ago, my wife started to become deaf. Since then, she has worn progressively more powerful hearing aids, allowing her to retain no more than a minimal level of hearing. There is a strong likelihood that my wife will become completely deaf, as did her mother. As a family, we decided to learn British Sign Language (BSL) so that we would have a means of communication in addition to verbal speech. Having always worked in the National Health Service (NHS), my wife spent several years supporting deaf pupils in a mainstream secondary school, before eventually returning to work in the NHS once more. Meanwhile, one of the patients in my London general practice became our sign language tutor. He encouraged other profoundly deaf people like himself to register with us, as they preferred to attend a comparatively deaf aware practice which had a signing nurse and a signing doctor.

In 2006 I joined the first cohort of part-time postgraduate students to study for a master's degree in Literature and Medicine at King's College London. When the time came to choose the topic of my dissertation, I selected "deaf characters in literature", and was surprised to find how little had been written about the subject. The research this entailed, combined with the experiences of the many wonderful deaf people that I encountered, prompted me to carry on this fascinating journey of discovery.

I want to thank Professor Brian Hurwitz and the Centre for the Humanities and Health at King's College who encouraged and guided my academic interests. I am indebted to Arun Krishna, our friend and BSL teacher, who patiently endures my attempts to sign, and constantly reminds me to "practise, practise, practise". I thank Jean, my wife, for her support during the prolonged task of bringing this book to completion, my daughters Anna and Sarah, and my son Jonathan, who persistently prompted me to begin the work in the first place, as well as advised on some of the layout. I thank my grandchildren who allowed the time and space to finish this project. Finally, I am grateful to the deaf patients and friends who enabled me to glimpse inside the deaf world.

ACKNOWLEDGEMENTS

I am indebted to many people and institutions. The British Library in particular deserves my thanks, as does that wonderful resource, the website archive.org. I acknowledge the inspiration gained from the excellent book *The Quiet Ear* compiled by Brian Grant. My gratitude is extended to Professor Brian Hurwitz, who not only graciously agreed to write the Foreword but enlightened and encouraged me at King's College London.

I appreciate the kind permission given to reproduce the following:

British Deaf History Society: Image of the fingerspelling alphabet chart from *The History of The Life and Adventures of Mr. Duncan Campbell*, 1720.

Getty Images: Photograph of the statue by Thomas Woolner entitled *Constance and Arthur*.

Pluin: the image of the poster from the film *Sign Gene*.

Deaf Life Press: excerpt from *On his deafness and other melodies unheard* by Robert Panara.

Gallaudet University Press: excerpts from *The Mute's Lament* by John Carlin, and excerpts from *Poetry of the deaf and dumb* by Luzerne Rey.

Penned in the Margins: *Echo Pt 3*, *After Reading 'Deaf School' by the Mississippi River, Dear Hearing World (after Danez Smith)*, all from *The Perseverance* by Raymond Antrobus.

INTRODUCTION

Comparatively little attention has been paid to the subject of deaf characters in literature. Much of the material that does exist tends to focus on the study of American sources, with fewer examples drawn from British authors. This probably reflects the origin of many of the researchers, as interest in deaf culture and history is more widespread in the United States. Nonetheless this is surprising, considering the long and extensive history of British literature that includes a moderate number of deaf characters. I have attempted to redress the balance by exploring examples of deaf characters originating from both sides of the Atlantic.

The first chapter, *Speakers and Signers-the History of Deaf Communication and Education* outlines themes that are crucially important in understanding the historical background and contemporary context of a fictional deaf character, and may be reflected to varying extents in the portrayal given by the author.

Chapter Two, *Goldilocks, Gifted, and Granny–the Portrayal of Deaf Characters in the English Novel* is the foundation of the book. The chapter addresses the representation of deaf characters in mainstream novels for a predominantly hearing audience and explores the existence of stereotypes and tropes. I should point out that I followed certain guidelines to help me focus on specific areas. The first of these is that I selected examples of deaf characters only found in British and American texts. Deaf characters can also be discovered in French and Russian novels that are readily available as translations, but books written originally in English contain the majority of deaf characters. More importantly, I am aware that the experience of authors, and the deaf people upon whom they might choose to base their characters, may differ quite considerably between different countries and cultures. This preserves some degree of historical and cultural continuity as British and American authors share a common language and elements of a common heritage. However, there remain significant differences between these two contexts, including a separately evolved deaf history, totally different sign languages, and a deaf community in the United States that is much bigger, more organised and strident, and possesses a more obvious and distinct identity, when compared with that in the UK. The chapter also largely avoids the plethora of material written for children, much of which is overtly educational and has the intention of being instructive and aspirational for deaf children or is designed to promote understanding and deaf awareness amongst hearing children. I could not even begin to duplicate the extensive review of children's books containing deaf characters that appears in Sharon Pajka's magnificent blog,[1] and encourage anyone interested to explore this excellent resource. Therefore, the chapter focuses on novels written primarily for adults. I have also excluded books written by deaf authors specifically for the deaf community, as the author and reader share a common experience that is probably unknown to the majority of the population, and the texts are unlikely to be intended for mainstream consumption. I am primarily interested in discovering more about how and why hearing authors should choose to write about deaf characters, how far the information and characteristics described reflect the experience of the writer, and whether this represents the attitudes of the hearing majority of which they are a part. The chapter also excludes short stories, as it is my belief that a novel gives the author more scope to include and develop deaf characters within the larger text.

Chapter Three, *Communication, Correction, and Community-Recurring Themes in the Portrayal of Deaf Characters in the English Novel* explores how such portrayals reflect the reality of deaf experience and refers to an alternative set of deaf narratives. The chapter considers themes that often appear in the context of deaf characters including the use of silence, modes of communication, education, medical involvement, and community, and provides a template for the exploration of deaf characters in the other types of literature studied later in the book.

The guidelines offered in Chapter Two continue in principle throughout the book, so that Chapter Four, *Stereotypes and Superheroes–Deaf Characters in Comics* considers only deaf characters created for English language comics and graphic novels and intended for a mainstream readership. That audience may of course include children, but comics generally, and especially those produced by DC and Marvel, tend to have an older clientele consisting mainly of teens and young adults. The chapter looks at how deafness is represented visually and the themes that deafness is used to convey. In particular, the chapter explores the portrayal of deaf superheroes and whether these depictions can be considered aspirational or simply become another type of stereotype, the 'supercrip'.

Chapter Five, *Verse and Video–Deaf Characters in Poetry* includes a number of autobiographical examples provided by deaf poets as well as characters created by hearing writers. Although this would appear to breach

---

[1] Sharon Pajka, "Deaf Characters in Adolescent Literature", accessed April 25, 2021, https://pajka.blogspot.com./

the guidelines outlined above, it is impossible to consider contemporary deaf poetry without including notable works that express the anxiety and anger of the deaf writer, and provide insights into their lived experience that are intended for a mainstream and largely hearing readership. The chapter also includes examples of visual poetry based entirely on sign language.

Chapter Six, *Sound, Subtitles, and Signing–Deaf Characters in Drama, Television, and Film* addresses issues related to a medium based in sound as well as vision. The representation of deaf characters in drama is considered, as is the move towards identifying deaf people increasingly as sign language users in television and film. I also consider the trend in visual media towards more authentic portrayals of the lives of deaf people as production companies employ more deaf advisors and deaf actors.

Throughout the book I use the term "deaf" to refer to all deaf people. There has been a relatively recent convention on both sides of the Atlantic to describe people as either deaf with a lower case "d" or Deaf with an upper case "D", depending on their personal histories and cultural affiliations. The deaf are likely to have become deafened later in life, continue to use verbal speech, and identify primarily with the hearing culture to which they have always belonged. The Deaf are usually born without hearing, or have become deaf early in life, tend to use sign language as their first language, and identify primarily with a signing-based culture.[2] When referring to both groups together the term d/Deaf is sometimes used. I have employed these distinctions in the past but have decided against their use in this book for a number of reasons. Many of the imaginative deaf characters were created before these terms existed making it inadvisable to ascribe them to either group in retrospect. In more contemporary examples the author may not have had the knowledge, or if they did, the intention, to categorise their character in this way. In real life it is for the deaf person to determine how they want to be identified and described. This may or may not be straightforward as the terms present two distinct ends of a wide spectrum of deaf life, rather than the complexity, subtlety, and overlap, that often reflects the individual's experience. The use of "deaf" referring to all deaf people is also considered to be more inclusive,[3] and avoids the danger of virtue signalling, an emotive subject for some deaf people,[4] in an academic context.

---

[2] Paddy Ladd, Understanding deaf culture: in search of deafhood (Clevedon, England: Multilingual Matters, 2003) xvii.

[3] H-Dirksen L. Baumann and Joseph Murray (eds), Deaf Gain (Minneapolis: University of Minnesota Press, 2014) xiii.

[4] See Chapter Six.

CHAPTER ONE

SPEAKERS AND SIGNERS – THE HISTORY OF DEAF COMMUNICATION AND EDUCATION

The ability to communicate is fundamental to human society. This may be through vocal speech or the use of visual forms. Vocal speech is actually more than just the exchange of meaningful sounds, and involves subtle visual cues produced and observed as body language and para-verbals.[1] These are largely sub-conscious, whereas gestures are more deliberate and are meant to emphasise or aid the understanding of what is being said. Sign languages are not simply glorified gestures or mime, but are sophisticated and codified forms of communication that have developed in different eras and in a wide variety of settings. For instance, signing is referred to in the Talmud, and was also used by monks during their periods of religious silence. Sign language developed, and was considered valuable, among indigenous peoples in Australia, southern Africa, and the Plains tribes of the United States.[2] The need for profoundly deaf people to use a visual form of communication will be obvious, and its existence was recognised by hearing observers. Plato wrote about deaf people using sign language, and Leonardo da Vinci advised artists to learn how to represent gestures in their subjects by studying the deaf.[3] However, throughout history, deaf people have lived an isolated existence within hearing societies, and were often misunderstood, mistreated, and marginalised. In ancient Greece and Rome, it was even permissible to kill deaf and dumb children up to the age of three, though under Jewish law deaf people were viewed as vulnerable people who needed protection. In most societies, deaf people had few or no legal rights and were not allowed to marry.[4] During the Middle Ages and the Industrial

---

[1] Dakin, Paul. "Speech without Sound: Signing as 'Body Talk'". In Body Talk in the Medical Humanities, ed. Jennifer Patterson and Francia Kinchington (Newcastle upon Tyne: Cambridge Scholars Publishing, 2019), 236-245.
[2] Dorothy Miles (ed), British Sign Language (London: BBC Books, 1988) 13.
[3] Nicholas Mirzoeff, "The Silent Mind: Learning from Deafness," History Today No. 7 (July 1992): 19-25.
[4] Jonathan Ree, I See A Voice (London: Harper Collins Publishers, 1999) 94-95.

Revolution, populations migrated increasingly from rural areas to towns and cities, allowing more profoundly deaf people to congregate together and formulate a common local sign language. It should be remembered that in every age there would have been far more deaf people who were moderately rather than profoundly deaf, and would not have purposefully sought out the company of other deaf people. They simply struggled to hear, and were pushed to the margins of conversations, family, and work. Because their plight was not so obvious or readily observable, they remained largely overlooked both by contemporary reports and historical examination.

The first mention of deaf people using signs appeared in England in 1450, in a book entitled *History of the Syon Monastery at Lisbon and Brentford*. Some of the signs identified are used today. The first description of people actually signing in England was in 1576 from the marriage of Thomas Tillsye, with the fact recorded in the marriage register. The earliest English reference to lip-reading and signing dates from 1602, when Richard Carew observed the deaf servant Edward Bone reading lips and signing to another deaf man in Cornwall.[5] Towards the end of the sixteenth century, the first known teacher of the deaf was working in Spain. Ponce de Leon, a Benedictine monk, was asked to teach deaf children born to Spanish noble families. The families experienced a high rate of hereditary deafness due to inter-marriage. The rights and inheritance of deaf people, even those who came from wealthy families, were severely limited by law, so powerful clans wanted their deaf children to write and speak well enough to satisfy the courts. Sir Kenelm Digby recorded the results of this teaching in 1623, as he had seen a deaf man reading lips and using vocal speech while visiting Spain.[6] In 1644 John Bulwer, a physician at Gray's Inn London, published a treatise entitled *Chirologia or the Natural Language of the Hand. Composed of the speaking motions, and discoursing gestures thereof.* The book was illustrated with the typical handshapes used by the profoundly deaf people he had encountered. Some of the signs are used in British Sign Language (BSL) today. Two years later, Bulmer produced *Philocorpus, or the Deaf and Dumb Man's Tutor*, dedicating it to two deaf brothers. The book inferred that specific education was needed to improve communication for deaf people. Bulwer wrote,

> What though you cannot express your minds in these verbal contrivances of man's invention; yet you want not Speech, who have your whole Body for a Tongue, having a language most natural and significant...[7]

[5] Peter W Jackson, Britain's Deaf Heritage (Edinburgh: Pentland Press, 1990) xiii.
[6] Ree, I See A Voice, 100
[7] Miles, British Sign Language, 15

Samuel Pepys wrote of meeting a deaf and dumb boy who signed, and Francis Bacon referred to sign language with the wonderfully evocative phrase "transitory hieroglyphics".[8] Reports from Spain about Ponce de Leon's methods and Bulwer's book stimulated interest in the ways in which deaf people could learn and communicate. Rev Dr William Holder (the brother-in-law of Sir Christopher Wren) taught speech exercises to deaf people. Thomas Dalgarno recognised a form of signing that was not based on spoken English in 1680. He had developed the standard two-handed signed alphabet by 1678, which was later systematised by Rev Dr John Wallis, a clergyman and Professor of Mathematics at Oxford.[9] Wallis had already produced a manual alphabet for spelling out words. Some of the signs he described remain in use today. The alphabet and teaching methods of Dr Wallis are referred to by Daniel Defoe in *Duncan Campbell*, written in 1720, the first novel to have a deaf man as its main character.

Bulwer identified the need for deaf education in 1646, but it wasn't until the following century that the first deaf school was founded. Before this time, teachers of the deaf like Ponce de Leon were independent pioneers. Another of these educators was Henry Baker, the man whom Daniel Defoe's daughter married in 1727. The first deaf school in the UK was established in 1760 by Thomas Braidwood, who taught oral and finger communication in Edinburgh. This private school was visited and enthusiastically described by the writer Samuel Johnson.[10] Braidwood later moved to London to set up another private school, and then the first charitable school in Bermondsey in 1792. The free school moved to Old Kent Road in 1803 and one of its teachers was Braidwood's nephew Joseph Watson.[11] Watson had been working for his uncle since 1784. Braidwood and his family taught both oral and finger communication and published *On the Education of the Deaf and Dumb* in 1809, in which they state their opposition to signed versions of the spoken language. Wilkie Collins' fictional deaf character Madonna attends The Deaf and Dumb School in the Old Kent Road, and Collins' great friend Charles Dickens followed his example by sending his deaf character Sophie to the same establishment.[12] A contemporary description notes that the Old Kent Road school accepted one hundred and

---

[8] Ree, I See A Voice, 122

[9] JJ Kitto D.D, "The lost senses. Part I. Deafness. The Land of Silence," Edinburgh Review, No. 207 (July 1855): 124-5.

[10] Macleod Yearsley, "Deafness in Literature," The Lancet, (April 14, 1925): 746-747.

[11] Jackson, Britain's Deaf Heritage, 23

[12] Paul Dakin, "Literary portrayals of deafness", Clinical Medicine, No. 3 (June 2009): 293-4

ten pupils in a twenty-four year period, while similar schools started to appeared elsewhere in the country.[13] Between 1800 and 1850, fifteen schools for deaf children started in the UK.[14] The founder of the school in Exeter, Mrs Charlotte Hippisley Tuckfield, wrote the book *Education for the People* in 1839 in which she extols the virtues of both signing and vocal exercises. This was typical of deaf education in England at the time. Schools encouraged a variety of methods of communication by teaching signing as well as exercises to encourage lip-reading and vocal speech, thus attending to the needs of a wide variety of deaf children.

There was a different emphasis in France. The great pioneer l'Abee de l'Epee, who became known as the "Father of the Deaf", had taught deaf students since the middle of the eighteenth century, and established a free deaf school in Paris in 1755. In l'Abee's school, pupils were taught mainly in sign language, as well as how to read and write, with some speech lessons only introduced in later years. l'Abee's methods, carried on by his successors, attracted wide interest, so that many teachers of the deaf visited Paris from all over Europe and beyond. In 1816, Thomas Gallaudet came to Europe from the United States to learn more about teaching the deaf. He first visited the Braidwoods in London and then travelled to Paris. Impressed by what he saw, Gallaudet invited Laurent Clerc, a deaf pupil who had become a teacher at the Paris school, to return with him to Connecticut. A great deal of historical information about the development of deaf education in Europe and America, including statistics from the United States, and illustrated with deaf biographies, can be found in a single volume.[15] In 1864, the school for the deaf that Gallaudet founded was finally established as a college in Washington DC, its charter having been granted by Abraham Lincoln. Gallaudet, named after its founder, remains the world's only deaf university. Gallaudet was critical of the emphasis on speech he had seen in the teaching provided by many European deaf schools, and at this time, the college used mainly sign language with a few speech exercises permitted.

The growth of deaf education, seen in different parts of the world, encouraged large numbers of deaf children to live together and learn to communicate with a shared language. This segregation from the hearing world forged a sense of community,[16] allowing groupings of deaf people to

---

[13] Rev W Fletcher, The Deaf and Dumb Boy (London: JW Parker, 1843).

[14] Jackson, Britain's Deaf Heritage, 38

[15] John R Burnet, Tales of the Deaf and Dumb, with miscellaneous poems (Newark: B Olds, 1835).

[16] Rosemarie Garland Thomson, Extraordinary Bodies (New York: Columbia University Press, 1997) 35-36.

develop and flourish in many towns and cities. As deaf people became better educated, they could find more skilled work with higher pay, and this new level of comparative prosperity allowed them to be regarded for the first time with some measure of greater esteem within hearing society. This in turn prompted a shift in legal recognition, so that the first interpreter for the deaf was used in court in Glasgow in 1817.[17] This rising self-confidence prompted a desire to mix in deaf social settings, with the first Mission club opening in Glasgow in 1823. It is interesting to note that at the end of the nineteenth century, signing was accorded royal approval when Queen Victoria learned how to finger spell in order to communicate with her daughter-in-law, later to become Queen Alexandra, who had been deaf since her teenage years. Queen Alexandra attended St Saviour's, the church for deaf people in Oxford Street. The vicar was Rev FWG Gilby, the hearing child of deaf parents who had learnt to sign as a boy.[18]

Unfortunately, approval and acceptance were not commonly experienced by deaf people. Ignorance and prejudice among the hearing were the norm, leading one commentator to write that

> …few groups in history have suffered such sustained and uncomprehending cruelty as the so-called 'deaf-and-dumb'[19]

and another from personal experience, that

> …the unconscious object of their charity neither hears nor answers their sarcasm.[20]

The emerging deaf community was even perceived to be threatening by some hearing people, who were worried that the deaf would live separately and become independent from the hearing world. Alexander Graham Bell is famous for inventing the telephone, a device designed so that his deaf wife could hear. The inventor's father was a teacher of the deaf, therefore Bell was familiar with the oral methods of teaching deaf children. Bell was deeply concerned that if deaf people continued to sign, they would distance themselves increasingly from the hearing world and would never fully integrate within hearing society. Bell was also influenced by some extreme eugenic beliefs which were in vogue at the end of the nineteenth century that encouraged him to call for a ban on deaf people marrying and having

---

[17] Jackson, Britain's Deaf Heritage, 81
[18] "History of British Sign Language", University College London, accessed May 11, 2023, https://www.ucl.ac.uk/british-sign-language-history/.
[19] Ree, I See A Voice, 85
[20] Kitto, "The lost senses. Part I. Deafness. The Land of Silence," 117.

children. We shall see in a later chapter that these views are reflected in the character of Dr Booth in *A Silent Handicap*. Bell believed that sign language was the key to the integrity of the deaf community and intent on undermining it, used his prestige and money to promote the sole use of oral methods of teaching that were already gaining ground in deaf education in the United States and Europe. This move coincided with the growing belief encouraged by colonialists that signing was associated with "uncivilised" parts of the world, that it was by its very nature primitive, and that it appealed to the degenerate animal emotions rather than to the intelligent mind. These arguments fuelled the pre-existing struggle for dominance between two conflicting strategies of deaf education, as deaf schools and teachers of the deaf had become increasingly aligned either with methods rooted in signing or those based on vocal exercises. This was a continuation of the public disagreements at the end of the previous century between l'Abee de l'Epee and Pereire, both influential French deaf educators who represented the signing and oral factions. The repercussions of this dispute were to profoundly affect the future of deaf education and the deaf community on both sides of the Atlantic up to the present day.

The considerable forces ranged against the use of signing culminated in 1880 at the notorious second international congress of deaf educators held in Milan. The conference was hardly international since ninety per cent of the delegates attending originated from either Italy or France. Deaf people who taught in schools were specifically banned from attending, so that the only deaf person who was actually present at the proceedings was a member of the small American delegation.[21] The oralist leaders had already signalled the outcome, so it was no surprise but still a shock, when the congress voted overwhelmingly in favour of a motion to teach deaf children exclusively by the use of vocal methods. This vote had far-reaching implications that reverberated throughout deaf schools in many countries. As a result, the Royal Commission of 1889 recommended that deaf children in the UK should be taught according to oralist methods. The 1893 Elementary Education (Deaf and Blind Children) Act accepted the Milan decision and provided the legal framework that allowed speech-led teaching to dominate in British deaf schools. Sign language was outlawed within educational establishments, and its use in the dormitories and playgrounds was punished. If students expressed their preference to continue to use signing, this was taken as a refusal to improve their inferior and unhealthy state and therefore morally suspect.[22] Since ninety per cent of deaf children are born

---

[21] Jackson, Britain's Deaf Heritage, 114
[22] Mirzoeff, "The Silent Mind: Learning from Deafness," 19-25

to hearing families, deaf schools had played an indispensable role in teaching, preserving, and passing on sign language. Signing was now used only at home within deaf families or secretly in schools, although it was still permitted within deaf clubs and promoted by deaf periodicals and the publication of illustrations of signs. Many deaf people were outraged. The British Deaf and Dumb Association was founded as a direct response to the decision of the Milan conference and the consequent attempt to eradicate sign language and undermine the integrity of the deaf community. At its first congress in 1890, the delegates defiantly declared,

> ...the Association indignantly protests against the imputation...that the finger and signed language is barbarous. We consider such a mode of exchanging our ideas most natural and indispensable. [23]

In the first half of the twentieth century, speech-led views in the UK became further entrenched, so that sign language was completely absent in deaf schools and deaf teachers were no longer able to practice. However, in the United States, signing was preserved largely because of the pre-eminence of Gallaudet as an educational institution. This regressive impact on the lives of generations of deaf people lasted until the 1970s, when it was shown by academic studies that oral methods alone produced limited results and were not as effective as had been first thought.[24] [25]

In the 1960s, William Stokoe's research at Gallaudet proved that American Sign Language (ASL) should be considered a true language from a linguistic standpoint.[26] He also codified ASL and laid the foundations for a new approach to deaf education. There was increasing recognition that deaf education should teach the whole spectrum of deaf children, some of whom would be profoundly deaf, while others wanted to retain their place within hearing families, some preferred to sign, and others used technological aids and looked to improve hearing and speech. In the 1960s, the Total Communication method of deaf education was launched in the United States which included learning by finger spelling, sign language, speech, reading, writing, and assistive technology. Since then, it has been common on both sides of the Atlantic to have a more liberal outlook that

---

[23] David Brien (ed), Dictionary of British Sign Language/English (London: Faber and Faber, 1992) x.

[24] Ladd, Paddy. "The Modern Deaf Community". In British Sign Language, ed. Dorothy Miles (London: BBC Books, 1988) 27-43.

[25] Mirzoeff, "The Silent Mind: Learning from Deafness," 19-25

[26] Petitto, Laura-Ann. "Three Revolutions: Language, Culture, and Biology". In Deaf Gain, ed. H-Dirksen Baumann and Joseph J. Murray (Minneapolis: University of Minnesota Press, 2014), 65-76.

advocates a combination of signing and oral-auditory approaches. This is thought by many deaf educators to give the majority of deaf children the best educational opportunities,[27] although this view has been challenged.[28] Some schools have sought to develop a "bilingual-bicultural" model that recognises the reality of living as a deaf minority within a hearing majority and seeks to negotiate the tensions that exist between the two.[29]

As signing developed over many years through consistent use and educational involvement, it became much more complex than the simpler and more common forms of visual expression. Sign language involves not only the hands, but also body posture, lip patterns, and facial expressions. One or both hands create shapes that flow into one another. Some signs are iconic and easily recognisable, while many are symbolic and require specific training to understand. Size, speed, and position of the hand shapes express variations and emphasis. Specific signs are still used for finger spelling and numbers. A variety of multi-channel signs change their meaning depending on shifts of body posture and facial expression. Sign languages, such as ASL or British Sign Language (BSL), the name adopted in the UK in 1975, have developed in many different parts of the world over many centuries.[30] They continue to evolve, and have very different styles, handshapes, syntax, and grammar, with regional variations existing within a national sign language.[31] Despite the popular opinion of hearing communities to the contrary, there is no universal and international sign language, although similarities exist between certain hand shapes in different systems.

Knowing the history of conflict between movements supporting oral speech or signing in deaf education explains why

---

[27] Evans, Lionel, "Total Communication". In Constructing Deafness, ed. Susan Gregory and Gillian M. Hartley (Milton Keynes: The Open University, 1991), 131-136.

[28] Lynas, Wendy, Alan Huntington and Ivan Tucker, "A Critical Examination of Different Approaches to Communication in the Education of Deaf Children". In Constructing Deafness, eds. Susan Gregory and Gillian M. Hartley (Milton Keynes: The Open University, 1991), 125-130.

[29] Padden, Carol, "From the Cultural to the Bicultural". In Cultural and Language Diversity and the Deaf Experience ed. Ila Parasnis (Cambridge: Cambridge University Press: 1996), 79-96.

[30] Brien, "Dictionary of British Sign Language/English", x

[31] Cath Smith, Signs Make Sense (London: Souvenir Press, 1994) 33.

...communication is *the* underlying issue with hearing loss, regardless of severity.[32]

As a result, it has become a potent, and at times, emotive cultural identifier for many deaf people. The choice of a deaf person to primarily use oral speech or sign language is inextricably linked to whether they see themselves to be part of the hearing majority or a signing based deaf culture. In general, deaf people can be thought of as two distinct groups, with the overwhelming majority having become deaf later in life and continuing to identify with the hearing world of which they have always been a part. They have been termed deaf with a lower case "d". The much smaller minority of deaf people, usually unable to hear from birth or early childhood, use sign language as their first language, and see themselves as belonging to a linguistic minority who share a specific culture. They have been termed Deaf with an upper case "D". This results in two very different types of stories about being deaf. The personal narratives of the deaf majority have been described as "wounded", with their history of deafness characterised by damage, loss, medicalisation, exclusion, and isolation. In contrast, the individual accounts of Deaf signers are described as "warrior", with their experience of deafness characterised by the struggle for identity, the use of war metaphors, rights, and citizenship, and an unwillingness to be defined in relation to the hearing world.[33] There is a striking divergence in how members of the two groups understand the significance of their deafness. The "deaf" perceive it as a regrettable and marginalising loss that needs to be fixed, whereas the "Deaf" regard it not only as a key to their identity and community, but also as a call for battle to be accepted as a linguistic and cultural minority. There is, of course, considerable overlap between the two groups. Many "Deaf" people who sign use hearing aids and vocal speech, if only to a limited extent. Some "deaf" individuals learn how to sign. Although "wounded" and "warrior" narratives represent two extremes of the experience of deafness, the reality is much more complex and nuanced, with many people finding themselves relating to elements of both.

---

[32] Zazove, Philip, Commentary on Lesley Jones and Robin Bunton, "Wounded or warrior? Stories of being or becoming deaf". In Narrative Research in Health and Illness, eds. Brian Hurwitz, Trisha Greenhalgh and Vieda Skultans (Oxford: Blackwell Publishers Ltd, 2002), 203.

[33] Jones, Lesley and Robin Bunton. "Wounded or Warrior? Stories of Being or Becoming Deaf". In Narrative Research in Health and Illness, eds. Brian Hurwitz, Trisha Greenhalgh and Vieda Skultans (Oxford: Blackwell Publishers Ltd, 2004) 187-204.

In recent years, there have been demands from Deaf people for sign languages to be accepted as distinct languages within their own countries. Following Stokoe's ground breaking work to prove that ASL had a syntax and grammar distinct from spoken English, many of the States of the USA have formally recognised ASL. In 1988 the momentum for recognition propelled a large number of deaf people to take part in the "Deaf President Now" demonstrations at Gallaudet University, demanding the appointment of the university's first deaf president in its one hundred-and twenty-four-year history. Demonstrations in the UK also succeeded in convincing the British Government to grant recognition of BSL in 2003, and legal standing in 2021. These instances of official acknowledgement were in response to the call from many deaf people that they should be accepted as a language group rather than as disabled, with some believing that they should be accorded a unique social status.[34] This is because some "Deaf" people believe that their culture, language, and community

…constitute a totally adequate, self-enclosed, and self-defining sub-nationality within the larger structure of the audist state,[35]

and that they have more in common with other disabled people than those who share gender or race.[36] Some believe that the

…shared sense of oppression of language, and hence of human potential, is at the very heart of British Deaf culture.[37]

There is a specific rejection of the medical model that perceives deafness as a condition requiring treatment, stating instead that it is only in matters of oral communication and education that deafness is a handicap,[38] as deafness cannot be considered to be a disability in a community that communicates exclusively by signing. Finkelstein's assertion that the "Deaf" have more in common with other disabled people seems strange considering that the basis of the argument supporting the ethnic model of deafness is built on a belief that deaf people are not in fact disabled. This

---

[34] Paddy Ladd, "Understanding Deaf Culture. In Search of Deafhood". (Clevedon: Multilingual Matters Ltd, 2003) 230.
[35] Lennard J. Davis, "Deafness and Insight: The Deafened Moment as a Critical Modality," College English, No. 8 (December 1995): 881-882.
[36] Finkelstein Vic, "'We' Are Not Disabled, 'You' Are". In Constructing Deafness, eds. Susan Gregory and Gillian M. Hartley (Milton Keynes: The Open University, 1991), 265-271.
[37] Brien, "Dictionary of British Sign Language/English", 2
[38] Mirzoeff, "The Silent Mind: Learning from Deafness," 19

seems to be rather disingenuous when many of those who claim a cultural and linguistic "Deaf" identity use hearing aids and cochlear implants, evidencing the medical model of deafness they oppose, with some receiving benefits and free bus passes based on an assessment of disability. I have no problem defending the right of any deaf individual to use technological aids or to be in receipt of benefits, but it appears that despite any activist rhetoric, many profoundly deaf people adopt a more pragmatic approach, and rather than preferring to remain "self-enclosed", are content to compromise with the "audist state" in which they live. For the profoundly deaf signing minority, the issue of which language is chosen as an individual's first language remains highly sensitive. Any attempt to challenge or change this may be perceived as threatening to individuals, to a deaf family, and as an attack on the signing community as a whole. This issue is highlighted by the forcefully held and opposing opinions regarding whether or not deaf families should accept cochlear implants in their young, that still erupts into controversy on both sides of the Atlantic.[39]

Although the issues raised are of tremendous significance, it is important to remember that people who use BSL as a first language represent only 1-2% of deaf people,[40] causing difficulties in adopting a purely ethnic minority model.[41] Such a model may apply to a significant but small minority of deaf people, however, the vast majority, even those with a profound loss, continue to identify with the hearing majority. Most deaf people are relatively untroubled by questions of identity and prefer to remain within the hearing community from which they originate. Their concerns are the everyday practicalities of trying to understand somebody speaking and not becoming isolated from their hearing families, friends, and colleagues. Results extrapolated from the 2021 census suggest there are seventy thousand deaf signers in the UK, with double that number, including family members, teachers, and interpreters, signing regularly.[42] This compares with eleven million people in the UK, nearly one in six of the total population, who are thought to be hard-of-hearing, with over one

---

[39] Paul Dakin, "A Cut Too Far? Cochlear Implants and Division among the Deaf," No. 1 (February 2017):1023-1025.
[40] "Facts and Figures", Royal National Institute for the Deaf, accessed May 12, 2023, https://rnid.org.uk/about-us/research-and-policy/facts-and-figures/.
[41] Parratt, David, and Brenda Tipping. "The State, Social Work and Deafness". In Constructing Deafness, eds. Susan Gregory and Gillian M. Hartley (Milton Keynes: The Open University, 1991), 247-252.
[42] "Work to be done on census figures for BSL", British Deaf Association, accessed November 30, 2022, https://bda.org.uk/bsl-census-figures-2022/.

million experiencing a profound loss.[43] Most of these people continue to use their voices to converse. Two million people use hearing aids,[44] and twenty thousand wear cochlear implants.[45] The statistics from the United States show a similar pattern. It is estimated that nearly thirty-eight million, or fifteen per cent, of the American population do not hear well, and there are one million who are profoundly deaf. The level of hearing at which profound loss is defined in the United States is lower than in the United Kingdom accounting for a smaller proportion. There are thought to be one million ASL users including family members, teachers, and translators. Nearly thirty million are prescribed hearing aids and one hundred and sixty thousand people wear cochlear implants.[46]

Despite these statistics demonstrating that large numbers of deaf people are known to exist within hearing societies, they are represented comparatively rarely within mainstream literature. The figures from both sides of the Atlantic clearly show a wide variety of deaf experience, and we shall discover in the next chapter whether this is reflected by the portrayal of deaf characters found in novels. It is only natural that the members of any group, hearing or deaf, should want to see depictions of themselves that are appropriate and realistic, rather than being represented by stereotypes that are perpetuated. Deaf people have remained hidden and largely silent over many years. This is particularly true for the profoundly deaf and signing community, many of whom already feel misunderstood and marginalised by a hearing society and its culture, and eagerly seek accurate portrayals that can be held up as aspirational role models for their young. The knowledge of the longstanding struggles of deaf people over matters of language and education help the hearing to understand why the representation of deaf people in literature is so significant to the deaf community.

---

[43] "Facts and Figures", Royal National Institute for the Deaf, accessed May 12, 2023, https://rnid.org.uk/about-us/research-and-policy/facts-and-figures/.

[44] Hearing Link, "Hearing loss statistics in the UK", British Academy of Audiology, accessed May 12, 2023, https://www.baaudiology.org/about/media-centre/facts-about-hearing-loss-and-deafness/.

[45] British Cochlear Implant Group, accessed May 12, 2023, https://www.bcig.org.uk/.

[46] "Quick Statistics about Hearing", National Institute on Deafness and Other Communication Disorders, accessed May 12, 2023, https://www.nidcd.nih.gov/health/statistics/quick-statistics-hearing.

CHAPTER TWO

GOLDILOCKS, GRANNY, AND GIFTED – DEAF CHARACTERS IN THE ENGLISH NOVEL

The relatively small number of deaf characters portrayed in literature tend to be based on misplaced assumptions made by hearing authors. This, in turn, has led deaf commentators to complain that the deaf have been neglected by established writers,[1] marginalised,[2] and described inaccurately.[3] The majority of authors who write for the mainstream are hearing, so that the representation of deaf people is from

> …an essentially hearing viewpoint, and the deaf characters who appear have rarely established themselves as credible people but are usually caricatures or useful devices within the story."[4]

Hearing authors are accused of appropriating deafness to their own ends,[5] and make the deaf person "sentimentalised or emblematic of some larger insight into humanity".[6] Even when hearing authors display empathy for deaf characters, they combine this with

---

[1] Robert Panara, "Deaf characters in fiction and drama". The Deaf American, May 1972, 3-8.

[2] Lennard J. Davis, "Deafness and Insight: The Deafened Moment as a Critical Modality," College English, No. 8 (December 1995): 881-900.

[3] FG Barnes, "The deaf in literature", Teacher of the Deaf, No.1 (1903): 42-45.

[4] Gregory, Susan. "Deafness in fiction". In Constructing Deafness, eds. Susan Gregory and Gillian M. Hartley (Milton Keynes: The Open University, 1991), 294-300.

[5] Susan Gregory and Gillian M. Hartley (eds), Constructing Deafness (Milton Keynes: The Open University, 1991), 295.

[6] Harman, Kristen. "On Deaf Literature" Bloomsbury Admin, January 18th 2019. Accessed January 18th, 2019,
https://bloomsburyliterarystudiesblog.com/continuum-literary-studie/2019/01/on-deaf-literature.html.

…a striking display of misconceptions and ignorance about them–for example, when they exaggerate the lip-reading and special abilities of their deaf characters.[7]

Although I believe these assessments to be largely true, especially when applied to older examples, there are some recent portrayals of deaf characters that more accurately reflect the reality of deaf experience, communication, and community. In forming this view, I have examined sixty-four novels that have been written in English over three hundred years for a predominantly hearing adult readership. Some books are well known, many forgotten, and a few are rare and difficult to access.

The subject of deaf characters in literature has received surprisingly little attention, particularly those created in novels written by British authors. There are only three included in what was probably the first attempt to document examples nearly a hundred years ago.[8] Forty years later, Guire lists a single minor British example alongside eight international characters, although it is only fair to point out that his primary reason for writing the article is to document Russian texts.[9] A decade later, Panara offers twelve, half of which are American, including the script of a play,[10] and Taylor reviews forty-two short stories that contain a deaf character rather than novels, commenting on only three of British origin.[11] Bergman writes an excellent and wide-ranging overview of fictional deaf characters from throughout the world for Gallaudet's influential encyclopaedia, but again includes only a handful of British as opposed to American portrayals.[12] Miller should be applauded for providing an annotated bibliography of one hundred and thirty-six works, but only eleven out of fifty-six adult reader novels are British.[13] *Angels and Outcasts* [14] described as "An Anthology of Deaf Characters in Literature" is often quoted. The authors arrange fourteen samples taken from factual accounts, novels, and children's books, in three

---

[7] Bergman, Eugene. "Literature, fictional characters". In Gallaudet Encyclopaedia of Deaf People and Deafness, Volume 2, ed. John V. Van Cleve (New York: McGraw Hill Book Company Inc, 1987), 172-175.

[8] Macleod Yearsley, "Deafness in Literature," The Lancet, April 14, 1925, 746-7.

[9] Oscar Guire, "Deaf characters in literature." The Silent Worker, August 1961, 3-6.

[10] Panara, "Deaf characters in fiction and drama", 3-8.

[11] Gladys M. Taylor "Deaf characters in short stories," The Deaf American, May1974, 6-8.

[12] Bergman, "Literature, fictional characters", 172-175.

[13] Jonathan Miller, "The Rustle of a Star: An Annotated Bibliography of Deaf Characters in Fiction", Library Trends, No.1 (Summer 1992): 42-60.

[14] Trent Batson and Eugene Bergman (eds), Angels and Outcasts, (Washington, DC: Gallaudet University Press, 2002).

sections depending on whether they originate from the nineteenth or twentieth centuries, and those written by deaf authors. There is only one excerpt taken from a British novel. In the extensive bibliography, there are eighty-six works that span a variety of novels, biographies, short stories, dramas, and poems. Only eight of the thirty-two books listed are by British authors. Even allowing for the fact that all of the reviewers except Yearsley are American, I am astonished at the omission of British sources. This is remedied to an extent by *The Quiet Ear*,[15] an anthology from a British compiler that lists thirty-seven stories, thirty-three of which are novels, including nineteen by British authors.

In my review, forty-nine of the sixty-four novels are written by British authors, with all but four of their stories set in the UK.[16] Two more have British settings, the first by the American author Elizabeth George, and the second by writers from New Zealand, Lance and James Morcan. The remaining thirteen are by American authors and set mainly in the United States.[17] Four of the characters that are sometimes referenced as being deaf should be discounted straightaway. Fenella in Sir Walter Scott's *Peveril of the Peak* (1823) pretends to be deaf in order to overhear conversations.[18] Her depiction cannot be used to tell us how the author would have represented deafness in an imaginary character intended to be genuinely deaf. Scott had previously used a deaf imposter as a literary device,[19] as had Tobias Smollett.[20] The idea of somebody hearing pretending to be deaf for their own ends was reprised by the "deaf and dumb Spaniard" in *The Adventures of Tom Sawyer* (1876).[21] That leaves sixty novels that include characters intended to be truly deaf. These characterisations divide easily into minor and major roles. Furthermore, I have previously proposed that many characters can be categorised as belonging to two iconic groups: the beautiful, intelligent victim rescued from abuse, who communicates through signs, that I describe as "Goldilocks"; and the elderly, humanely and humorously treated individual, who is usually communicated with by

---

[15] Brian Grant (ed), The Quiet Ear (London: Andre Deutsch Ltd, 1987).

[16] The exceptions are *Under Western Eyes*, *The Scapegoat*, *The Cretan*, and *Hotel du Lac*.

[17] The exceptions are *The Prince of India*, *For Whom the Bell Tolls*, and *Gorky Park*.

[18] Sir Walter Scott, Peveril of the Peak (1823; London: Thomas Nelson and Sons, 1905), 704.

[19] Sir Walter Scott, (1825; New York: Dodd, Meade & Co, 1943), 303.

[20] Tobias Smollett, Peregrine Pickle (1751; London: George Routledge & Sons, 1929), 224.

[21] Mark Twain, The Adventures of Tom Sawyer (1876: London: Dean & Sons Ltd) 1980, 153.

shouting, whom I have termed "Granny".[22] I should stress this classification is my own invention, does not originate from the deaf community, and is not used by deaf people. I wanted to create a convenient way of referring to two types of deaf character that are found repeatedly and consistently within novels. The idea of summarising obvious characteristics was used by deaf commentators Batson and Bergman in the title of their popular anthology *Angels and Outcasts* mentioned above. The "Angel" description would easily match that of Goldilocks, but features attributed to the "Outcasts" are represented in my view by more than one type of character. I would like to add a "Gifted" group to my two original categories, as a number of deaf characters found in crime novels exist simply because of their amazing ability to read lips at a distance.

This chapter gives a brief overview of each of the novels under consideration, and is arranged chronologically to show how the portrayal of deaf characters has evolved over time. The next chapter examines specific themes that become apparent when studying their depiction. Some of these themes are already present in the original deaf character, who in other ways, could be described as being quite unique, defying easy classification into any of the more obvious categories outlined above.

Duncan Campbell

In 1720, the first deaf character in an English novel appeared in *The History of the Life and Adventures of Mr. Duncan Campbell*. Although the book is traditionally attributed to Daniel Defoe, the authorship is debated, with some suggesting William Bond as the likely writer.[23] The story is based on a true account of a handsome, intelligent, "deaf and dumb boy" who rises from an obscure background to enjoy fame and popularity among a fashionable society fascinated by novelty. This change in fortunes is ascribed to Campbell having been taught according to Dr Wallis' "method of teaching deaf and dumb persons to write, read, and understand a language",[24] that is referred to in Chapter One. Campbell is shown to finger spell Wallis' alphabet that includes many of the same signs used in modern

---

[22] Paul Dakin, "Goldilocks or Granny? Portrayals of deafness in the English novel" Journal of Medical Biography No. 4 (November 2015): 227-37.
[23] "The History of the Life and Adventures of Mr. Duncan Campbell", British Deaf History Society, accessed n/d, http://www.bdhs.org.uk/timeline/the-history-of-the-life-and-adventures-of-mr-duncan-campbell-by-daniel-defoe/.
[24] Daniel Defoe, The History of the Life and Adventures of Mr. Duncan Campbell, (1720; London: J.M. Dent & Co, 1895), 21.

British Sign Language (BSL).[25] In fact, the original publication contained a manual alphabet chart to inform its readers; this is reproduced in the illustration on the next page. However, the book reveals another theme as Campbell possesses an inherited ability to prophesy the future,[26] a very desirable commodity in exalted circles, particularly when predicting husbands for wealthy young ladies. We might be inclined to associate eighteenth century England with prejudice, misunderstanding, and exclusion, but the novel reveals Campbell to be treated humanely by an accepting society. The character is dealt with sympathetically by the author who ensures Campbell's redemption through his ability to communicate by writing and signing. The author was evidently an enthusiastic supporter of Wallis and his methods, with the novel asserting that deaf people in general are capable of understanding a language and communicating with the hearing majority. Panara, a deaf reviewer, considers Campbell to be an important literary figure, with the image of deaf people enhanced by the book. He argues favourably for what he sees as Defoe's pioneering approach, but believes Campbell's exploits to be "too sensational and exaggerated."[27] In contrast, Bergman, another deaf reviewer, dismisses the "vast stretches of sanctimonious prose".[28] To his credit, the author chose to write a novel about an unusual and less obvious subject who would normally have been ignored by the reading classes. If Defoe was indeed the author, the innovative idea of writing about a deaf man may have appealed to him because he wrote about other characters who existed beyond the margins of society, such as a castaway and a courtesan. Four years after the publication of *Duncan Campbell,* Defoe met Henry Baker, an educator of deaf children, who married Defoe's daughter Sophia in 1727.[29]

Although much of the volume consists of discussion concerning Wallis' methods, two thirds are actually taken up with philosophical speculations about the origin of Campbell's "special powers". The book states that these are bestowed as divine compensation for his loss of hearing. The book's originality and inclusive approach is likely to have been considered quite extraordinary at the time and should be commended. But as is so often true of a pioneering work, the story cannot be perceived as faultless when viewed with the benefit of history and changed perspectives.

---

[25] Defoe, The History of the Life and Adventures of Mr. Duncan Campbell, 23
[26] Defoe, The History of the Life and Adventures of Mr. Duncan Campbell, 44
[27] Panara, "Deaf characters in fiction and drama", 3-8
[28] Bergman, "Literature, fictional characters", 172-175
[29] Maximillian E. Novak, "Daniel Defoe: Master of Fictions: His Life and Work" (New York: Oxford University Press, 2001), 648.

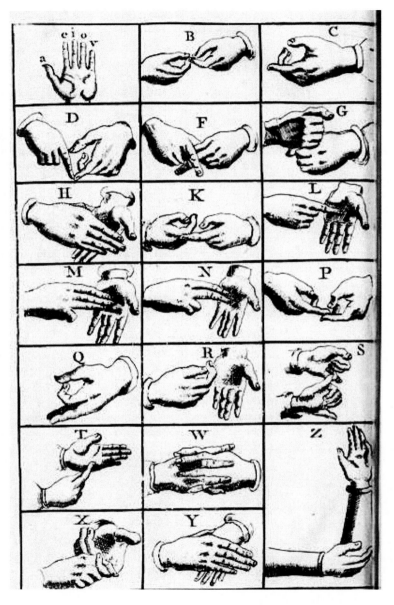

Figure 2-1: Image of the fingerspelling alphabet chart from The History of The Life and Adventures of Mr. Duncan Campbell, 1720. British Deaf History Society.

Let's not be over-critical. The writer succeeded in creating a deaf man as his major character and treated him in a way that would have been exceptional at the time. But he also set an unfortunate precedent for many of the depictions of deaf characters yet to be written, with two major issues inherent in the book that the author could not have recognised and would only become apparent with time. The first is that although Campbell is shown to possess a considerable prowess in finger signing, the fact of his deafness is completely overshadowed by the importance ascribed to his supernatural gift to predict the future. This power is given as compensation for his deafness. The implication is that to be deaf makes a person incomplete, that being deaf is not enough and *needs* compensating, that some form of additional ability is required for a deaf person to be valuable and accepted within a hearing society. As a result, the author unwittingly pointed the way for many deaf characters yet to come who would need to be enhanced or "made whole" rather than simply received as interesting in their own right. The second issue is that Campbell is a character against whom the attitudes and desires of many hearing characters are made known. He is the focus around which theological points are made and philosophical speculations revolve. In other words, even though Campbell is the main figure of the book, he is a catalyst who aids the development of the hearing characters, and a ficelle through whom the reader discovers more about the hearing characters and their attitudes.

Deaf characters in the nineteenth century

These two features evident in *Duncan Campbell* are continued by examples of deaf characters that originate in nineteenth century novels. Although there are deaf characters that are ascribed compensating gifts, this is a trope more commonly associated with comics of the superhero variety that are reviewed in Chapter Four. The majority of deaf characters are given either the role of a plot device or act as a "sounding board" against whom are displayed the emotions and values of the hearing characters around them.

For instance, Mrs Bates in Jane Austen's *Emma* (1815) exists merely to reflect the kindness of the hearing characters who surround her, in particular her daughter. The elderly lady is described as gentle, quiet, and deaf, the widow of the town's former vicar. The amiable Miss Bates says that her mother's deafness is

> …very trifling you see—just nothing at all. By only raising my voice, and saying any thing two or three times over, she is sure to hear; but then she is

used to my voice. But it is very remarkable that she should always hear Jane
better than she does me. Jane speaks so distinct![30]

Although communication is made possible by repetition and shouting,
this is selective as conversations and correspondence are censored to
prevent distress.[31] Pairing the loquacious Miss Bates with her deaf mother
has been said to make both into objects of derision,[32] but I disagree. Both
are accorded a status that their poverty might deny, and they are treated with
generosity and respect by their neighbours. I have previously described Mrs
Bates as the prototype Granny character.[33] Granny characters are minor and
peripheral to the plot. They are elderly, isolated, and shouted at by their
hearing counterparts. They are mostly treated kindly, sympathetically, and
often with humour. They struggle to remain part of the hearing community
with which they identify. Granny characters do not have the typical
attributes associated with claiming a deaf identity, such as being able to
sign, having had a deaf education, and belonging to a deaf community. This
stereotype is recognisable and familiar to many hearing readers, possibly
through having elderly deaf relatives who share at least some of these
characteristics.

Another Granny character appears in *The Posthumous Papers of the
Pickwick Club* (1836). Mr Wardle's mother is the first of at least six deaf
characters that Dickens includes in his works. The elderly lady, who is
treated with kindness, is described as "rather cross, and by consequence,
most particularly deaf",[34] perhaps inferring an element of wilfulness that
caused the old woman to exaggerate her difficulties in hearing people speak.
Mr Wardle's mother, and two more of Dickens' deaf creations described
below, are used to demonstrate the virtues of hearing characters in their
familial circles and help provide an atmosphere of domestic cosiness.

This is also partly true of the unnamed "deaf gentleman" in *Master
Humphrey's Clock* (1840), an anonymous but major character who submits
manuscripts to an informal literary society. He is delightful and charming,
and is able to read lips and speak. Mr Pickwick communicates with him by

---

[30] Jane Austen, Emma (1815; London: MacMillan and Co Ltd: 1896,) 137.

[31] Austen, Emma, 151

[32] Davis, "Deafness and Insight: The Deafened Moment as a Critical Modality," 881-
900.

[33] Dakin, "Goldilocks or Granny? Portrayals of deafness in the English novel", 227-
37.

[34] Charles Dickens, The Posthumous Papers of the Pickwick Club (1836; London:
Chapman & Hall Ltd, 1910), 455.

finger spelling and writing on slates.[35] The plot was reviewed favourably for a deaf magazine that references Dickens' familiarity with deaf people by mentioning his visit to the Asylum for the Deaf in Connecticut.[36]

Another type of plot device, not uncommonly associated with deaf characters, is the provision of amusement. The first of these is Theodore Hook's novel *Gilbert Gurney* (1841), which includes a humorous episode about a deaf judge trying to administer justice. He and the barristers are constantly instructing the defendants and witnesses to speak louder.[37]

In 1852, however, Dickens wrote tragically of Caddy Jellyby's baby, a pathetic deaf infant who appears briefly in *Bleak House*. Once again, the character reflects the attributes of a hearing character by being portrayed as the object of a selfless maternal devotion that contrasts with the oblivious neglect shown to Caddy by her own mother.[38]

Two years later, Dickens' close friend, Wilkie Collins, portrayed the original of a Goldilocks character in *Hide and Seek* (1854). I have described Goldilocks characters as young, beautiful, intelligent girls that are unable to speak and communicate by signing. They are positioned as main characters in the plot, and after being rescued from abuse by hearing people, they are educated, and become paragons of morality and saintly behaviour. The concept of Goldilocks takes further the reference to "inspirationally disadvantaged" deaf characters in Miller's bibliography.[39] The story concerns Mary Grice, a young illegitimate orphan, later known as Madonna, who is deafened after falling from a circus horse. Traumatic deafness, as we shall see, is a convenient plot device favoured by hearing authors. Mary is treated badly by Jubber, the circus owner, and is rescued from the abusive situation by an artist and his wife. Mr Blyth, the artist, calls her 'Madonna' because in appearance she reminds him of a Renaissance Virgin. A physician examines Madonna with "a sort of queer spy-glass thing",[40] and refers her to the Asylum for the Deaf and Dumb where she learns the manual alphabet. The themes of medical involvement and deaf education, the first time that both are seen in the representation of a deaf character, become

---

[35] Charles Dickens, The Mystery of Edwin Drood / Master Humphrey's Clock (1840; London: Chapman & Hall Ltd, 1911,) 346.

[36] Toivo Lindholm, "A Deaf Character in Charles Dickens' Master Humphrey's Clock" The Silent Worker April 1963, 11.

[37] Theodore Hook, Gilbert Gurney (London: Richard Bentley, 1841), 176-192.

[38] Charles Dickens, Bleak House. (1852; London: Pan Books 1976), 292.

[39] Miller, "The Rustle of a Star: An Annotated Bibliography of Deaf Characters in Fiction", 42-60.

[40] Wilkie Collins, Hide and Seek (1854; London: Sampson Low, Son & Co, 1861), 73.

more consistent and achieve even greater prominence in later novels. Collins is sympathetic about the isolation of deafness, writing that "No deprivation attending their affliction is more severely felt".[41] The angelic and aptly named Madonna arises from obscurity to be redeemed through learning to sign, just like Duncan Campbell. It is hard to imagine that Collins was unfamiliar with Defoe's work, and so it is astonishing when he declares,

> I do not know that any attempt has yet been made in English fiction to draw the character of a Deaf Mute.[42]

Collins is well known for having introduced original female characters into his novels that include a detective, a villain, and a woman who is wrongly incarcerated, and I expect the idea of writing about a deaf young girl would have interested him. The character he created provides the template for Goldilocks characters. She escapes not only from abuse, but also from her original silent state by virtue of her education and signing, a transition implied by the evolution from suffering Mary into saintly Madonna. His main character was reportedly modelled on a case of Dr Kitto, [43] and Collins took most of the details about her deafness from Dr Kitto's *The Lost Senses*, including the moral traits that allowed Madonna to survive "the deprivation from which she is suffering."[44] A deaf educator wrote that she was pleased the author made a deaf girl the main character, but criticises the unlikely cause of Madonna's speech and hearing loss, [45] even though Collins stated that he studied several medical examples. She also disapproves of Madonna's renowned intelligence, dependence on slate writing, and the absence of lip-reading, clearly believing that despite Collins' attempts to bring credibility to his character through appropriate research, Madonna did not reflect the reality familiar to many deaf people. It would be unusual, even during the era in which Collins was writing, for a completely deaf person not to show some ability in reading lips, but the other features are suggestive of Madonna being made to appear more than realistic. Perhaps her creator was according Madonna a level of mental and moral success that raised the character above the mundane as compensation for her deafness. Another deaf writer is more complimentary, believing that Madonna is a demonstration of progress and adjustment through

---

[41] Collins, Hide and Seek, 114
[42] Collins, Hide and Seek, note to Chapter Seven
[43] Collins, Hide and Seek, vii
[44] Collins, Hide and Seek, note to Chapter Seven
[45] Barnes, "The deaf in literature", 42-45

communication.[46] In common with most Goldilocks characters, Madonna strikes me as being rather too good to be true, but my impression is that Collins tried to describe accurately and sympathetically, a situation and style of education that would have been largely unknown to most of his readers.

In contrast, when Thackeray wrote about the elderly village lady in *The Virginians* four year after Madonna, his Granny character would have been familiar to a hearing readership. Kindly attitudes are extended towards her by the main hearing characters with only superficial mention of the issues related to her hearing (1858).[47]

Deaf characters are often employed as plot devices with the intention of moving the story forward. These can range from quite trivial depictions that are almost incidental to crucial roles that have a major impact on the story. In *A Tale of Two Cities* (1859) Dickens records an unusual instance of temporary and traumatic deafness when a gun is fired next to Miss Pross during a struggle. She requires visual prompting from her companions until her hearing recovers.[48] The fight with the villainess and the shock of the sudden deafness are more important to the plot than the deafness itself.

The same is true of Wemmick's father, another of Dickens' minor deaf characters, whose deafness is less important than the effect he has, and the emotions he engenders in the hearing characters around him. Found in *Great Expectations* (1861), Wemmick's father is another Granny character despite his gender, and serves much the same purpose as Mr Wardle's mother. The elderly man is dependent on visual cues and affirmation.[49] It is suggested that this simple form of communication is a demonstration of filial affection.[50]

Dickens and Collins often discussed their ideas and works in progress, so it is hardly surprising that within ten years of the publication of *Hide and Seek*, Dickens had created his own version of Madonna. Sophy is one of the most significant and widely referenced examples of a deaf character in any novel, and appears in *Dr Marigold* (1863), one of Dickens' popular Christmas stories. The similarity to Madonna is immediately apparent. Sophy is a beautiful, intelligent orphan who is rescued from abuse by the

---

[46] Panara, "Deaf characters in fiction and drama", 3-8.

[47] W.M. Thackerary, The Virginians (1858; London: Henry Froude, 1911), 191.

[48] Charles Dickens, A Tale of Two Cities (1859; London: JM Dent & Sons Ltd, 1979) 364.

[49] Charles Dickens, Great Expectations (1861; London: Chapman & Hall Ltd, 1911) 241.

[50] Davis, "Deafness and Insight: The Deafened Moment as a Critical Modality," 881-900

itinerant tinker known as Dr Marigold. He teaches her to read from
signposts and invents finger signs so they can communicate on their travels.
When Sophy is older, Dr Marigold takes her to be educated at the Deaf and
Dumb establishment in London, enabling her to learn how to sign properly
and so that she can meet other deaf people.[51] Dickens emphasises the
importance of sign language, and for the first time in fiction, there is
mention of the existence of a signing community.[52] Sophy meets and
marries a deaf man, allowing Dickens to foreshadow a major concern of the
modern deaf community, frequently expressed in novels, by expressing
fears about whether their baby will be deaf or hearing. In fact, the child is
able to hear, and through the efforts of Dr Marigold and the boy's parents,
he becomes the first fictional character to be bilingual in speech and
signing.[53] Sophy is the most frequently quoted instance of a deaf character
that I have come across, partly, I assume, because of the renown of her
author, as well as the interesting features of her character and the engaging
plot. Dr Marigold was described as "one of the prettiest stories about the
deaf and dumb" by an anonymous reviewer in an American newspaper for
the deaf nearly thirty years after publication,[54] and is considered to be a
sympathetic study of deafness in an English medical periodical.[55] A deaf
commentator believed that Collins and Dickens accurately reflected societal
attitudes towards the deaf,[56] although it remains to be seen how far the
creations of an author can act as a proxy for public perspectives. Sophy has
also been described more negatively, as a catalyst who transforms lives
around her while having no life of her own.[57] Another reviewer was also
unimpressed, labelling Sophy as a "prop" who made others happy,
especially when she gave birth to a hearing child.[58] This is, I think, a
reasonable criticism, although the idea of a hearing child being born to, and
looked after, by deaf parents would have been shocking for many of
Dickens' readers in an age when people were worried about the inheritance
of what were seen as imperfections and were likely to conflate deafness with
idiocy. Indeed, the legal framework of the day may have prevented such a

---

[51] Charles Dickens, Dr Marigold in Christmas Stories. Volume II (1863; London:
Chapman & Hall Ltd, 1911), 98.
[52] Jonathan Ree, I See A Voice. A Philosophical History of Language, Deafness and
the Senses (London: Harper Collins, 1999) 23-5.
[53] Dickens, Dr Marigold, 125-6.
[54] Anonymous, "Dr Marigold", The Silent Worker, January 30, 1890, 1.
[55] Yearsley, "Deafness in Literature", 746-747
[56] Panara, "Deaf characters in fiction and drama", 3-8
[57] Gregory, "Deafness in fiction", 294-300
[58] Bergman, "Literature, fictional characters", 172-175

family from existing. But in my view, Sophy is hardly a prop. She does not exist simply to provide a sounding board for the hearing characters like so many examples of deaf representation, nor can she be viewed as just a catalyst with no life of her own in order to make the hearing characters happy. Sophy is one of the two main characters in the novel, and through her experiences we discover more about the experience of deafness, the value of signing, the importance of deaf education, and for the first time in a novel, the existence and benefits of a signing community. These features must surely commend Sophy to deaf readers. She expands the scope of a deaf character considerably when compared with Madonna. It should be said, however, that Sophy is treated with extreme sentimentality, an aspect of writing not unknown with Dickens, and one that is mocked in the poem *Doctor Marigold Re-evaluated* written by a modern deaf poet.[59]

The first deaf character created by an American author is also treated with great sentimentality but is definitely not a moral paragon or a Goldilocks figure. Cathy Garth appears in *The Silent Partner* (1871) by Elizabeth Stuart Phelps, one hundred and fifty years after Duncan Campbell. Her role is that of the unwilling and undeserving recipient of the main character's charity. Perley Kelso, the "silent partner" of the title, inherits her father's cotton mill in Massachusetts and vigorously tries to improve the conditions of the workers. Her protégé is a mill hand whose sister, Cathy, was born deaf, and was beaten by their drunken father. Cathy is able to speak a little and "talks on her fingers".[60] Simple-minded, wayward, and immoral, Cathy dies in a freak accident in a floodtide of timber. The deaf character is portrayed as mentally and morally lacking, the undeserving object of Perley's benevolence that serves her philanthropic ideals. Perley's involvement with Cathy is motivated by her religious beliefs and a genuine desire to help, but her platitudes, typical of the time, come across as rather patronising when read today. We learn little of Cathy's experience of deafness other than it is said to exacerbate her failings. To be fair to the author, the book is primarily concerned with harsh industrial conditions and social injustice. The story also includes Bijah Mudge, a more peripheral character who is deafened from long exposure to the machines in the mill, testifying to the awful working conditions.[61] The title has nothing to do with the deaf characters but refers instead to Perley's supposed role in her

---

[59] Raymond Antrobus, The Perseverance (London: Penned in the Margins, 2018), 51-52.

[60] Elizabeth Stuart Phelps, The Silent Partner (Boston: JR Osgood and Company, 1871), 52.

[61] Stuart Phelps, The Silent Partner, 166

father's business. Hearing authors are sometimes a little too ready in attributing bad attitudes and moral failure to their deaf creations.

Stuart Phelps' character was followed by two further American examples. Mark Twain briefly mentions a deaf girl in *The Adventures of Huckleberry Finn* (1884). She is used purely as a plot device. Jim's daughter 'Lizabeth developed scarlet fever at the age of four and was left without hearing.[62] Jim tells Huck that he hit 'Lizabeth for not responding to his command only to discover that she could not hear. He felt sad and humbled by this misunderstanding. The purpose of the reminiscence is that Jim is hoping Huck will re-evaluate Jim's behaviour and forgive him in the same way Jim understood 'Lizabeth's lack of response and forgave her.

Lew Wallace employs deaf characters as a plot device in *The Prince of India* (1893). The silent obedience of the two "deaf mutes" that serve The Prince instils a sense of awe and mystery in the visitors to his residence. The prince is able to sign with servants Syama and Nilo but prefers them to read his lips as it is quicker.[63]

Two "deaf and dumb" characters are also included in Rider Haggard's *Joan Haste* (1895). The eponymous main hearing character lodges at Mrs Bird's house in London. The landlady's "paralytic'" husband and their young daughter are both deaf, but Joan is told not "to think them stupid".[64] It is refreshing to find in this story that deafness does not equate with stupidity, a trope that is all too evident in many other works. In fact, husband and daughter are shown to read and write, read lips, and sign. The care with which Mrs Bird looks after them testifies to her understanding and compassion, qualities that Joan must later rely upon when informing Mrs Bird that she is pregnant with an illegitimate child.

The nineteenth century saw the creation of tropes that would become used more frequently. We have seen the first examples of Goldilocks and Granny, an instance of a deaf character being used for humour, and others provided with histories of deafness initiated by trauma. The majority of deaf characters, with two notable exceptions, play minor roles, making situations familiar and comfortable to the hearing reader. They are positioned mainly as plot devices or to highlight the attitudes and behaviour of hearing characters considered to be more important by the author. Some have been employed as lessons in morality or develop significant themes such as abuse, mistreatment, and working conditions, that would fit with the general

---

[62] Mark Twain, The Adventures of Huckleberry Finn (London: Chatto & Windus, 1884), 233.

[63] Lew Wallace, The Prince of India (1895; Philadelphia: Polyglot Press, 2005), 18.

[64] Sir Henry Rider Haggard, Joan Haste (New York: Longmans, Green, and Co, 1895), 294.

tenor of contemporary literature. Most nineteenth century deaf characters tell us little about the actual experience of being deaf. There are some early indications of features that have come to be associated more with later portrayals, in particular the importance of different forms of communication, deaf education, medical involvement, and the emerging deaf community.

Deaf characters in the twentieth century

The Goldilocks trope seemingly has an appeal for authors as Mrs Fred Reynolds reinstated it when she wrote about Psyche in her novel *In Silence* (1902). Interestingly, this is the first of quite a few twentieth century novels that indicate the supposed "silence" of its deaf characters by including the concept in the title. Psyche is described as a beautiful and romantic rural primitive who, content to remain in idyllic isolation, uses a form of sign language when trying to communicate with hearing people.[65] Her innocent happiness is spoiled after she is adopted and sent to an oralist deaf school where she is taught how to read books, read lips, and speak. She is devastated to come across Khayam's words, "did the Hand of the Potter shake?" leading her to think that she may be God's mistake.[66] Psyche misunderstands spoken words, is gauche and inexperienced, and, unable to follow social cues, is nearly seduced by an unscrupulous man. As a result, Psyche becomes desperate to hear, and rejects the love and acceptance of a decent fellow who happens to be an ear specialist, preferring instead to travel abroad in search of a possible treatment. The therapy fails, and acknowledging that she will always be deaf, Psyche rediscovers her lost state of contentment. Once again, she sacrifices the prospect of romance, but this time to run a home for deaf children. *In Silence* is a fable, a morality tale, in which Psyche preserves her purity after nearly falling into moral disaster through innocence rather than choice. She is another example of an attractive orphan who, apparently rescued through education, actually becomes dissatisfied when exposed to the hearing world. Psyche yearns to become hearing through fear and misunderstanding, but like any Goldilocks character who seems too good to be true, she resists and remains strong. The story is resolved when Psyche realises that she is not imperfectly formed and rediscovers her intrinsic worth. Through renunciation and service, the desire for romance is supplanted by educational mission and the support of the deaf community. It surprises me that deaf commentators have not

---

[65] Mrs Fred Reynolds, In Silence (London: Hurst & Blackett, 1906), 31.
[66] Reynolds, In Silence, 110

discovered Psyche and referred to her as a powerful exemplar of deaf identity.

The central character of Conrad's *Under Western Eyes* (1911) is hearing until the last few pages. Beginning in St Petersburg, the social misfit Razumov is recruited as a Tsarist spy and sent to Geneva. He is attacked by revolutionaries, one of whom deafens him with blows to the sides of his head.[67] Unable to hear a tram, he is knocked down and severely injured. Razumov's eventual deafness is used to exemplify his social isolation by estranging him even further from other people, and causing him to be reliant on the help of another.

Deaf characters are often used to develop specific themes, some of which are rooted in the realistic details of the lives of deaf people. Such characterisations are usually found in books of more recent origin in response to the gathering demands of deaf people for more accurate portrayals and a greater awareness of the varieties of deafness that includes the recognition of a signing community. However, the prototype appears much earlier. *King Silence* (1919) is a very rare book. It is written by Arnold Payne and consists of a collection of chapters that concentrate on multiple deaf characters said to be the "slaves'" of King Silence. Many of the tales and characters are inter-connected. Some of the stories are said to be factual, others are fiction, particularly those invented episodes that include the Gordons. Mr and Mrs Gordon teach at Sinton Down, a deaf school. Mr Gordon is the principal. He is deaf. The Gordons value both oral speech and signing, and are criticised by other deaf educators and doctors who tell parents not to let their children sign. They gradually substitute their pupils' signing with signed English and vocal speech as they believe that the acquisition of English language should be their primary goal. One of their alumni studies at an American deaf university (Gallaudet thinly disguised as "Sicard College") and detailed statistics are given about deafness in the United States.[68] Mr Gordon discusses whether deaf people should marry[69] and refers to hereditary deafness as a "defect" that "may be stamped out". [70] Although these passages highlight some of the views commonly held by Victorian society that were touched on in Chapter One, I was surprised that they are voiced by the deaf principal. Being deaf is believed not to be an inevitable handicap to future prospects, but is nonetheless viewed as a state of loss and imperfection. The situation in the UK is compared with that in

---

[67] Joseph Conrad, Under Western Eyes (New York: Harper & Brothers, 1911), 364-365.
[68] Arnold Hill Payne, King Silence (London: Jarrolds, 1919), 139.
[69] Hill Payne, King Silence, 129
[70] Hill Payne, King Silence, 141.

Germany, where teaching is "pure oral" and the deaf are not permitted to marry.[71] There is an addendum entitled "The case against the German method." The novel extols the value of a mixed form of deaf education, and is dedicated to the author's parents "after devoting your lives to the deaf". Arnold was the hearing son of Benjamin Payne, the deaf principal of the Cambrian Institution for the Deaf and Dumb in Swansea.[72] Even the fictional chapters are largely based on his parents' teaching methods, opinions, and students. The volume provides valuable insight into the lives of deaf people and deaf education, and appears to be written as a vindication of the educational approach adopted by Payne's parents.

By contrast Naomi, the major deaf character in Hall Caine's *The Scapegoat* (1921) is a plot device. She is designed to be the actual embodiment of the central theme. Naomi is unique in being blind, as well as mute and deaf, prompting her father's description of her as a "scapegoat" and "a monument of sin that was not her own".[73] Naomi's parents are Jewish and live in nineteenth century Morocco. Her father acts as administrator to an unpopular ruler and becomes an object of contempt by carrying out his harsh commands. Naomi grows up in silent and darkened isolation, but filled with pity, her father repents of his sin and bitterness and reads the scriptures to his unhearing daughter. There is a trivial attempt at medical intervention but it is prayer that miraculously cures Naomi, allowing her to speak, hear and see in three stages. Naomi is tricked when she tries to save her father from prison, but eventually he is released. The character is fairly well-developed if rather implausible, but remains little more than a romantic plot device that represents her father's wickedness and enables his redemption.

The Goldilocks trope was reiterated by Ann Denman in the character of Mary, an illegitimate and orphaned deaf and dumb gipsy in *A Silent Handicap* (1927). Mary attends a deaf school where two hundred residents are taught skills such as mending shoes and dressmaking. Vocal exercises are preferred to finger spelling which is thought to be "backward".[74] The young residents continue to sign secretly. Sympathetic staff encourage the students to sit examinations as well as to enjoy outings, sports days, and holidays. There is mention of the 1870 Elementary Education Act, Poor

---

[71] Hill Payne, King Silence, 178
[72] Lesley Hulonce, "King Silence – the lives of Victorian deaf children" British Library untold lives blog, accessed 15th September 2014, https://britishlibrary.typepad.co.uk/untoldlives/2014/09/king-silence-the-lives-of-victorian-deaf-children.html
[73] Sir Hall Caine, The Scapegoat (London: William Heinemann, 1921), 60.
[74] Ann Denman, A Silent Handicap (London: Edward Arnold & Co, 1927), 36.

Law officers, officials from the Department of Health, and the National Association of Teachers of the Deaf. Mary is told by the odious Dr Booth that her deafness originates from secondary syphilis, stigmatising both her and her parents. Dr Booth believes deaf people should be segregated, sterilised, and sent to a lethal chamber. Mary is married at the Church for the Deaf in a ceremony conducted by a finger spelling Missioner. Her friend Sally, the daughter of a baronet, is treated with respect when she is admitted to Cambridge University. There is the inclusion of 'Gaudelet' (Gallaudet).[75] The novel's message is stated clearly on the final page, "higher education for the deaf justified itself. Here was proof positive."[76] This is a crusading book that allows deaf characters to overcome themes of prejudice and horrible stereotypes. Like *King Silence*, which preceded *A Silent Handicap* by only eight years, the book proclaims the merits of adequately funded and humane education, and reflects the prevailing educational approach that believed speech was ultimately preferable to signing. It is unfortunate that the overwhelmingly affirming nature of the book should be undermined by a title that reiterates the contemporary perception of deafness as a disability. These examples of Goldilocks characters portray an idealised innocence hidden by the "defect" of deafness. The characters have the quality of a fairy tale princess who is rescued from an undeserved destitution. They are pure, silent, and isolated, resembling an aural virgin who waits for the doctor or educator as Prince Charming, with the happy ending achieved through restoration to the hearing community. Goldilocks characters have little or nothing in common with the reality of deafness, and neither deaf nor hearing readers are likely to have encountered one. Goldilocks characters behave according to the conventions of morality fables and fairy tales, reminding readers that the virtues of patience and forbearance will be recognised and rewarded, and encouraging them to act kindly to those who are less fortunate. Interestingly, all of these iconic idealised characters are penned by British authors, making me wonder whether the concept is peculiar to British literature.

The main role in Florence Riddell's *Silent World* (1934) is also occupied by a character who needs inner strength but doesn't always show it. Christopher is deafened by a gas explosion. His well-intentioned parents believe that the deaf are likely to be neglected, and send Christopher to a residential institution to encourage him to speak orally and to learn how to sign.[77] After nearly being seduced, because his deafness has left Christopher ignorant rather like Psyche in *In Silence*, he marries Dawn who is

---

[75] Denman, A Silent Handicap, 180
[76] Denman, A Silent Handicap, 313
[77] Florence Riddell, Silent World (London: Geoffrey Bles, 1934), 32.

profoundly deaf. Their families hope that the couple will be childless rather than give birth to a deaf baby. Christopher's hearing returns after an operation, and he begins an adulterous liaison with a hearing neighbour only to discover that Dawn is pregnant. When the baby is born, Dawn appears to be the first literary example of a deaf parent rejoicing that her child cannot hear. The presumptions and prejudices of hearing relatives are compared with the wishes and feelings of the deaf characters. Christopher's purity is threatened by coming into contact with, and ultimately re-joining, the hearing world. The character is exposed as imperfect through his deception, rather than being treated with a patronising sentimentality just because he began life as deaf. This book provides another example of a fable through which themes of innocence and ignorance are explored.

The minor character of El Sordo "The Deaf" is found in *For Whom the Bell Tolls* (1940). He is a hardy guerrilla leader fighting in the Spanish Civil War, and his comrades need to shout in one ear in order for him to hear.[78] The deafness is shown to accentuate his natural stubbornness when taking important decisions with little, if any, discussion.

Some deaf characters are composed to reveal the more unpleasant attitudes of their hearing counterparts. These include hostility, prejudice, abuse, and violence. Flora Thompson's *Candleford Green* (1943) is a semi-autobiographical novel set in an Oxfordshire village at the end of the nineteenth century. Luney Joe is a "village idiot in the form of a young man who had been born a deaf mute."[79] He is largely shunned and feared by the villagers because of his deafness and the strange vocal noises that he makes. His isolation and agitation lead to episodes of erratic and misconstrued behaviour. Joe's mother had invented a rough form of signing to communicate with him, but after she died, the young man was committed to the County Asylum. Joe is one of a wide range of colourful and eccentric characters shown to populate the village, but his portrayal confirms how easily hearing people may assume the worst by misunderstanding the consequences of being deaf.

The main character of Caron McCuller's *The Heart is a Lonely Hunter* (1943) is a vital constant around which the hearing characters revolve. John Singer is a deaf silver engraver living in a mill town in Georgia. The story concerns the effect his silent "listening" acceptance has on the people he encounters. These include his only true friend Antonapoulos, an unpleasant deaf man who is committed to an asylum by his cousin; a taciturn bar owner who closely observes his customers including Singer; a drunk union

---

[78] Ernest Hemingway, For Whom the Bell Tolls (1940 Thorndike, Maine: GK Hall & Co, 1994), 215.

[79] Flora Thompson, Candleford Green (Oxford: Oxford University Press, 1943), 49.

organiser; the black physician civil rights activist Dr Copland; and an adolescent girl whose family runs the boarding house in which the deaf man lives. Singer does not speak and carries a card that reads,

> I am a deaf-mute, but I read the lips and understand what is said to me. Please do not shout.[80]

Singer has been deaf since infancy, and grew up in an institution where he learned to sign. He is a non-judgemental figure to whom people go with their problems and share their future plans. Safe from interruptions or questions, the cathartic one-sided conversations leave individuals such as Dr Copland changed, so that visiting Singer "blunted the feeling of loneliness in him".[81] He is bestowed with a mystic quality by his hearing friends, so that rumours spread about his origins and wisdom, allowing each of them to describe Singer "as he wished him to be."[82] After Antonapoulos dies, Singer shoots himself, an event that catalyses his friends to re-evaluate their lives and act on the ideas they shared with him. The book's title infers the isolation of the characters who are seeking fulfilment. Singer is a prime example of a ficelle through whom we can explore the innermost thoughts and wishes of the major hearing characters. He is a well-developed character who exists as much more than just a plot prop. A deaf reviewer states Singer "does not inspire admiration" and "instead brings despair",[83] perhaps because deaf characters are often used to symbolise isolation, and Singer appears to be detached even when he is with his hearing acquaintances. Nonetheless, there is a contented acquiescence seen in Singer's silence and independence and he has little interaction with deaf people other than Antonapoulos. Paradoxically it is the hearing characters that are shown to be lonely and estranged from their families, community, and one another.

The next example is radically different. In *The Mating Season* (1944), P.G. Wodehouse relates Wooster's embarrassment when telling an unfortunate anecdote about two deaf men to a group of elderly aunts. It falls flat as one of the aunts relies on a hearing trumpet and needs the joke carefully explaining.[84] Although she is treated kindly and with great respect,

---

[80] Carson McCuller, The Heart is a Lonely Hunter (1943; London: Penguin Books Ltd, 1981), 52.

[81] McCuller, The Heart is a Lonely Hunter, 133

[82] McCuller, The Heart is a Lonely Hunter, 197

[83] Trent Batson and Eugene Bergman (eds), Angels and Outcasts, 138

[84] P.G. Wodehouse, The Mating Season (1944; London: Evergreen Publishers plc, 2001), 57-58.

the episode reveals a frequently held readiness to regard deaf people as an easy source of humour for the hearing.

Deaf characters are also used as objects of misplaced anger. This can be found in Ivy Compton Burnett's novel *Manservant and Maidservant* (1947). It is set before the First World War, with Sarah as one of the main characters. She is intelligent and beautiful, able to speak and can read lips. Sarah's father is a violent bully who accuses her of obstinacy and manipulation rather than acknowledging her difficulties in understanding speech.[85] The book presents themes of prejudice and hopeful expectations, cleverly contrasting Sarah's obvious deafness with the hidden shame of a family friend's illiteracy.

A deaf character develops a parallel between the loss of hearing and the loss of vision in *The Day is Ours* (1947) by Hilda Lewis. The book starts with a dedication to Irene Ewing "She makes the deaf to hear, the dumb to speak."[86] Mrs Ewing was a popular British pioneer in audiology and deaf education in the early twentieth century.[87] As might be expected from such a beginning, the book makes speech the prominent goal of deaf education. Tamsie is a young girl who is mistreated by her mother and feels isolated because of her deafness. She attends a deaf school and is taught how to vocalise by copying lip patterns and sensing vibrations. Tamsie then studies at art college and finds satisfaction in working at a children's hospital during the Blitz. There she meets and falls in love with Andrew, a young man who has developed hysterical blindness. This interesting plot device permits a comparison between the experiences of deafness and blindness. The couple explore their histories of loneliness, self-pity, and rejection, as well as their fear about possibly having a deaf child. The book provides a very sentimental story that treats deafness as a disability, discusses the impact of deafness on the family, and mentions in passing the value of belonging to the deaf community. It shows that the oralist approach to deaf education was still very much in vogue in the mid-twentieth century.

Holden Caulfield fantasises briefly about pretending to be a "deaf-mute" in *The Catcher in the Rye* (1951).

If anybody wanted to tell me something, they'd have to write it on a piece of paper and shove it over to me. They'd get bored as hell doing that after a

---

[85] Ivy Compton Burnett, Manservant and Maidservant (London: Victor Gollancz, 1947), 45.

[86] Hilda Lewis, The Day is Ours (London: Jarrolds, 1947).

[87] Laura Dawes. "The Ewings and paediatric audiology". ENT and Audiology News, March 3, 2021. https://www.entandaudiologynews.com/features/ent-features/post/the-ewings-and-paediatric-audiology.

while, and then I'd be through with having conversations for the rest of my life.[88]

His imagination shows how much he wants to escape from being pressurised by other people.

Mervyn Peake inserted a deaf cook into his comic fantasy novel *Mr Pye* (1953). Ka-Ka is completely deaf, blind in one eye, and has a cleft palate.[89] She is shown to sign but exists only as an object of fun.

Nest-egg for the Baron (1954) was written under the pseudonym Anthony Martin by the author better known as John Creasey. Deaf, beautiful, blonde Miranda experiences a psychosomatic loss of speech and hearing. Both return after the shock of witnessing a shooting.[90] In this crime novel Miranda is repeatedly accused of being "truly dumb",[91] leading to the demeaning title of the 1961 re-issue *Deaf, Dumb and Blonde*. She provides a plot device as a possible suspect who is unable to prove her innocence.

Detective fiction may also include deaf characters with superb lip-reading skills that make them valuable plot devices. I have termed them "Gifted" as the ability is usually exaggerated well beyond the limits of what is actually possible. A competent lip-reader without residual hearing can only understand thirty per cent of a conversation.[92] Such characters appear frequently enough for a deaf commentator to suggest the creation of a sub-genre "who-heard-it" as opposed to "whodunit". He looks forward to the development of a deaf villain and a deaf detective to broaden the range of depictions.[93] Since we are describing deaf characters who read lips, it would be more accurate to label the category "who-saw-it" rather than "who-heard-it." The first example is found in Patricia Wentworth's intriguingly entitled *The Listening Eye* (1957), in which Patricia Payne, deafened from a bomb blast, understands part of a private conversation by reading the lips of the speakers from a distance. Patricia informs a renowned amateur detective that a robbery and murder are planned,[94] but is then killed in a convenient road accident, leaving the sleuth to reconstruct the conversation.

---

[88] J.D. Salinger, The Catcher in the Rye (1951; Harmondsworth: Penguin, 1958), Loc 3107, Kindle.

[89] Mervyn Peake, Mr. Pye (1953; Harmondsworth: Penguin, 1972), 26.

[90] Anthony Martin, Nest-egg for the Baron (London: Hodder & Stoughton, 1954), 177.

[91] Anthony Martin, Nest-egg for the Baron, 19

[92] Neil Baumann, "Speechreading (Lip-Reading)", Center for Hearing Loss Help, December 2011, revised August, 2020).
http://hearinglosshelp.com/blog/speechreading-lip-reading/.

[93] Philip Murphy, "Whodunit? Who heard it?" SHHH Journal, 14 (3), 1993: 5-6.

[94] Patricia Wentworth, The Listening Eye (London: Hodder & Stoughton, 1957), 31.

Doreen's mother in Alan Sillitoe's *Saturday Night and Sunday Morning* (1958) is a very minor character having little effect on the outcome of the novel. Doreen is shown to shout at her deaf mother,[95] and she and her boyfriend are able to enjoy amorous encounters downstairs knowing that she is unable to hear them from her bedroom.

A very different type of deaf character is found in Prudence Andrew's *Ordeal by Silence* (1961), a historical novel set in the early Middle Ages. We follow the life of Philip of Evesham through witness testimonies, as a Cardinal is appointed to determine whether the deaf and dumb man is worthy of being canonised.[96] Philip's deafness and silence adds to the aura of his personal holiness.

The main protagonist in the second of three inter-related sections of William Faulkner's *The Mansion* (1962) is a strong deaf woman. Linda Kohl Snopes is an exotic and troubling personality for a small town in Mississippi. She lost her hearing in an explosion when volunteering as an ambulance driver in the Spanish Civil War. Linda is not only known as a war hero, she is also the daughter of the local racist banker, widow of a Jewish sculptor, mistress of a wealthy lawyer, and suspected of being a communist. Linda carries a pad and pen for people to write on and is able to speak but with a distorted sound. Considered by herself and others to be an outsider, Linda is isolated from people by her deafness and from social conventions by choice. She is aptly described as "the bride of quietude and silence inviolate in the isolation of unhearing".[97] Linda wants to improve the level of education for local black families but misses the inter-personal cues that signify resistance to her well-intentioned strategies. After moving to California during the Second World War to work on aircraft engines, Linda returns to the family home and is complicit in the escape of her father's murderer. Like Singer, Linda stands as a pivot at the centre of the story, with the words and actions of the hearing characters moving around her. She supplies a constant source of unmoved principle against which others act and react, her deafness and temperament keeping her aloof from small town society and family intrigues.

Casting a deaf character in the main role of a book is a means of amplifying particular themes or attributes the author wants to develop. For example, the theme of obstinacy is revealed in Elisabeth Ayrton's first-person narrative *The Cretan* (1963). The American version of the book is known as *Silence in Crete*. Arkas was deafened by an explosion during the

---

[95] Alan Sillitoe, Saturday night and Sunday morning (1958; London: Panther Books, Granada Publishing Ltd, 1985), 245.

[96] Prudence Andrew, Ordeal by Silence (London: Hutchinson, 1961), 35.

[97] William Faulkner The Mansion (1961; London: The Reprint Society, 1962), 214.

War and believes people are unwilling to communicate with somebody who cannot hear. Although he continues to speak easily, Arkas lacks confidence in his ability to read lips, and so disguises his deafness at business meetings by asking his hearing sister to write down all the details.[98] Arkas manages the family estate very well but is consumed with anger at being deaf and refuses other forms of help. His repressed rage and impulsive nature allow Arkas to be misled by criminals. He is imprisoned, and after an inner struggle, overcomes his irritation, depression, and pride. Following his release, Arkas reluctantly learns to read lips and reconciles himself with the idea of living as a deaf person in a hearing world. It is interesting to speculate whether the inclusion of the word "Cretan" in the English title is a word-play on "cretin" as other characters in the book assume that deaf people, including Arkas, are stupid. In a letter to the editor of *The Quiet Ear* the author wrote that she wanted to base the book around a hero-figure with a disability. Settling on the idea of a deaf character, she then researched deafness. Ayrton believed that an angry man in the circumstances experienced by the main character would feel "an even greater despair than the deaf almost always feel," and created Arkas whose "helpless rage" was so great he refused help.[99] Arkas is shown to overcome the obstacles set before him, but first passes through a period of suffering of his own making.

Margaret Kennedy's *Not in the Calendar* (1964) is the story of a friendship between a wealthy hearing girl Myra, and Wynn, the profoundly deaf daughter of one of the servants. Myra's father, Lord Seddon, adopts Wynn. There is a note of thanks at the beginning of the book for the advice given to the author by the Librarian to the Royal National Institute for the Deaf (RNID).[100] Wynn is taught to read lips and sign by a member of the Seddon family. She learns to speak orally with fluency. The plot spans several decades around the turn of the century during which Wynn becomes a talented artist and inherits Myra's estate. The family's home becomes a pre-school for deaf children. Wynn is honoured by the King for her services to art and to deaf children. There is an element of Wynn being compensated for her deafness by achieving an extraordinary level of artistic ability. American deaf education is mentioned and the use of "Oracles", electric hearing aids that were brought from the US to the UK in the 1940s.[101] Kennedy evidently took care to be informed about the salient features of deafness and deaf history that are incorporated into the story. The theme of

---

[98] Elisabeth Ayrton, The Cretan (London: Hodder and Stoughton, 1963), 8.
[99] Grant, The Quiet Ear, 151
[100] Now known as the Royal Institute for Deaf People
[101]Margaret Kennedy, Not in the Calendar (London: MacMillan & Co, 1964), 239.

friendship, that remains the focus of the book, is permeated with this information.

Elizabeth Bowen's eponymous main character *Eva Trout* (1965) has a "deaf mute" son Jeremy.[102] Relatives and friends find him unsettling and wonder what he is thinking. Eva uses Jeremy as an excuse to limit her social obligations, and comments made about him by hearing characters tell the reader about their attitudes and values. The boy consistently refuses treatment until he is pressured to receive tutoring in oral speech from a French doctor. Jeremy can read lips and enjoys watching silent films. He is content to keep everything in his life the same. The story ends at Victoria Station when Eva pretends to be married and Jeremy shoots her with the faux groom's gun. There is an underlying theme in the book of incomplete communication with many important issues partially discussed or left unsaid. Jeremy's silence helps to bring this into focus.

In This Sign (1970) by Joanne Greenberg is a very different type of book. Two of the main characters are completely deaf. The novel is an epic story of Abel and Janice Ryder's family that spans four generations starting at the end of the nineteen twenties. The story begins with the newly married couple appearing in court. Abel had failed to understand the contract when he bought a car due to his poor standard of reading. The sign language interpreter brought into the court is prejudiced against them because of their low level of education and poverty. This event, and the ongoing repayments of the debt and the fine imposed by the court, shapes both their future and their perception of the hearing world. Abel and Janice both had a deaf parent, and both attended deaf school where they were taught the rudiments of vocal speech. Abel discovered illicit signing and "was made free in a language learned in spite of watchful teachers".[103] The school offered Abel an apprenticeship in printing and Janice another in cap making. After leaving school, they discovered that hearing people didn't care about them and they were sometimes called "freaks" and "dummies". When Janice discovers she is pregnant, Abel worries that a hearing baby may eventually leave them. They have a daughter, Margaret, who is hearing. Margaret attends a mainstream school, but her progress is inhibited by having to translate for her mother at the clinic, and having learned poor verbal grammar from her parents. Margaret's younger brother Bradley dies after falling down the stairs. She is horrified by the prospect of helping her parents choose a coffin. Margaret becomes angry and frustrated and the reader is given insights into the difficulties of a child growing up with deaf

---

[102] Elizabeth Bowen, Eva Trout (New York: Alfred A Knopf, 1968), 165.
[103] Joanne Greenberg, In This Sign (1970; New York: Henry Holt and Company, 1984), 10.

parents. Abel and Janice become more prosperous and buy a new house. Margaret marries a hearing man. At the wedding breakfast Abel asks Margaret to translate his speech in which he declares,

> When the hearing child leaves the House of the Deaf, their mouths are also taken away from them and their ears are taken away, and the child also, whom they love.'[104]

Janice burns her arm on the coffee pot despite a warning from Margaret's new mother-in-law who is stunned to realise the extent of Janice's deafness and her silent existence. Margaret eventually has a son who shocks his mother by referring to his grandparents as "the deafies". Gallaudet is spoken of as being rather elite, and the family attend a deaf church where Abel and Janice are impressed by the elegant signing. When Janice finally retires, the interpreter shockingly tells her that "Nothing has changed for the Deaf since long before you were born."[105] After years of repressed rage and frustration, Margaret proclaims 'I am the afflicted'.[106] Margaret is embarrassed and her parents confused when, having struggled for decades to escape the effects of their early poverty, Margaret's son abandons his college course to identify with poor black farmers in the South. The book ends with Margaret and her parents united by laughing at the bitter irony. The book documents years of debt, misunderstanding, and hard work, against the backdrop of momentous changes in American society. Deafness is presented as creating a constant barrier for the Ryders. Signing has given them their only source of hope, as it enables them to communicate with each other, their hearing daughter and grandson, and the deaf community. The novel presents a deaf family as the main characters, describing their existence in great detail with sensitivity rather than sentimentality. The Ryders are presented as the focal point of prejudice and poverty that in turn illuminates the wider historical and social setting. The narrative uncovers their emotions and demonstrates for the first time the specific pressures and continuing despair of being a Child of Deaf Adults (CODA). This ground-breaking book was described by a deaf reviewer as an "unflinching and compassionate account of the world of the deaf"'.[107]

The Listening Silence (1970) is a romantic tale written by Helen Lillie, a former Second World War intelligence officer. The main character,

---

[104] Joanne Greenberg, In This Sign, 176
[105] Joanne Greenberg, In This Sign, 239
[106] Joanne Greenberg, In This Sign, 258
[107] Loraine J Pietro," Reviewed Work: In This Sign," American Annals of the Deaf, No.1 (February 1971): 15-17.

Margaret Schuyler nee Drummond, returns to Scotland following the drowning of her sister. Schuyler is diagnosed with otosclerosis and is offered surgery.[108] There is a strong history of deafness in the Drummond family, making her fearful that she will not be able to marry a politician whom she has always loved. Margaret's uncle uses an ancient hearing aid with a head piece and batteries, and a cousin reads lips so well that Margaret does not realise she is deaf. The story is resolved when Margaret's lover accepts her as she is, but she chooses to have an operation to improve her hearing anyway. Margaret's family history is the most potent theme of the book. This includes the inherited deafness that provides impetus to the story, and includes the possibility that her sister was unable to hear the mill race in which she drowned.

Dinah is a minor deaf character in C.P. Snow's *Last Things* (1970) whom Maurice is planning to marry. Dinah's deafness is believed by some of his family to have made her "backward" and isolated as a child. She is described as having a rather puzzled look when people are speaking around her, and those who want to talk to her need to shout to make themselves understood. After Maurice's relatives have been introduced to Dinah for the first time, one asks "Is that a real marriage?"[109] The prejudice against her continues so that when a baby is born to the couple, the family are concerned as to whether or not the child will be deaf.

The Gifted trope of another superb lip-reader being put at risk is repeated in Scott Corbett's *Dead Before Docking* (1972). The young boy, Jeff Wister, boards a freighter bound from New York to Callao to join his father. He has a twenty per cent hearing loss in one ear following an operation and has worked hard to master lip-reading. Before the boat sails, the young lad slips ashore and witnesses an unknown man saying "he'll be dead before they reach port".[110] Jeff is horrified to see the same man on the ship talking to one of the passengers, and tries to discover the identities of both the intended victim and the assassin. Jeff nearly becomes a victim himself, but the assassin is caught and the plot exposed. I assume the book is intended for older children or teenagers as it consists of one hundred and thirty-four pages with twelve illustrations. The limitations of lip-reading are described but Jeff knows he can discover information from watching the body language of the passengers. A deaf community is recognised by mention of a deaf school and a passenger having worked with deaf children. There is a suggestion of compensatory heightened senses when Jeff identifies the

---

[108] Helen Lillie, The Listening Silence (London: Arrow Books, 1970), 17.

[109] CP Snow, Last Things (1970 Harmondsworth: Penguin Books, 1972), 265.

[110] Scott Corbett, Dead Before Docking (Boston: An Atlantic Monthly Press Book. Little, Brown & Co, 1972), 21.

lingering smell of a particular tobacco. The relatively detailed account of Jeff's experience is explained by the book's dedication "To Dr Francis B Sargent MD with appreciation for his help". Dr Sargent is known to have established a language and speech centre for deaf children in Rhode Island where the author lived.[111]

Deafness exaggerates the rudeness, dogged certainty, and alienation, of Sampson Trehune, the main character in *The Acupuncture Murders* (1973), a crime novel by Dwight Steward. Trehune is a short-tempered book dealer who lost all his hearing as a boy due to scarlet fever.[112] He speaks with a very loud voice, communicates by signing and reading lips, and wears a redundant hearing aid to emphasise his deafness. Trehune reluctantly allows a renowned acupuncturist an attempt to treat his deafness. Afterwards his hearing seems to return fleetingly. A fellow patient is murdered, and Trehune investigates. Throughout the book, he is shown to have a low opinion of what he terms "the Hearers", mainly because he feels angry, marginalised, and misunderstood. His friend Dr Abel shares the misconceptions of many Hearers by asking whether Trehune wants to be "normal" again,[113] and asserts that "cases of hysterical deafness are not uncommon".[114] Trehune later expresses the exasperation of many deaf people by arguing,

> Aristotle would have labelled me mentally defective and dropped me in a river…Saint Augustine would damn me to hell because, he said, 'knowledge of God comes only through hearing.' [115]

Trehune is not very representative of deaf people in that he is rich and has no deaf friends. The character's bad temper and persistent grumpiness are exacerbated by a deaf man's irritation with all the Hearers. The frontispiece states that the author researched at the National Theatre of the Deaf. The preface explains the limitations of lip-reading, as well as the practice of signing. Despite this, Trehune is given a remarkable facility to read lips, but this skill is not used to "over-see" a conversation.

In Catherine Cookson's *The Mallen Girl* (1973) we learn little of the title character's experience of deafness other than her irritation with sign language. Barbara is young and beautiful and progressively loses her

---

[111] "About Sargent", The Sargent Center, accessed n/d, https://www.sargentcenter.org/about_sargent.
[112] Dwight Steward, The Acupuncture Murders (1973; Harmondsworth: Penguin Books, 1977), 30.
[113] Steward, The Acupuncture Murders, 17
[114] Steward, The Acupuncture Murders, 10
[115] Steward, The Acupuncture Murders, 110

hearing but retains vocal pitch and exaggerated lip movements. She reflects the ignorant views of her hearing family by perceiving deafness as an embarrassing "disease".[116] Barbara's deafness is not as important to the plot as the fact of her illegitimate birth. There is mention of Abbe de L'Epee, the pioneering educator of the deaf.

Sharpe's elderly Chaplain in *Porterhouse Blue* (1974) is another minor character whose deafness is exploited for amusement. The Chaplain is often insulted without his knowledge, and he invites a student to shout at him through a loudhailer.[117]

Cookson described another eponymous "deaf and dumb" character in *Our John Willie* (1977). He is considered by many of his hearing counterparts to be "an idiot"[118] and is often the focus of their prejudice, anger and abuse. John Willie is one of two main figures in the book and provides his hearing brother with an object of care and protection.

Alison Rowland's novel *Light My Candle* (1977) revolves around the successful writer Rex who was deafened as a result of shell-shock. He is aware of his limitations and not defined by them. Rex describes his embarrassment at misunderstanding the words of people who then think him stupid. A friend complains,

> if he were blind he would get all of everybody's sympathy…But the deaf!
> Are they not completely overlooked and ignored? [119]

Creating Rex as deaf reveals more of his strength as he overcomes a variety of obstacles and opposition.

In the Inspector Morse mystery, *The Silent World of Nicholas Quinn* (1978), Colin Dexter sets Quinn up as a Gifted character, by writing that the deaf historian "could lip-read so brilliantly" he uncovers the crooked scheme of an academic colleague.[120] He wears a hearing aid and cannot use the telephone properly. Quinn is shown to experience prejudice and exclusion by hearing colleagues. Unfortunately, the staggering lip-reading skills lead to Quinn's murder. Colin Dexter is well-known to be deafened, and his familiarity with hearing aids is apparent from the descriptions of Quinn's struggles with them.

---

[116] Catherine Cookson, The Mallen Girl (Geneva: Edito-Service S.A, 1973), 22-23.

[117] Tom Sharpe, Porterhouse *Blue* (1974; London: Arrow Books, 2002), 72.

[118] Catherine, Cookson, Our John Willie (London: George Prior, 1977), 6.

[119] Alison Rowland, Light My Candle (Ilfracombe: Arthur H Stockwood Ltd, 1977), 37

[120] Colin Dexter, The Silent World of Nicholas Quinn (London: Pan, 1978), 170.

Another crime novel, *Gorky Park* (1981), has an elderly lady who is classed as disabled, having lost her hearing in the artillery during the War. Her job in the park is playing records at the skating rink. Because she is deaf, she plays them very loud, allowing the gunshots of a murder to pass unnoticed.[121]

Annabel Dexter created an international opera singer who gradually loses her hearing in *Kilcaraig* (1982).[122] Isabella is a minor character forced to retire because of painful tinnitus. She is sensitively described as coping with the effects of her deafness and the problems associated with hearing aids, but it is the impact of her withdrawal from public life on the hearing characters that matters most.

Sally Barnes is the main character of Marie Joseph's *The Listening Silence* (1983) set during the Second World War. Sally is nearly killed by a van she cannot hear and threatened with sexual assault because the assailant knows she cannot scream. The main point of including Sally in the book, however, is her ability to read lips. This becomes a valuable attribute when David, her pilot boyfriend, loses the ability to speak after a flying accident.[123] The equality in relationship that is then established between David and Sally is criticised as being achievable only by disabling the main hearing character rather than through empathy and understanding.[124]

Mme de Bonneil is described as being "stone deaf" in Brookner's *Hotel du Lac* (1984).[125] She is a dignified elderly lady living in the Swiss hotel who is offered as an object of curiosity and treated solicitously by the hearing characters. Madame's stoic acceptance of her unchanging situation is used to magnify the contrasting internal turmoil of the main hearing character forced to choose between unsatisfactory options.

The only example of an apparently deaf villain that I can find in detective fiction appears in Ed McBain's *87th Precinct* series. A number of the books in the set involve a serial killer known as the Deaf Man who taunts the police. For instance, in *Eight Black Horses* (1985) the detectives receive a letter with a picture of an ear crossed through and believe this is a self-disclosed clue to the murderer's identity.[126] He is described by witnesses as wearing a hearing aid and uses pseudonyms based on the translation of "deaf

---

[121] Martin Cruz Smith, Gorky Park (1981; London: Pan, 1996), 47.

[122] Annabel Dexter, Kilcaraig (London: Heinemann, 1982).

[123] Marie Joseph, The Listening Silence (London: Hutchinson, 1983), 14.

[124] Gregory, "Deafness in fiction", 294-300

[125] Anita Brookner, Hotel du Lac (1984 New York: E.P. Dutton, 1986), 71.

[126] Ed McBain, Eight Black Horses (Seattle: Thomas & Mercer, 1985) Loc 114, Kindle.

man" in several languages.[127] Whether the assassin is actually deaf is a subject of debate among the investigators. His character provides no information regarding what it is like to be deaf. However, there is a truly deaf character in the book. Detective Carella, the Deaf Man's nemesis, has an intelligent and strong-willed "deaf-mute" wife. Although she plays a minor role, we learn how she communicates easily with her husband by signing.[128] There is no trace of sentimentality in the portrayal of the deaf psychopath or Carella's wife. It seems to me that casting the representative of a minority in the role of a villain is an important step that signifies a measure of acceptance by the general public.

The last of the twentieth century examples is the first book to display aspects of a more contemporary signing identity and deaf culture. The eponymous main character is the murder victim in Elizabeth George's thriller *For the Sake of Elena* (1992). Elena is a student at Cambridge University, and is able to sign, read lips, and speak. Elena's parents didn't want her to be deaf and forbade her from signing at home. However, she chooses to identify with a signing deaf culture and as a result, feels as if she was "caught between two worlds…she wasn't brought up to fit completely into either".[129] Elena believed deafness to be "a culture in itself rather than a handicap",[130] as opposed to her parents who agonised over the possible deafness of Elena's unborn child. Issues of deaf culture and conflict between the hearing and non-hearing worlds are well described with Elena's deaf ex-boyfriend wanting hearing people to "see us as people as good as they are."[131] George writes at length about deaf language, deaf culture, and deaf societies including the Deaf Students' Union. She also includes many recent and valuable forms of assistance for deaf people that include a visual cell phone which would have been unusual at the time of writing, signed translations available in lectures, and the use of a BSL interpreter in police interviews. The detail and approach of the book suggest a level of research and understanding that seeks to inform rather than patronise.

Many of the deaf characters found in twentieth century novels remain peripheral to the plot, and are devices and props that are used to develop themes or express the natures of the hearing characters. There are an increasing number of major deaf characters, many of which include details of deaf schools and medical treatment, aspects that became more prominent in a century that increasingly valued the provision of education and health

---

[127] McBain, Eight Black Horses, Loc 836, Kindle.
[128] McBain, Eight Black Horses, Loc 1292, Kindle.
[129] Elizabeth George, For the Sake of Elena, (London: Bantam Press, 1992), 74.
[130] George, For the Sake of Elena, 73
[131] George, For the Sake of Elena, 243

care. As detective fiction grew in popularity, there are examples of deaf characters appearing in the genre, some of them presented as Gifted because of their superb lip-reading skills. There is evidence of a rising awareness and interest in the existence of deaf communities that extend beyond educational establishments, culminating in the descriptions given in *For the Sake of Elena*. As we continue into the twenty-first century, these features become more strongly developed, with much more detail included in novels about the deaf experience, sign language, and deaf identity.

Deaf characters in the twenty-first century

The first example provides more information about living with hearing aids than any other book. *Deaf Sentence* (2008) concerns the exploits of a Professor of English Literature who loses his hearing late in life. It is a humorous story, as implied by the title, and is based on the author's own experiences of becoming deaf. Professor Bates misconstrues what is said by colleagues at cocktail parties, fiddles with the awkward batteries that need replacing in his hearing aids, and becomes increasingly isolated. He sees himself as "a damper on every party, a dud at every dinner table"[132] Lodge avoids the obvious pitfalls of making fun out of deafness by creating humour and pathos out of real-life occurrences familiar to anyone who use hearing aids. Deaf people have told me that they find the book to be very funny, implying that it is not being the source of humour they consider to be objectionable, but the way the humour is portrayed.

The theme of deaf community is clearly expressed in *Silent Fear* (2018) from New Zealand authors Lance and James Morcan. This novel is a whodunit set almost entirely in a fictional deaf university in London. The classic closed environment of the genre is provided by a total lockdown of students and staff inside the building when a potentially fatal viral infection is discovered. This is remarkably prescient considering that it was published over a year before the Covid outbreak, although the methods of controlling it, with soldiers who operate a shoot to kill policy and plastic sheeting sealing off the building, owe more to sensational films than the rather mundane reality we actually experienced during the pandemic. The main protagonist is police detective Valerie Crowther, a CODA fluent in BSL. The plot develops from Crowther's perspective. The character combines the ability to investigate the crimes professionally with a knowledge of signing that enables her to conduct interviews with the deaf students and staff. There is frequent mention of features associated with deaf people living in

---

[132] David Lodge, Deaf Sentence (London: Penguin Books, 2008), 160.

community, the unnaturally quiet common room filled with lots of signers, expensive lighting to facilitate signed conversations, organisations familiar to deaf people such as SignHealth, and deaf students praying together in BSL. Some characters wear hearing aids, many speak, and the majority are able to read lips and communicate in a variety of national sign languages. This is the first novel to include people who wear cochlear implants. The killer murders five people by exploiting the fact that they are unable to hear his approach and people nearby cannot hear the victims scream. He is ultimately revealed to have adopted the identity of his deceased twin brother and pretended to be deaf in order to access the university and secure a sizeable legacy. There are some interesting observations including a student who declares that cochlear implants are 'highly political and traitorous',[133] and that for deaf people going blind would be the "final cruelty".[134] The book starts with a dedication to "the many millions of deaf people around the world", and a statement that it was inspired by "the murders of deaf students at Gallaudet University." There was indeed a murder at Gallaudet in 1980, and another two in the early 2000's, but the events are entirely unrelated to the plot. The authors acknowledge the help of Brent McPherson, "a member of the deaf community", who describes the book as "an important addition to the dearth of literature that exists about Deaf people and Deaf culture."[135] I agree with both points. It is rare that hearing authors relate the dynamics within the deaf community quite so clearly. I particularly approve of the inclusion of a CODA and the variety of sign languages from different countries. The deaf students and staff are treated as ordinary people who happen to be deaf, and are allowed to express emotions, endure personality clashes, and erupt into arguments. There is no hint of patronising sentimentality.

The notion of writing about a deaf community is taken further by Nell Pattison in her first book *The Silent House* (2020). Relatively few authors that have written about deaf characters are themselves deaf, making Pattison, who became deaf as an adult, an exception. Paige Northwood, the main character, is a CODA, and a BSL interpreter. She is asked to assist with a murder inquiry after the daughter of deaf parents is found dead. The book recounts experiences familiar to many deaf people, including being surrounded by "hearing people making demands she didn't understand

---

[133] Lance and James Morcan, Silent Fear (Bay of Plenty NZ; Sterling Gate Books, 2018), Loc 207 Kindle.
[134] Morcan and Morcan, Silent Fear, Loc 4758 Kindle
[135] Morcan and Morcan, Silent Fear, Loc 12682 Kindle

because they weren't using her language",[136] the frequent riposte 'I'm deaf, not stupid',[137] and exclusion by hearing people from conversations that have a direct impact on the deaf individual.[138] Set almost entirely within the deaf community of a small northern town, there is mention of hearing aids, a school for the deaf, communication support workers, a deaf football team, and video calls used to chat in BSL. A wide range of communication by deaf characters is used including signing and speech, and the limitations of lip-reading are indicated.[139] The story stresses the crucial role of the deaf club within the local deaf community. The reader is told that being deaf is

> …a cultural identity, not simply a term for hearing loss. You can have full hearing and still be considered part of the Deaf community."[140]

An added dimension to the story is the insight into the work of a BSL translator. Northwood stresses the need for privacy, especially within a closed enquiring community and the value of observing facial expression and body language to accurately interpret what is being signed.[141] She attempts to translate the "angry sarcasm" of a deaf subject's body language with her tone of voice,[142] and does not want to be more specific without using the words of the questioner.[143] Northwood explains that

> BSL has a very different grammatical structure from English, and the meaning of a sign can change depending on how it's signed or the facial expression used.[144]

Creating the main character as a BSL interpreter is an interesting and successful plot device as she already knows most of the people questioned by the Police through deaf club, and is privy to the details of the investigations through translating the interviews. The convention of printing signed speech in italics and without speech marks distinguishes it from verbal speech. There is mention of violence, threats, drugs, criminality, and

---

[136] Nell Pattison, The Silent House (London: Avon; Harper Collins Publishers Ltd, 2020), Loc 134, Kindle.
[137] Pattison, The Silent House, Loc 214, Kindle
[138] Pattison, The Silent House, Loc 689, Kindle
[139] Pattison, The Silent House, Loc 1498, Kindle
[140] Pattison, The Silent House, Loc 341, Kindle
[141] Pattison, The Silent House, Loc 248, Kindle
[142] Pattison, The Silent House, Loc 413, Kindle
[143] Pattison, The Silent House, Loc 595, Kindle
[144] Pattison, The Silent House, Loc 990, Kindle

social problems within the deaf community that has a strong sense of its own identity.

Pattison continued the Paige Northwood series with *Silent Night* (2020). The headteacher of a residential Deaf School is murdered during a trip away. Five deaf teenagers are snowed in and one is missing. Paige Northwood is brought in to interpret for the Police. Northwood educates officers drafted in for the investigation by indicating the wide variety of communication methods used by deaf people. She outlines how to work best with BSL interpreters, pointing out the similarities and differences between their previous experience cooperating with interpreters of spoken foreign languages.[145] Information is given about the arrangements of a deaf school, with much written about the need for safeguarding, the vulnerability of deaf students, and the potential for manipulation. The importance of mobile phone use by deaf students is stressed. The book is set almost exclusively within a relatively closed deaf world and the majority of characters are deaf. The strengths and failings of students and staff are observed without any trace of sentimentality. The book includes a brief biography of the author that states she became a teacher and specialised in deaf education. Pattison lost hearing in her twenties, and now wears hearing aids.[146] Her professional experience in deaf education illuminates the entire book, not only in details of the situations described, but in attitude and approach.

The Northwood series was interrupted briefly when Pattison wrote *Hide* (2021). The thriller's main deaf character is Emily who has worn cochlear implants since being deafened by childhood meningitis.[147] Emily's sister Lauren works at a nature reserve and organises a night visit for a group that includes Emily. Lauren blames her sister for their mother's inability to cope. This led to the girls being forced into foster care. Lauren also resents the wealth and success that Emily enjoys after she develops an app for deaf people. A member of the group is shot and killed in a hide. The survivors split up and attempt to reach the reserve's headquarters through treacherous marsh and woods while the weather is worsening. Emily loses one of her implants and is afraid to switch on a torch to read lips. Emily is terrified at being abandoned, and because she cannot hear, does not know whether the murderer is close by in the darkness. Emily becomes increasingly reliant on other senses, so that she feels the vibration of a train, and stays alert to movement in her peripheral vision. The limitations of cochlear implants are

---

[145] Nell Pattison, Silent Night (London: Avon; Harper Collins Publishers Ltd, 2020), Loc 729, Kindle.

[146] Pattison, Silent Night, Loc 4794, Kindle

[147] Nell Pattison, Hide (London: Avon; Harper Collins Publishers Ltd, 2021), Loc 128, Kindle.

explained as well as technical procedures such as connecting the processor to a mobile phone via Bluetooth.[148] Emily has been made to feel guilty throughout her life, culminating in the plea to her sister "to forgive me for being deaf."[149] Emily's character is well constructed and realistic. She is shown to have flaws and make mistakes. Hearing characters are shown to react to Emily's personality, not just to the fact of her being deaf. Emily's deafness is used very well to accentuate her fear of hiding in the darkness. In effect the character becomes temporarily bereft of both sound and sight.

Pattison then returned to Paige Northwood and published, what is at the current time the third and last of the series, *The Silent Suspect* (2021). The Police enlist Northwood's help once more when a deaf man is arrested following the discovery of his wife's body in their burnt-out house. The suspect is portrayed as "silent" in two ways—he is unable to speak verbally, and mysteriously chooses not to answer the questions translated by Northwood. The situation becomes more complex when a deaf social worker asks her to continue digging for information after the translator is excluded from some of the official investigations. Northwood is disgusted when a neighbour uses the phrase "deaf and dumb",[150] indicating how times have changed since deaf characters were portrayed in the nineteenth and early twentieth centuries. She explains how deaf people are often afraid of hearing people who occupy positions of authority. As a consequence of the communication difficulties, they may meekly agree to what is expected of them.[151]

True Biz (2022) is a novel intended for young adults written by Sara Novic, a deaf American author. The plot centres on River Valley School for the Deaf and portrays multiple deaf characters. These include head teacher February Walters, who became deaf after she jabbed a pencil in her ear as a child, and two students Charlie and Austin. Charlie has a cochlear implant, reads lips, and uses sign language, speech, and an interpreter for her hospital appointments. Austin comes from the fifth generation of deaf people in a family well known for its hereditary deafness. Walters is shocked when she learns that the school is going to close due to financial constraints. Charlie and Austin become involved with a group of hearing political activists and bomb the bionics company that make Charlie's failed implants. The story is concerned with the personal histories of the characters, their family backgrounds, and the interactions within the stifling

---

[148] Pattison, Hide, Loc 460, Kindle
[149] Pattison, Hide, Loc 3962, Kindle
[150] Nell Pattison, The Silent Suspect (London: Avon; Harper Collins Publishers Ltd, 2021), Loc 1067, Kindle.
[151] Pattison, The Silent Suspect, Loc 1883, Kindle

environment of a residential school. The deaf characters are treated realistically with the younger ones conveying the qualities of ordinary teenagers. Adolescent surliness is a prominent feature of the book, as are pre-occupying interests associated with teenagers such as fashion, sex, music, and alcohol. There is a strong emphasis on issues of identity and belonging. When Austin's girlfriend has his baby it "flunks the deaf test"[152] by being proved to be hearing. Black American Sign Language is mentioned.[153] The book informs hearing young people about the realities of deaf experience and allows deaf young people to identify with different aspects of deaf education and the characters described. The book consists of short chapters interspersed with fact sheets about people, concepts or events that are referenced in the story. These include aspects of deaf culture such as the Milan congress and ASL grammar, as well as subjects of wider interest such as anarchy and Robespierre. There are illustrations of sign language handshapes, and finger spelling. Novic dedicates the book to four named deaf schools and "for deaf people everywhere". At the end of the novel, there is an author's note that speaks against the closure of deaf schools and lists those in the United States that have been shut down. There is a clear message about the need to preserve deaf education.

The seven examples that exist at this early stage of the twenty-first century already show a marked shift from the depictions of their predecessors. Increasingly accurate details of deaf life are represented. These include the reality of living with technological aids, the wide variety of modes of communication available, the narrowing opportunities for deaf education, and the search for identity within a widely defined deaf community. Interestingly, and significantly, three of the authors, Lodge, Pattison, and Novic, are themselves deaf. Despite these changes there remain certain themes, metaphors, and features that have persisted in the portrayal of deaf characters throughout the three hundred years since Duncan Campbell first appeared.

---

[152] Sara Novic, True Biz (London: Little, Brown, 2022), 163.8/584, e-book.
[153] Novic, True Biz, 419.7/584, e-book

CHAPTER THREE

COMMUNICATION, CORRECTION, AND COMMUNITY – RECURRING THEMES IN THE PORTRAYAL OF DEAF CHARACTERS IN THE ENGLISH NOVEL

The use of silence

The majority of the novels considered in Chapter Two depict silence as part of the experience of their deaf characters. Twelve of the works have "Silent" or "Silence" in the title. These books all have deaf characters who are major or who are crucial to the story, implying the importance of this facet of their existence to the construction of the plot. The only exception is that of *The Silent Partner* in which the title refers to the business role of the main hearing character. It should be remembered that silence is not simply a trope or a plot device, it is a fact of life for a person who is deaf, although not necessarily experienced in the same way as hearing people. The renowned "deaf-mute" Dr Kitto mentioned by Collins and Dickens, writes about his experience of "silent loneliness" in terms of the separation that it brings between him and other people.[1] For anyone who becomes deafened later in life, the absence of familiar sounds must be terrifying, but the concept of auditory silence will mean nothing to those who have been born deaf or deafened from an early age, making a discussion of silence inappropriate from their perspective.[2] I would imagine the nearest sensation to sound that a profoundly deaf person can experience is that of feeling vibrations, but the absence of vibrations is not the same as the absence of sound. Care then should be taken by hearing authors in using concepts that the real-life equivalents of their characters would have difficulty in understanding. The

---

[1] J. Kitto D.D., "The Lost Senses. Part I. Deafness. The Land of Silence," Edinburgh Review, July, 1855, 116-147.
[2] Davis, "Deafness and Insight: The Deafened Moment as a Critical Modality", 881-900

popularity of the word with authors is likely to arise from the belief that people who live in silence are cut off from their hearing family and friends, and like Dr Kitto, are forced to live in isolation. This may be experienced by people of any age, so that Professor Bates in *Deaf Sentence* is unable to follow conversations and feels lonely even when surrounded by lots of hearing people. Such a situation is likely to make a deaf person feel depressed, and even devastated, and their hearing friends may soon tire of shouting and repeating themselves. This happens frequently in the portrayals of typical Granny characters. As a result of deaf people being excluded from conversations and activities, characters that represent them may be intended as symbols of alienation.[3] Silence is then imbued with a significance that marks an isolated character who has lost their place within society. Duncan Campbell is considered to be the original of the alienated deaf character:

> Defoe's protagonists all explore aspects of society by occupying the place of the other – a man deprived of all society, a criminal, a prostitute, and logically then a deaf man.[4]

But there is another aspect to the way in which the words are used. Deaf people are thought to be "silent" because they are unable to demonstrate the human attribute of vocal speech. By extension, deafness is perceived to embody the absence of any sort of language, so that the deaf are considered to be "not us".[5] There are examples of silence being used as a metaphor for alienation and marginalisation including Madonna and Sophy. The non-verbal Cathy in *The Silent Partner* is avoided due to her immoral behaviour and violent outbursts, Luney Joe from *Candleford Green* is shunned and incarcerated, and silent Jeremy who appears in *Eva Trout*, instils fear in the people he meets. Deafness is perceived as "different" in nineteenth-century children's literature,[6] and one of the two iconic categories of deaf people described in the title of the anthology edited by Batson and Bergman is that of the "outcast". But surely these roles are conferred upon deaf characters when authors write about them as existing within a purely hearing context?

---

[3] Miller, "The Rustle of a Star: An Annotated Bibliography of Deaf Characters in Fiction", 42-60

[4] Davis, "Deafness and Insight: The Deafened Moment as a Critical Modality", 881-900

[5] Davis, "Deafness and Insight: The Deafened Moment as a Critical Modality", 881-900

[6] Ian F.W.K. Davidson, Gary Woodill, and Elizabeth Bredberg, "Images of Disability in 19th Century British Children's Literature", Disability & Society, No.1 (1994): 33-45.

People who are deaf are likely to experience isolation only when those around them communicate exclusively by verbal speech. The reality for most deaf people, however, is that they "do not lead lives of isolation."[7] Representations of marginalised individuals ignore the existence of a viable sign-based deaf community and the possibility of communication by non-vocal means. A reading of the more recently written novels by George, the Morcans, Pattison, and Novic, reveals that deaf characters no longer need to be seen as symbols of alienation unless they leave the deaf community and cross by themselves into the hearing world.

The silence of a deaf non-verbal person is often rendered, particularly in older books, by the words "mute" and "dumb". There are in fact only ten examples of deaf characters in the novels examined above who have no vocal speech whatsoever.[8] Including a non-verbal character is a plot device that adds an aura of mystery or distance to a character, evidences imbecility, or signifies innocence. A study of nineteenth century children's literature concludes that muteness tends to be depicted as the most unfortunate aspect of being deaf, presumably because deaf children appear as silent paragons that elicit the most reaction from concerned adults.[9] There is no need for the children to speak from the point of view of their portrayal, as their silence enhances the condition that evokes so much pity from onlookers. Adult deaf characters such as Madonna and Sophy are portrayed in much the same way, but although they may be innocent, they are not idiots. The problem associated with, and offence caused by using the word "dumb", is the bias revealed in the double connotation of "dumb" as being either non-speaking or stupid, a notion that has been quite rightly criticised.[10] Thankfully writers no longer use such a term, unless their story takes place in the nineteenth or early twentieth century. The author of *Not in the Calendar* records that it was only in 1930, a comparatively recent date, that "Deaf Mutes" were no longer automatically classed with imbeciles, signalling a great advance in the public attitude towards them.[11] In recent years, the vocabulary used in

---

[7] Batson and Bergman (eds), Angels and Outcasts, xii

[8] Duncan Campbell, Madonna (*Hide and Seek*), Sophy (*Dr Marigold*), the servants (*Prince of India*), Mrs Bird's husband and daughter (*Joan Haste*), Luney Joe (*Candleford Green*), Singer (*The Heart is a Lonely Hunter*), Philip of Evesham *(Ordeal by Silence)*, and Jeremy (*Eva Trout*).

[9] Davidson, Woodill, and Bredberg, "Images of Disability in 19th Century British Children's Literature", 33-45

[10] Davis, "Deafness and Insight: The Deafened Moment as a Critical Modality", 881-900

[11] Kennedy, Not in the Calendar, 212

connection with deaf people and deaf characters has evolved,[12] so that "dumb", with its implications of deaf people as stupid, has fallen out of favour. This may indicate a change in attitude from the majority of the public, but deaf individuals maintain that hearing people often assume their lack of response to spoken words is due to stupidity. Perhaps the use of the words "silent" and "silence" with the connotations of lack of communication should be reconsidered in certain contexts as well.

Modes of communication

Deaf people are of course not silent. They have as much to say as a hearing person but may not use verbal speech. Most characters that become deaf in later life, many of them minor examples of the Granny type, use verbal speech and are shouted at by hearing companions. There is a mixture of non-signing and signing examples found in novels originating from the nineteenth and twentieth century, although virtually all of the characters created during the last twenty years are shown to sign fluently. As I pointed out in Chapter One, communication is the "underlying issue with hearing loss, regardless of severity".[13] Whether characters are born deaf or become deafened at a later date is likely to determine their use of vocal speech or signing. The type of education they are said to receive, if any, may be shown to compound or discourage that initial preference. It is therefore important to bear in mind the role of specialist deaf education, mentioned in quite a few books, that may influence whether the character ends up using verbal speech or sign language.

Most deaf characters who sign from an early age attend a deaf school or institution, even though signing may not have been encouraged. Duncan Campbell is educated according to the methods of Dr Wallis, and Madonna and Sophy are sent to the Deaf and Dumb establishment in London. Although children's novels were not included in my study, interesting insights into the teaching methods offered by Dr Watson from 1792 are recorded in Fletcher's historical fiction. A contemporary of Dickens and Collins, the author describes the Old Kent Road Asylum that had treated eleven hundred deaf pupils in twenty-four years, noting the existence of

---

[12] Miller, "The rustle of a star. An Annotated Bibliography of Deaf Characters in Fiction", 42-60.
[13] Philip Zazove, Commentary on Lesley Jones and Robin Bunton, "Wounded or warrior? Stories of being or becoming deaf" in *Narrative Research in Health and Illness* eds Brian Hurwitz, Trisha Greenhalgh, Vieda Skultans (Oxford: Blackwell Publishers Ltd, 2002, 203.

similar establishments elsewhere in the UK.[14] *King Silence* is a thinly veiled, and historically valuable, fictional account of the teaching methods of the author's parents, who uniquely championed both signing and verbal speech. Psyche, Mary, Tamsie, Christopher, Abel, Janice, and Singer all attend specialist deaf schools. Many of the earlier examples of deaf characters are taught, in keeping with their real-life contemporaries, according to the prevailing oralist beliefs. In this at least, fiction appears to reflect fact. Singer, who learned to sign at school, is an exception, perhaps reflecting a more liberal American deaf education, although The Riders, who appear in *In This Sign,* had been punished for signing at their establishment. *Not in the Calendar* shows Wynn educated by private tutor. She then attends art school and becomes a famous painter. Futile attempts are made by a French tutor to teach Jeremy how to speak in *Eva Trout*. Both Jeff in *Dead Before Docking* and Nicholas Quinn attend lip-reading classes. Most of these are relatively major deaf characters whose roles are crucial to the plot, and so their back-stories including their education, take on a greater importance. In general, their histories reflect educational practice at the time, with many continuing to sign despite being punished, even though they are taught vocal exercises and oral skills. Mary's experience in *A Silent Handicap* yields a lot of detailed information about British deaf education in the 1920s. This includes training not only in verbal speech, but also in artisan skills, so that the deaf can become useful working members of society. The children are encouraged to sit national examinations but their futures are likely to be limited. Mary's wealthy friend exceeds expectations by attending Cambridge University. The book was written fifty-seven years after the 1870 Elementary Education Act that ossified the teaching of deaf pupils with its verbal programmes and a perspective that deafness was a medical defect. The book emphasises the control wielded by state officials who regulate the educational process in order to make deaf children fit for work in a hearing world. A similar experience is given to Abel and Janice from *In This Sign* in an American context of oralist schooling and apprenticeship. The educational experiences of the more recently devised characters in *For the Sake of Elena*, *Silent Fear*, the Paige Northwood novels, and *True Biz,* show how deaf education has changed on both sides of the Atlantic, leading to a much greater level of social and professional expectations. Most instances of educational intervention are shown to have some value, even though later generations may view many of the attitudes expressed towards deaf children as paternalistic. But for Psyche from *In Silence* and Christopher in *Silent World*, innocent contentment is ruined by the enforced

---

[14] Rev W Fletcher, The Deaf and Dumb Boy (London: JW Parker, 1843).

entry into the hearing world mediated via their experiences of specialist deaf education.

Twenty-four of the books studied have deaf characters who use sign language. The characters that are said to have been born deaf are all signers.[15] The exception is Naomi, found in *The Scapegoat*, who was also born blind. The elderly gentleman of *Master Humphrey's Clock*, Madonna from *Hide and Seek*, Mrs Bird's husband in *Joan Haste*, Christopher from *Silent World*, and Trehune found in *The Acupuncture Murders,* all learned to sign as older children or adults. There is no information as to when the elderly gentleman learned to sign. Although the great majority of deaf people have become so later in life, and continue to use verbal speech rather than sign language, very few employ a single method of communication exclusively. This is reflected in the variety of methods used to converse by deaf fictional characters.

As we know the majority of deaf people have some degree of verbal speech, and are not in any case "silent" or 'dumb' when they are writing or signing. All the characters surveyed who are old enough, except Cathy in *The Silent Partner* and Luney Joe in *Candleford Green*, both of whom are considered to be incapable of education, communicate by reading and writing. There is particular mention of the elderly gentleman's slates in *Master Humphrey's Clock*, Linda's use of a pad and pen in *The Mansion*, Sally's writing in *The Listening Silence*, and the hand-written cards that Singer from *The Heart is a Lonely Hunter* shows to people. Ironically

> It is only in the 20th century, …that the average person (who should be even more literate than his 19th century forebears) finds it both inconvenient and embarrassing to communicate with the deaf by pad and pencil.[16]

Many deaf characters are given the ability to read lips, often surprisingly and unrealistically well. Almost all have this skill with the exception of a few of the Granny characters such as Jane Austen's Mrs Bates. Four Gifted characters, all drawn from the crime genre, are endowed with a phenomenal and almost super-human level of accuracy in reading lips at a distance,

---

[15] Duncan Campbell, Sophy (*Dr Marigold*), Mrs Bird's daughter (*Joan Haste*), Cathy (*The Silent Partner*), Psyche (*In Silence*), the two servants (*The Prince of India*), Mary (*A Silent Handicap*), Christopher (*Silent World*), Luney Joe (*Candleford Green*), Singer (*The Heart is a Lonely Hunter*), Ka-Ka (*Mr Pye*), Wynn (*Not in the Calendar*), The Ryders (*In This Sign*), Barbara (*The Mallen Girl*), Mrs Carella (*Eight Black Horses*), and Elena (*For the Sake of Elena*). Many of those represented within *King Silence* and the deaf communities created by Morcan, Pattison, and Novic use BSL or ASL as their first language.

[16] Panara, "Deaf characters in fiction and drama", 3-8

enabling them to "oversee" rather than "overhear" private conversations.[17] This is quite a recent convention, with the first, Patricia Payne appearing in 1957 in *The Listening Eye*. Although it provides a useful plot device in detective fiction, it was not in vogue for very long, presumably because it is not realistic, and has been omitted in the more recent crime novels of George, the Morcans, and Pattison.

Hearing aids developed throughout the twentieth century and so we only find them being worn by characters appearing in later books. A hearing trumpet is mentioned by P.G. Wodehouse and ancient aids are referenced in *Not in the Calendar* and *The Listening Silence*. It is surprising that the first account of a character wearing a contemporary hearing aid, Nicholas Quinn, was as late as 1978. There are further examples found in *Kilcaraig*, *The Acupuncture Murders*, and *Deaf Sentence*. Hearing aids and cochlear implants are worn by various members of the deaf communities mentioned by Morcan, Pattison, and Novic, but the only main characters to have cochlear implants are Emily in *Hide* and Charlie from *True Biz*. Authors often write of characters wearing spectacles, but hearing aids, that are also commonplace devices, are largely ignored. Considering the incidence of people who wear hearing aids in the general population, I'm very surprised that there aren't more characters in mainstream fiction who use them incidentally. The six novels that include and follow *For the Sake of Elena* (1992) show deaf people making the most of modern technology such as computers and mobile phones. These are now used universally by deaf people who can easily read, send, and respond to messages. The most recent five stories show the frequent use of video calls, a mode of communication that grants the caller the considerable advantage of being able to read lips and see signed conversations.

Medical intervention

The provision of hearing aids and cochlear implants involves medical professionals. From the eighteenth century onwards, doctors have also examined, diagnosed, and treated problems related to hearing. This emphasis on medical intervention signified a shift away from the belief that deafness is a state ordained by divine providence and deserving of compensation, to that of a defect, illness, or condition that could be alleviated, not only by specialist education, but potentially treatable or even

---

[17] Patricia Payne in *The Listening Silence*; Jeff in *Dead before Docking*; Trehune in *The Acupuncture Murders*; Quinn in *The Silent World of Nicholas Quinn*.

curable.[18]   Certainly in the nineteenth and the first three-quarters of the twentieth century, medical intervention was thought to be desirable, if not always possible or successful. Writing in 1837, Rev W Fletcher refers to treatments for deafness at the London Dispensary for Diseases of the Ear.[19] Madonna in *Hide and Seek* was examined by a physician and Tamsie from *The Day is Ours* received medical treatment. Doctors proscribe signing in *King Silence*. Psyche from *In Silence* and Naomi in *The Scapegoat* are offered treatment by doctors. Mary is subjected to the appalling and discriminatory opinions of Dr Booth and is offered an operation that fails in *A Silent Handicap*. Christopher, found in *Silent World,* has his hearing restored after an operation, an event that leads him to abandon his deaf wife for a hearing neighbour. Psyche from *In Silence* rejects a possible cure and regains her composure, with an identity and future rooted in the deaf community. Trehune in *The Acupuncture Murders* reluctantly submits to acupuncture. Jeremy from *Eva Trout* receives treatment from a French doctor. Margaret in *The Listening Silence* is offered and eventually accepts surgery. Jeff in *Dead Before Docking* has a history of failed surgery. A young girl is offered cochlear implant surgery in *Silent Night*, and Emily (*Hide*) and Charlie (*True Biz*) have had implant procedures performed.

The reader is provided with medical diagnoses that explain the deafness of seven characters. Mrs Bird's husband is "paralytic", presumably paralysed following a stroke in *Joan Haste*. Annabel has tinnitus in *Kilcaraig*, and Margaret from *The Listening Silence* is given a diagnosis of otosclerosis. Jeff developed postoperative complications in *Dead Before Docking*. 'Lizabeth from *The Adventures of Huckleberry Finn,* and Trehune of *The Acupuncture Murders* suffered from childhood scarlet fever. Emily in *Hide* became deaf after suffering from meningitis. Bijah Mudge, a minor character found in *The Silent Partner*, had an industrial disease, deafened from years of continued exposure to loud machines. Physical trauma is given as the cause of deafness in eight characters.[20] Two characters experience deafness from psychological causes, Rex from *Light My Candle* following shell shock and Miranda in *Nest-Egg for the Baron* after witnessing a murder. One of the doctors whom Margaret Schuyler visits in *The Listening Silence* thinks her deafness may be psychosomatic, but his

---

[18] Nicholas Mirzoeff, "The Silent Mind: Learning from Deafness," History Today No. 7 (July 1992): 19-25.

[19] Fletcher, The Deaf and Dumb Boy.

[20] Madonna is deafened from a fall, Miss Pross from a gunshot (*A Tale of Two Cities*), Razumov (*Under Western Eyes*) and Walters (*True Biz*) have eardrums perforated by foreign objects, and Christopher (*Silent World*), Linda (*The Mansion*) Arkas (*The Cretan*) and the elderly lady in *Gorky Park* from explosions.

opinion is rightly ignored by the surgeon. Persistent severe post-traumatic deafness from any cause, physical or psychosomatic, is not common.[21] But the sudden onset which may involve an event vital to the plot, and its potential reversibility, provide a useful device for the author. The overwhelming majority of people who become deaf in later life have far more prosaic diagnoses if indeed it is possible to indicate a specific cause.

Hearing authors may attempt to define deaf characters in terms of order and chaos relative to the hearing world with equilibrium regained only after hearing is restored.[22]   Six characters are shown to recover at least some degree of hearing: Miss Pross in *A Tale of Two Cities*; Miranda in *Nest-Egg for the Baron*, who recovers from the effects of psychological trauma; Naomi in *The Scapegoat* after prayer; Christopher in *Silent World*, and Margaret from *The Listening Silence* following operations; and Trehune recovers briefly after treatment in *The Acupuncture Murders*. The majority of doctors are shown to be sympathetic towards their deaf patients with the notable exception of Dr Booth who appears in *A Silent Handicap*. He has a pejorative view of Mary's deafness, believing it to be caused by a sexually transmitted infection, and espouses the views of the eugenics movement of the late nineteenth century by supporting the segregation, sterilisation, and euthanasia of deaf people. It is rare that such a prejudiced perspective about deafness is shown in a novel, although I'm convinced that this reflects some of the more extreme views in vogue at the turn of the nineteenth century. It did however, remain true well into the twentieth century, that hearing authors were much more likely to construe deafness as a physical impairment rather than view it in a social context.[23] This perspective seems to be changing, as although more modern characters are shown to live with hearing aids and cochlear implants, we read very little about the input of hospitals and clinics in ensuring these technological prostheses are properly prescribed and managed. *True Biz* is the only book that records details about a character's appointment at the hospital.

---

[21] Hamid Djalilian, Adwight Risbud, Ariel Lee and Mehdi Abouzari, "Symptom: Traumatic Deafness" The Hearing Journal, No.12 (December 2020): 31-34.

[22] Lesley Jones and Robin Bunton, "Wounded or warrior? Stories of being or becoming deaf" in *Narrative Research in Health and Illness* eds Brian Hurwitz, Trisha Greenhalgh, Vieda Skultans (Oxford: Blackwell Publishers Ltd, 2002, 187-204.

[23] Frederic W Hafferty and Susan Foster, "Decontextualising disability in the crime mystery genre: the case of the invisible handicap", Disability & Society, No.2, (1994): 185-206.

Deaf communities

The relative lack of information about medical intervention in more recent works corresponds with the evolution in understanding of deafness from a distinctly medical to a more ethnic model. The experiences of specialist education and proficiency in sign language that deaf people share allow informed authors to develop characters that demonstrate aspects of a wider deaf culture and community. When a deaf character is allowed significant interaction with other deaf characters, there are likely to be features of a deaf community described, if only in the context of a deaf school, even in the older novels. More recent stories recount details of a much wider and more pervasive deaf community based on sign language. Sixteen of the novels studied refer to a deaf community,[24] starting with Sophy who meets and marries a deaf man who has watched her signing at a distance in *Dr Marigold*. Sophy becomes pregnant and the family is worried about whether the baby will be deaf or hearing. Remarkably, Dickens identified a concern that remains a source of anxiety among deaf people today. The baby is born hearing and learns to speak with his voice and by finger spelling, thus becoming the first literary example of a character bilingual by birth in vocal speech and sign language. Mr Gordon evaluates whether deaf people should marry and have children in *King Silence*. Family concerns are expressed about whether Dinah's baby will be born deaf in *Last Things*. In contrast, Christopher's deaf wife Dawn of *Silent World* is delighted to discover that her baby is deaf. Their families would have preferred the couple to be childless but she wants to bring up her child in the deaf community with which she identifies. Tamsie from *The Day is Ours* is in contact with other deaf people and agonises over what will happen if her baby is deaf. Austin's baby in *True Biz* demonstrates he is hearing by flunking "the deaf test."

Mary in *A Silent Handicap* is married by a signing Missioner in a deaf church. Deaf missions often provided the only place where deaf people could meet and engage in social activities. They eventually evolved into deaf clubs. Abel and Janice appearing in American novel *In This Sign* were educated in a deaf school. They attend a deaf church where they meet many more deaf people, many of whom are able to sign more elegantly than they. A pre-school for deaf children is established in *Not in the Calendar*. Psyche from *In Silence* runs a home for deaf children. There is passing mention of a deaf community in *Dead Before Docking*. It is interesting to note that the

---

[24] These are *Dr Marigold, In Silence, King Silence, A Silent Handicap, Silent World, The Heat is a Lonely Hunter, The Day is Ours, Not in the Calendar, In This Sign, Dead Before Docking, For the Sake of Elena, Silent Fear, Silent House, Silent Night, The Silent Suspect,* and *True Biz.*

public demonstrations organised by deaf people during the seventies and eighties on both sides of the Atlantic in support of deaf rights and the recognition of sign language, are not overtly referenced in any of the books studied apart from retrospectively in *True Biz*. Perhaps they influenced authors in more subtle ways. More recent accounts, including those of Elena and the settings of *Silent Fear*, the Pattison books, especially *Silent Night,* and *True Biz*, demonstrate the provision of supported attendance in mainstream schools, contemporary specialist deaf education, and the range of technology that make learning accessible to deaf students today. Students are taught in BSL and in ASL. The future of the students concerned is limited only by their educational abilities and inclinations, with support and access shown to be provided by signing teachers, note-takers, translators, and social workers. We discover the existence of clubs, societies, magazines, political activism, and an expansive social network that provides characters with a realistic backdrop to living as a deaf person.

Representations of deafness

There are therefore signs of some progress since the observation thirty years ago that

> …there has been little fictional writing which has shown an awareness of sign language and Deaf culture which are significant issues for the Deaf community today.[25]

Nonetheless when examining the majority of books that include a deaf character, there remain relatively few representations of deafness that truly reflect the reality of deaf experience. I suspect that most hearing authors are ignorant of many aspects of living with deafness rather than intentionally designing their deaf characters to be unrealistic, and others perhaps genuinely believe that their inadequate characterisations are true. I doubt whether hearing authors deliberately go out of their way to misrepresent deaf people in their books, although there may be examples of characters intended to be ironic or humorous who are meant to be outlandish and unbelievable. Sharpe's chaplain in *Porterhouse Blue* springs to mind. Most authors want their characters to be recognisable and comprehensible to their audience, which is largely hearing, except perhaps when writing in specific genres such as fantasy and horror. This allows the plot to evolve within a credible imaginary world, inviting the readers to care enough about the characters to have an appropriate emotional reaction evoked and to carry on

---

[25] Gregory, "Deafness in Fiction", 294-300

reading. Most hearing people have had some contact with deaf individuals. They have seen relatives raise their voices when talking to an elderly relative, witnessed strangers fiddling with hearing aids, or perhaps watched a signed conversation. These observations are made from a hearing perspective and tell us very little about living, thinking, and feeling as a deaf person.

It is reasonable to assume that those authors who are themselves deaf, have known deaf people well, or have troubled themselves to find out more about them, will produce a more realistic and detailed account. Collins modelled his main character on a case of Dr Kitto. Dickens was impacted by his visits to an American deaf institution twenty-three years before the publication of *Dr Marigold*,[26] which is thought to have influenced contemporary biographies of deaf people.[27] Lewis, Corbett, Payne, Kennedy, Steward, and the Morcans acknowledge deaf educators and professionals. Dexter, Lodge, Pattison, and Novic are known to be deaf. Denman and George include so much accurate information that it is likely that they conducted careful research. As a result, some of these authors, though not all, have created deaf characters that are much more realistic than their peers. Due to their personal experience, or encouraged by research, they are largely responsible for the twenty novels in which the main character is deaf,[28] and nine additional works portraying deaf characters that are absolutely crucial to the plot,[29] as well as the novels set largely in deaf communities that have multiple deaf characters–*Silent Fear, Silent House, Silent Night, The Silent Suspect,* and *True Biz.*

Portrayals of deaf people do not have to be limited to either of the two distinct and radically different extreme tropes-the ignored verbal Granny or the glorified signing Goldilocks. But many characters, even those that occupy pivotal or major positions within the novel, can be reduced in essence to a caricature or a plot device that exists to benefit the hearing

---

[26] Ree, I See A Voice, 219

[27] Elisabeth Gitter, The Imprisoned Guest (New York: Picador 2001), 120-125.

[28] Duncan Campbell, Madonna (*Hide and Seek*), Sophy (*Dr Marigold*), Mr Gordon (*King Silence*), Psyche (*In Silence*), Mary (*A Silent Handicap*), Christopher (*Silent World*), Singer (*The Heart is a Lonely Hunter*), Tamsie (*The Day is Ours*), Arkas (*The Cretan*), Rex (*Light My Candle*), Abel and Janice (*In This Sign*), Margaret (*The Listening Silence*), Sally (*The Listening Silence*), Professor Bates (*Deaf Sentence*), Jeff (*Dead Before Docking*), Trehune (*The Acupuncture Murders*), Elena (*For the Sake of Elena*), Emily (*Hide*), February (*True Biz*).

[29] Naomi (*The Scapegoat*), Linda (*The Mansion*), Sarah (*Manservant and Maidservant*), Patricia (*The Listening Eye*), Barbara (*The Mallen Girl*), Miranda (*Nest-Egg for the Baron*), Nicholas Quinn, Philip of Evesham (*Ordeal by Silence*), and Wynn (Not in the Calendar).

characters written around them. As a result, there is a risk that deafness becomes the focal and perhaps only point of their identity, thus preventing any further meaningful character development. It is the deafness itself that is important to the story, not the individual character. In addition to using deafness to symbolise loneliness and alienation, these are some of the specific ways in which authors have used deaf characters to further the plot – as a demonstration of special powers (*Duncan Campbell,* Wynn in *Not in the Calendar)*; objects of kindness and devotion (*Emma, Dr Marigold, Great Expectations, Bleak House, Joan Haste, The Silent Partner)*; sources of comfortable geniality (*Pickwick Papers, Master Humphrey's Clock, Great Expectations)*; an example of stoic acceptance (*Hotel du Lac)*; hereditary deafness preventing marriage (*The Listening Silence)*; exaggerating stubbornness (*For Whom the Bell Tolls, The Acupuncture Murders)*; dramatic devices (*A Tale of Two Cities, Nest-Egg for the Baron, Gorky Park)*; renunciation in a fable (*In Silence)*; a morality tale (*Silent World)*; a polemic (*King Silence, A Silent Handicap* and *True Biz)*; redemption for another (*The Scapegoat)*; revealing attitudes of hearing characters (*The Adventures of Huckleberry Finn; The Virginians, Candleford Green, Manservant and Maidservant, Eva Trout, Last Things, The Mallen Girl, Our John Willie, Saturday Night and Sunday Morning)*; to highlight inadequate communication (*Eva Trout)*; prompting humour (*Gilbert Gurney, The Mating Season, Mr Pye, Porterhouse Blue, Deaf Sentence);* to create an air of mystic distance (*Prince of India, The Heart is a Lonely Hunter, The Mansion, Ordeal by Silence)*; symbols of inner struggle (*The Cretan; Kilcaraig; Light My Candle);* highlighting shame (*The Mallen Girl)*; stigmatising a social misfit (*Under Western Eyes)*; transformation and redemption (*Hide and Seek, Dr Marigold, The Day is Ours, The Listening Silence);* possessing superb lip-reading skills (*The Listening Eye, Dead Before Docking, The Silent World of Nicholas Quinn)*; a statement of friendship (*Not in the Calendar)*; to contrast conflicting worlds (*For the Sake of Elena)*; to highlight parallels (*The Listening Silence, The Day is Ours)*; providing a reason for a closed environment (*Silent Fear)*; heightening fear (*Hide)*; and expressing community (*The Silent House, Silent Night, The Silent Suspect)*. Some of these characters have been relatively well developed, but not as well as those appearing in *In This Sign, The Silent House, Silent Night, Silent Suspect* and *True Biz.*

The use of deaf characters as a plot device is not the only way in which they can be seen to be unrepresentative. The absence of deaf characters from minority ethnic backgrounds is strikingly obvious apart from the brief mention of 'Lizabeth in *The Adventures of Huckleberry Finn.* All major deaf characters are white British or white American with the exception of Arkas in *The Cretan*. Naomi from *The Scapegoat* lives in Morocco, but is of British Jewish heritage. There are a few minor or peripheral deaf characters that represent other ethnicities—Spanish in *For Whom the Bell Tolls*, African- American in *The Heart is a Lonely Hunter,* Polish in *The Silent Suspect,* and students with a range of European and non-European nationalities in *Silent Fear*. Characters from earlier books may be expected to share a uniform ethnicity as they reflect the age and society in which they were written, but it is regrettable that novels of more recent origin should continue this omission. I assume that it is a function of the comparatively similar origins of the authors and so I look forward to a deaf author from an ethnic minority creating deaf characters who share their background.

The creation of superficially developed deaf characters by hearing authors has encouraged deaf people to believe in "the utter ignorance displayed by the general public" about them,[30] and that "society treats people with a hearing loss poorly".[31] This view presupposes that hearing authors reflect the ignorance and attitudes of the society from which they originate. This notion is supported by the comments of Panara, a deaf commentator, who writes,

> Collins and Dickens were most honest and realistic in reflecting the attitudes of society toward the deaf and the prevailing methods of educating the deaf.[32]

He continues by reporting that this stressed "the importance of learning to read and write as a means of developing language skills", an assertion verified by the details of deaf education given in a number of books and advocated particularly in King Silence." Panara concludes by stating that significantly society "did not expect the deaf to speak their own language", no doubt referring to the attitudes reflected in the oralist approach. Although it remains unclear as to how far an author can be said to be a mouthpiece for society,

> …the depiction of physical impairments in popular culture reflects as well as shapes public attitudes towards persons with disabilities.[33]

---

[30] Barnes, "The deaf in literature", 42-45
[31] Zazove, Commentary on Lesley Jones and Robin Bunton, "Wounded or warrior? Stories of being or becoming deaf", 203-204
[32] Panara, "Deaf characters in fiction and drama", 3-8
[33] Hafferty and Foster, 'Decontextualising disability in the crime mystery genre: the case of the invisible handicap', 185-206.

Deaf people certainly believe that the deaf characters created by a hearing writer provide inferences about the perspectives of the hearing,[34] reflect contemporary attitudes about deaf people,[35] and inform about "misconceptions which may influence popular notions of deafness".[36] In particular, deaf people believe they are treated very differently from those who are blind, even though "to be born deaf is infinitely more serious than to be born blind".[37] This may seem to be a strange assertion to some, even though Helen Keller, who was herself both deaf and blind, agreed that being deaf was "a much worse misfortune".[38] She is also quoted as saying that "blindness cuts us off from things, but deafness cuts us off from people".[39] The impression gained by deaf people is that the hearing public find it "easier to sympathise with the more obvious problems of the blind".[40] It is true that in a novel blind characters are unlikely to be accused of obstinacy like Sarah in *Manservant and Maidservant*, called "backward" like Diana in *Last Things*, or assumed that her sensory deficit is exacerbated by temper as happens to Mr Wardle's mother in *Pickwick Papers*. Cathy is deemed to be mentally and morally deficient in *The Silent Partner* and Luney Joe from *Candleford Green* is supposed mad. Perhaps because of these signs of unwitting prejudice against deaf people there is no literary parallel to the "blind sage" who is held in high regard, granted heightened hearing, and acquires "second sight" as a result of blindness.[41] The nearest that an author comes to conferring a similar status to a deaf character is when they use deafness to add to the sense of awe or mystery, but that has a much less interesting and profound effect. Deaf people in novels are not bestowed with enhanced eyesight and, with the notable exception of Duncan Campbell, do not experience supernatural phenomena. Although misconceptions about deaf people abound, and undoubtedly these are revealed in the characters that hearing authors create, I do not think there is any intention to "debase or ridicule the infirmity of deafness".[42] Deaf characters are not deliberately

---

[34] Batson and Bergman (eds), Angels and Outcasts, ix

[35] Mirzoeff, "The Silent Mind: Learning from Deafness," 19-25

[36] Gregory, "Deafness in fiction", 294-300

[37] Oliver Sacks, Seeing Voices. A Journey into the World of the Deaf (1989; London: Picador, 1991), 8.

[38] Helen Keller, quoted in Grant, The Quiet Ear, 36.

[39] Helen Keller quoted in Lai Meng Looi, Detlev Ganten, Peter F McGrath, Manfred Gross, George E Griffin, "Hearing loss: a global issue", The Lancet, No.9972 (March 14, 2015): 943-944. https://doi.org/10.1016/S0140-6736(15)60208-2.

[40] Zazove, Commentary on Lesley Jones and Robin Bunton, "Wounded or warrior? Stories of being or becoming deaf", 203-204

[41] Gregory, "Deafness in fiction", 294-300

[42] Panara, "Deaf characters in fiction and drama", 3-8

mocked in novels, unless by hearing characters that are shown to be unpleasant and prejudiced. Abuse is always condemned, characters guilty of mistreatment criticised, and sympathetic consideration is widespread.

Although I chose not to include novels written by deaf authors for deaf readers, or biographies written by deaf people, there may be insights that can be gained from an alternative set of narratives. These arise from the recognition of how for some people

> ...becoming deaf is an interruption of their story. For others being deaf becomes the point of the story itself.[43]

These first-person accounts originating from deaf people are divided into two categories. Those described as "Warrior" narratives are characterised by a struggle for identity, the hope of attainment, and belonging to a strong cohesive community. They use war metaphors, speak of rights and citizenship, and express an unwillingness to be defined in relation to the hearing world. In contrast, "Wounded" narratives are typified by damage, loss, medical involvement, exclusion and isolation, a continuing reliance on oral speech, and the desire to remain part of the hearing community.[44] In a different context, Ladd explores the difference between those people he terms "deaf" with a lower case "d" and "Deaf" with an upper case "D". He defines "deaf" people as having experienced a primarily audiological experience in later life, and enjoying little contact with signers, continue to identify with hearing culture. Whereas those who are categorised as "Deaf" have little or no experience of hearing from birth or early childhood, use BSL preferentially, and identify with a deaf culture.[45] This then allows Ladd to propose that the "Deaf", a predominantly signing subculture, should be viewed as a language group rather than as being disabled, as an ethnic group that enjoys a unique social status with their own culture.[46] The descriptions of "Warrior" and "Wounded" narratives correspond with Ladd's definitions of "Deaf" and "deaf" respectively. Deafness in literature, therefore, should be more than just character portrayal, and take into account more of the narrative and context that

---

[43] Jones and Bunton, "Wounded or Warrior? Stories of being or becoming deaf", 187-204

[44] Jones and Bunton, "Wounded or Warrior? Stories of being or becoming deaf", 187-204

[45] Paddy Ladd, Understanding Deaf Culture. In Search of Deafhood (Clevedon: Multilingual Matters Ltd, 2003), xvii.

[46] Ladd, Understanding Deaf Culture. In Search of Deafhood, 230

identifies the character's experience of being deaf.[47] Apart from George, the Morcans, Pattison, and Novic, all of whom use "Deaf" to identify a signing culture and community, mainstream authors appear to have little awareness of these distinctions, or were writing before their existence, and rather like health professionals, are inclined to view all deaf people as having similar experiences irrespective of the degree of loss, their origin or identity.[48] Most of the characters I have found in novels are given the wish to speak, or at least to integrate to an extent with the hearing world, and like Singer display no desire to seek out and join a signing community. Their geographical location or previous specialist schooling may, of course, may be said to give rise to that decision, but nonetheless their stories fall neatly into the "Wounded" category. Similarly, Psyche from *In Silence* and Mary in *A Silent Handicap,* stay within deaf institutions and relate primarily with deaf people, but their identities remain defined by loss. There are however, important exceptions, including some of the characters in *King Silence*, the university campus described in *Silent Fear*, the school in *True Biz*, the local deaf communities in the Pattison novels, Abel and Janice Ryder, Elena, and possibly Dawn, Christopher's wife. We can attribute elements of "Warrior" narratives to these characters, whether or not their creators were familiar with the concept, and even if the characters were written before such narratives existed, so that according to Ladd's paradigm, we can identify them as "Deaf".

Deaf authors would reasonably be expected to demonstrate aspects related to deaf life more extensively, and be more accurate in the development of deaf characters. They are less likely to stress problems related to deafness, unless it is to make a particular point regarding communication difficulties as we read in *Deaf Sentence* that was written by an author who wears hearing aids. A deaf author originating from the signing community is more likely to reject disability models that major on victimhood, and construct characters who embrace deaf culture. Pattison and Novic are probably the only such authors writing books for mainstream reading, and although Pattison is deafened and signs, it is not her first language. Deaf authors may believe that a majority hearing readership would reject signing deaf characters as being too unfamiliar, or they may have failed in their attempts to convince hearing agents and publishers to recognise their work. Deaf commentators indicate qualitative differences in texts written by deaf authors that make them unusual to a hearing reader,

---

[47] Davis, "Deafness and Insight: The Deafened Moment as a Critical Modality", 881-900

[48] Jones and Bunton, "Wounded or Warrior? Stories of being or becoming deaf", 187-204

and potentially difficult to access, although it is possible that hearing readers can learn about a reality quite different from their own experiences. Most deaf authors naturally draw heavily on their personal narratives and their own formative experiences.[49] The resulting "Deaf Literature" is described as written by deaf people for deaf people, and concentrates on their shared experiences often given in sign language.[50] These narratives may prove to be a fruitful source of information when a hearing author begins the process of creating a deaf character. There are limitations however, as the same writer wonders how well sign language can be conveyed in words. As she points out signing necessitates movement, includes body language and facial expression, and contains inflexions and layering. Deaf literature therefore, according to these defining qualities, tends to be multimodal, visual and kinetic, as opposed to hearing literature which is described as aural, linear, and focussed narrowly on language.[51]Another deaf commentator adds to these words of caution by noting the importance of the spatial relations between signing characters and the potential difficulties caused when the hands are occupied with other activities.[52] In addition, other differences in experience unfamiliar to a hearing reader may include altered acoustic representations and extra-acoustic descriptions of sound.[53] It may not be straightforward then, for a deaf or hearing author to faithfully render all the features that would create an accurate portrayal of a deaf character in mainstream books. In Chapter Four, we shall see that comics and graphic novels are capable of providing at least a limited, though static, visual representation of signs that are capable of being understood, the meanings of which are not so easily conveyed through printed words.

This then begs the question as to how far an author wants to pursue, or should pursue, a representation deemed to be accurate by a deaf person. As I have already stated, the vast majority of deaf people still use vocal speech and try to live as much as possible within a hearing community. Issues

---

[49] Michael Skyer quoted in Yi Shun Lai, "Broadening the Bookshelves: Getting to know deaf literature", The Writer. June 23, 2022.
https://www.writermag.com/writing-inspiration/essay-about-writing/broadening-the -bookshelves-getting-to-know-deaf-literature/.

[50] Kristen Harmon, "On Deaf Literature", Bloomsbury Admin, January 18, 2019.
https://bloomsburyliterarystudiesblog.com/continuum-literary-studie/2019/01/on-deaf-literature.html.

[51] Michael Skyer quoted in Yi Shun Lai," Broadening the Bookshelves: Getting to know deaf literature".

[52] Beacom quoted in Yi Shun Lai, "Broadening the Bookshelves: Getting to know deaf literature".

[53] Russell S Rosen, "Representations of Sound in American Deaf Literature", Journal of Deaf Studies and Deaf Education, No. 4 (Fall 2007): 552-565.

related to the rendering of signing for them are less important. They are more likely to be interested in whether the deaf character, as a person, is developed well, made to appear interesting, has some well-known features of deaf life described such as changing hearing aid batteries, and is not included as a minor prop or plot device. The minority of deaf people who do sign are likely to share those views, and would want to see features of deaf communities and reports of sign language conversations appearing in mainstream literature, even if signing is inadequately conveyed by the written form. I would suggest that for most deaf people it is the essence of the character itself, and the way it is used, that makes the character appealing. Perhaps surprisingly, one small study looking at the portrayal of deaf characters in a sample of adolescent literature found that deaf participants preferred the books written by hearing writers, and believed their representations of deaf characters to be more realistic than those created by deaf authors.[54] This may reflect a broader spectrum of deaf characters created by hearing writers as opposed to a potentially narrower variety of examples based on the personal experiences of a deaf author or more consistent with "deaf literature".

In conclusion, the representation of deaf characters in novels has evolved considerably since *Duncan Campbell* was published three hundred years ago. Defoe's work provides the single major eighteenth century example, but the inference is clear. Campbell's deafness was providential in origin and compensated for by a divine enhancement of his inherited ability to predict the future. By the nineteenth century deaf characters are presumed to be born with a defect or develop a medical condition that confers a silent victimhood often marked by abuse and injustice. As paragons of virtu, they arouse our sympathy and pity, while waiting patiently for release into the hearing world through oralist intervention. In the twentieth century deaf characters start to occupy a wider variety of roles and are educated and apprenticed to take their place in hearing society. No longer just idiots or moral exemplars, they are viewed through the lens of more modern thought, and reflect post-War uncertainties with characters used as symbols of alienation, loneliness, and isolation. Although there are important exceptions, the majority of deaf characters nonetheless continue to act as props and ficelles for the better developed hearing characters, and are frequently invented to take their place as a plot device. This was starting to change by the end of the twentieth century, so that in the last twenty years, most deaf characters have become more representative of real-life

---

[54] Sharon Pajka-West, "Representations of deafness and deaf people in young adult fiction", M/C Journal, 13 (3), 2010. https://doi.org/10.5204/mcj.261.

narratives. This is true for those characters shown to identify with the hearing community and for those who take their place within a signing subgroup. All deaf characters are shown to communicate and no longer live in isolation. More deaf authors are writing for the mainstream, and hearing authors tend to research in much greater depth. As a result, a wider variety of deaf characters are now displayed, including signers, vocal speakers, people who wear hearing aids or cochlear implants, are educated in either specialist or mainstream schools, and may or may not belong to deaf communities. There is less polarisation of characters into extreme tropes, with many possessing a unique mix of the features of deaf life described. Deaf characters are increasingly portrayed as people who happen to be deaf rather than being defined simply as devices by their lack of hearing.

CHAPTER FOUR

STEREOTYPES AND SUPERHEROES – DEAF CHARACTERS IN COMICS

We are all familiar with comics but probably spend little time in thinking about what makes them different from other literary forms. A comic is a story expressed and related through illustrations usually in serialised stages. Graphic novels tend to be longer and contain the entire story. Both types of visual narrative provide an immediate impact from looking at the page. The artwork conveys appearance, gesture, mood, and movement, often in a direct and obvious way that tends to be immersive and interactive. The artist and writer determine the structure of the layout, the position, size, angle and point of view of the illustrations, and the pace of progress of the narrative, intending to draw us further into their imaginary universe. Characters are created with distinguishing visual features that remain consistent and recognisable. Certain types of character, notably superheroes, are specifically associated with comics. Words may or may not be used as dialogue or narration. These aspects make graphic literary forms accessible and appealing to older children and young people, so the majority of Marvel comic readers for instance, range from eighteen to twenty-nine years.[1] Stories and themes are chosen and designed to be relevant to the target audience.

There is remarkably little academic work concerning deaf characters in comics. My very brief article on deaf super-heroes is one of the few sources available.[2] This is not due to a complete lack of material, as I have been able to discover eighteen examples, written in English and intended for a mainstream readership, including some from the iconic superhero comics issued by Marvel and DC. The majority of the comics and graphic novels are created by American artists, with two British, and two other exceptions.

---

[1] "Share of adults who are fans of Marvel Comics in the United State as of April 2019, by age group", Statista., accessed December 18, 2019.
https://www.statista.com/statistics/1005265/marvel-comics-fans-us-by-age/
[2] Paul Dakin, "'Super' heroes – special powers in deaf characters" Hektoen International, Summer 2014.

As would be expected, since comics are a relatively recent genre of literature when compared with novels, most of the works originate from the last sixty years. As comics and graphic novels tend to have a younger readership, I have included examples of deaf characters from publications intended for children as well as young adults. The works are examined in chronological order before discussing the themes revealed.

Review of deaf characters

As I noted in Chapters Two and Three, a common feature of deaf characters in novels is their use as catalysts to help develop a plot. They may be reduced to non-hearing sounding boards against whom the more significant hearing characters demonstrate their animosity, sympathy, or sense of humour.[3] The same is true in comics. An obvious catalyst is Professor Calculus in the *Tintin* stories created by the Belgian author Herge in 1944, and translated from the original French into English. Calculus is the oldest example that I have found of a deaf character in comics. He is portrayed as an elderly cantankerous figure who denies having problems with hearing. In the example I have chosen, *Tintin – Destination Moon*, the Professor struggles to use an ancient hearing trumpet, even though electronic aids had been available for decades, with the consequent misunderstandings leading to confusion and chaos.[4] This representation, exaggerating what may be considered to be identifiably "humorous" features for many hearing readers, is typical of the Granny trope that conveys little about the reality of living as a deaf person.[5] Such caricatures are meant to cause amusement in the context of the publication in which they appear. They are not intended to be taken seriously and are not designed to cause offence. Nevertheless, portrayals like this are often seen as insulting by deaf people for whom such misunderstandings are a constant source of upset and embarrassment. Deaf people frequently report that when trying to explain they are deaf to a hearing person they've not met before, the reply will often be a trivial comment thought to be "funny" such as "Pardon?!" The response may well be a misguided attempt to hide embarrassment, but this type of experience reinforces a view commonly held by deaf people, that although most hearing

---

[3] Susan Gregory, "Deafness in Fiction". In Constructing Deafness, ed. Susan Gregory and Gillian Hartley (Milton Keynes: The Open University, 1991), 294-300.
[4] Herge, The Adventures of Tintin: Destination Moon (London: Egmont UK Ltd, 1981).
[5] Paul Dakin. "Goldilocks or Granny?: Portrayals of deafness in the English novel." Journal of Medical Biography. No.4 (November 2015): 227-237.

individuals would consider mocking those without sight as unacceptable, it is quite alright to make fun of the deaf.[6] The famous writer Dr Kitto, who was deaf and blind and evaluated the effects of both, described the separation from people caused by his deafness as far more serious than problems related to lack of sight, despite the latter attracting much more sympathy.[7] The same perspective that belittled the impact of deafness two hundred years ago still seems to prevail in the minds of some people today.

The first instance of a deaf character to be granted superpowers is DC's Allegro (1979). He performs the role of a prop. Traumatic hearing loss, a convenient plot device for writers, provokes the superhero into becoming deranged and dangerous, turning him into a super-villain.[8] Allegro's deafness is simply an easy way in which to explain his change of status from hero to bad-guy. It is unfortunate that deafness is used as a literary tool to trigger madness and criminality.

There are two examples of well-developed and sophisticated deaf superheroes appearing in comics. The first, Hawkeye, did not start life as a character who was either deaf or well-developed. When Hawkeye was originally introduced by Marvel in 1964, he was hearing. The deaf version did not appear until a sonic arrow blast from Crossfire destroyed his hearing nearly twenty years later in 1983.[9] As a result of this assault, Hawkeye is shown to misunderstand the words of his superhero colleagues. He is afraid to acknowledge that he is deaf, believing deafness to be a weakness, and although he needs to wear hearing aids, conceals the fact of his deafness by hiding the aids underneath his costume. Hawkeye's exceptional sensory awareness, particularly his keen eyesight, had already made him a gifted marksman, but after becoming deaf, he develops other heightened senses, including the ability to feel vibrations. This follows the notion first seen in *Duncan Campbell* that a deaf person should be compensated by extra powers for losing their hearing. This turns Hawkeye into a "supercrip", a stereotype associated with "disabled" superheroes.[10] Supercrips are disabled individuals who are represented as struggling to overcome a perceived deficit in order to attain a level of achievement often assumed to be beyond

---

[6] This is considered in more detail in Chapter Three.

[7] Rev Dr. John Kitto. "The Lost Senses. Part I. Deafness. The Land of Silence." Edinburgh Review, July 1855, 116-147.

[8] Gerry Conway Dick Dillin, Justice League of America #163 (New York: DC Comics Inc, 1973).

[9] Mark Gruenwald, Bob Layton, Hawkeye 1 #4 (New York: Marvel Worldwide, Inc, 1983).

[10] Jose Alaniz, Death, Disability, and the Superhero: The Silver Age and Beyond (Jackson: University Press of Mississippi, 2014), 31.

them. Such characters possess exaggerated powers to compensate for a
perceived loss of ability or sensation. By this definition, Chapter Two
contains a number of fictional deaf characters appearing in novels that are
readily identifiable as supercrips including Duncan Campbell. In comics the
existence of the supercrip is made even more obvious, especially in those of
the superhero genre, as superheroes by their very nature possess some form
of extraordinary ability. The portrayal of a superhero who wears hearing
aids is a welcome representation, but very little was made of Hawkeye's
deafness at the time. The early Hawkeye potentially reaffirms three
stereotypes–that deafness should be hidden and denied; that medical
intervention is necessary to "cure" deafness by provision of the aids; and
that Hawkeye has become a supercrip. However, I can imagine that the
embarrassment expressed by Hawkeye, and the difficulty he faces in
coming to terms with the effects of the trauma, will resonate with some
readers as relating a realistic experience of sudden deafness. It is also quite
natural that a character who has always lived within the hearing world
should seek the enhancement of hearing aids. As I discuss later in the
chapter, the accusation that a deaf character is a supercrip may not be
entirely appropriate.

Four years later, DC created their first deaf superhero, Jericho, in 1987.
He is also the first super-hero to use American Sign Language (ASL), with
hand shapes clearly visible in a few panels.[11] Because a deaf character uses
sign language does not by itself guarantee a portrayal that is either realistic
or without stereotype. Unfortunately, the significance for deaf culture of the
first signing superhero was undermined by the character not actually being
deaf. There are instances of hearing characters in novels pretending to be
deaf but Jericho is not an imposter. He sustains a throat injury that renders
him incapable of verbal speech forcing him to discover an alternative mode
of communication. Jericho consequently learns ASL at a "School for the
Hearing   Impaired".   Most   deaf   people   would   encourage   the
acknowledgment of sign language by hearing individuals whatever the
circumstances, and so the introduction of ASL into the pages of a superhero
comic should be commended. The possibility of Jericho becoming a role
model for deaf young people however, never existed. It might also be
construed   that   because   Jericho   is   compelled   to   use   non-verbal
communication rather than through his own volition, this encourages the
view that sign language is second-rate when compared to oral speech. This
remains a very emotive issue.[12] At least there is recognition of the frequent

---

[11] John Byrne and Dick Giordano. Action Comics 1 #584 (New York: DC Comics
Inc, 1987).
[12] This is discussed in greater detail in Chapter One.

complaint from within the deaf community that hearing people assume a deaf person's lack of response to verbal speech is due to stupidity rather than lack of hearing. A pupil at the deaf school wears a t-shirt proclaiming "Deaf kids ain't dummies." It is interesting to note that Jericho was created at a time when deaf communities on both sides of the Atlantic, particularly in the United States, became increasingly visible, motivated, and politicised. This may perhaps have prompted DC to include ASL in a comic book. Although the US Government recognised ASL as a language in 1964, well ahead of the UK Government's recognition of British Sign Language (BSL) in 2003, it was another twenty-three years before ASL appeared in a superhero comic.

Issues of communication and loneliness are explored in the paradoxically entitled *The Listener* (1997). This British graphic novel aimed at older children is illustrated with black and white panels. The deaf main character is neither a stereotype nor a superhero. Shelley is a deaf girl staying at her hearing brother's house in the countryside. She witnesses Gavin, a hearing boy, arrive at the front door. Gavin has found his grandmother injured in the snow and needs to use the telephone to call for help. Because of a misunderstanding between the hearing people Gavin is shooed away. Shelley has read Gavin's lips and recognises the urgency of the situation. She takes charge, making it possible for the elderly lady to be rescued and removed to hospital. Shelley and Gavin become friends. Shelley has poor speech due to her early experience of deafness, but she can read lips reasonably well and signs fluently. Shelley and her brother communicate through signing, but outside the home Shelley is isolated, especially from hearing children at school. Gavin quickly learns to face Shelley when he speaks so that she can read his lips. After watching Shelley and her brother having a signed conversation Gavin wishes "that he could do sign language too. It looked cool".[13] Gavin compliments Shelley, "You may not be able to hear...but you're the best listener".[14] This statement, reiterating the book's title, is based on Shelley's ability to display emotional empathy, even when she experiences difficulties in communication and can't always understand everything that happens around her. Shelley takes responsibility and makes good decisions irrespective of her silent existence and sense of loneliness. She is not patronised by hearing characters and is not granted any unusual powers. The character is treated sympathetically by the author without being inordinately sentimentalised. I note from the author's biographical details that her son was severely disabled, and her

---

[13] Elizabeth Laird, The Listener (London: A&C Black, 1997), 74.
[14] Laird, The Listener, 80

books explore emotional and psychological issues that often involve characters set in difficult circumstances.[15] *The Listener* has a straightforward engaging plot that conveys universal themes of family, friendship, and domestic tensions. It gently informs a hearing readership of issues related to deafness, and is likely to allow deaf youngsters to identify with a realistic depiction. Shelley is the earliest example I can discover of a strongly defined and well developed graphic deaf character.

By comparison Hope Hibbert (1998) is rather disappointing. Hope is the deaf neighbour of Spider-Man, aka Peter Parker, and appears in nine Marvel issues. Hope is an African-American girl who makes friends with Parker's Aunt Anna. She attends a specialist deaf school but is reluctant to practice signing. In the appropriately titled "Signs of the Times" Aunt Anna helps Hope practice ASL.[16] Peter Parker learns a few signs that become crucial when the bus carrying Hope and her classmates is attacked by Rhino. After Spider-Man arrives on the scene he tries to reassure Hope, but the children cannot hear Spider-Man's words and are unable to read his lips because of his mask. Spider-Man demonstrates the sign for "friend" and settles the rising panic.[17] Deaf youngsters might identify with Hope as in the comic she is literally "the girl next door" and shares similar signing and educational experiences with many deaf youngsters. These features allowed Hope to be greeted enthusiastically by a deaf blogger who discovered that the scriptwriter had gained ideas from having worked with a deaf man.[18] She does not possess any superhuman power, and shows no sign of a compensatory gift, but she is treated in an excessively sentimental way. There are some remarkable features about Hope's portrayal. She is the first truly deaf character in superhero comics to use ASL, unlike Jericho who was actually hearing. She is also the first deaf character in the genre from an ethnic background. These are aspects of Hope's portrayal that should be applauded, but she is treated in a rather patronising way, and needs a hearing character to help her practice sign language. Hope remains undeveloped as a character and reflects very little of her ethnic background, deaf education, or deaf culture.

---

[15] "10 Facts About Elizabeth Laird", Fact File, accessed September 18, 2018. https://factfile.org/10-facts-about-elizabeth-laird.

[16] Todd Degazo and Andrew Hennessy, Sensational Spider-Man #26 (New York: Marvel Worldwide, Inc, 1998).

[17] Todd Degazo and Mike Wieringo, Sensational Spider-Man #31 (New York: Marvel Worldwide, Inc, 1998).

[18] Josh Lothridge, "Comic Star", Rave, SpiderFan.org, accessed 1998, http://www.spiderfan.org/rave/01085.htmlhridge.

The second example of a well-developed deaf superhero is Echo. Although she appears as a minor character in a number of Marvel comics, Echo has two major story arcs devoted to her origin, progress, and redemption. I propose to introduce her at the beginning of the first six-part arc entitled *Parts of a Hole* (1999).[19] The opening artwork is unique and striking, and consists of small framed images that surround Matt Murdock, aka Daredevil, as he is pictured playing the piano. A twisting musical fret emerges with pictorial memories that replace notes. A few pages later Maya is also shown playing a piano. She is surrounded by writing superimposed on images and boxes containing words that explain she cannot hear the music because she is deaf. Maya is shown to have a mixed Native American and Hispanic heritage. She reads lips and uses both ASL and Plains American sign language. Maya's father was a gangster who worked for Daredevil's nemesis, Wilson Fisk aka Kingpin. Fisk shot Maya's father. While he was dying, Maya's father reached out to his daughter and left the bloodstained imprint of his hand on her face. This event led Maya to invent the superhero persona of Echo. Maya was unaware of the identity of her father's murderer and allowed Fisk to send her to an expensive school for children with "learning disabilities". Maya had already discovered her superhuman powers as a child. These powers consist of an unerringly accurate visual memory combined with a sensitivity to vibrations, enabling her to mimic complex physical activities such as piano playing, acrobatics, dance, and martial arts. Maya's speech is not slurred because she is able to replicate vocal movements observed in others. This is shown to be in direct contrast with Matt's hearing client Lenny, whose speech impediment makes him unintelligible. Maya is deaf and can speak well whereas Lenny is hearing and unable to speak properly. This comparison emphasises Maya's ability to communicate, a facility accomplished by use of her superpowers. There is another parallel. Lenny smears fresh paint on Matt's door and leaves a print of his hand. This foreshadows what is to become the distinguishing mark of Echo's appearance, a handprint painted on her face "echoing" the bloodstain left by her dying father. Matt and Maya eventually fall in love unaware of one another's alter egos. Fisk wants Echo to kill Daredevil and tells Maya that Daredevil killed her father. Before their first fight Echo learns how to copy Daredevil's moves. Daredevil recognises Maya's scent and heartbeat and escapes by breaking the lights when he realises that Echo depends on sight. Echo uses a similar strategy to favour their next encounter by choosing a noisy and smoky environment that

---

[19] David Mack and Joe Quesada, Daredevil #9-15 (New York: Marvel Worldwide Inc, 1999).

cancels out Daredevil's senses of hearing and smell. The story is resolved when Echo realises the truth about her father's death and shoots Fisk. Echo's complexity and origins generate intricate and innovative artwork involving many visual parallels and "echoiing" of one character by another, reiterating the concept inherent in the superhero's name. Although describing an auditory phenomenon the character is unable to hear, the name Echo is appropriate, as she is able to "echo" the skills of others. Maya also explains how painful memories make her feel that she exists only as an "echo" of her true self. The tragic sense of loss and incompleteness felt by Maya is described succinctly by the story arc's title *Parts of a Hole*.

In an interview, the artist David Mack said he created Echo with Daredevil in mind. Daredevil is blind and deciphers his world in a unique way. Mack thought that Daredevil would have a unique interaction with a character that also views their world through a completely different perspective. Mack read the stories of people who had grown up deaf from childhood, and allowed these accounts to influence the depiction of Echo who had

> …learned to decipher all the visual cues of the world as a language she pieced together by an acute pattern recognition".[20]

Daredevil minimises the impact of his blindness through a heightened sense of hearing and echo-location. The problem of representing Matt's blindness visually, and showing how his mutated senses overcome it, was addressed in early issues of *Daredevil*. [21] It is shown visually in the comics by the presence of concentric rings that represent soundwaves or radar, and ECG images when the character senses another person nearby. Echo's deafness is represented mainly through showing words and pictures of her thoughts, as well as images of signing handshapes, rather than empty speech bubbles. Echo's internal commentary is vital to the plot rather than just relying on her communication with other people. The parallels between Maya and Matt are shown to extend beyond sharing the usual supercrip tropes of compensating senses and awesome abilities, although they certainly exist. Both Maya and Matt have extensive and complex back stories with powerful childhood experiences and internal conflicts, making

---

[20] David Mack, "An interview with Creator (David Mack) of one of my favorite Deaf characters (Echo)". Interview by Sharon Pajka. Deaf Characters in Adolescent Literature, accessed September 15, 2007, http://pajka.blogspot.com/2007/09/interview-with-creator-david-mack-of.html.
[21] Paul Young, Frank Miller's Daredevil and the ends of heroism (New Brunswick: Rutgers University Press, 2016), 32.

their characters more relevant, and raising the possibility that they could become role models.

Natalie Rodriguez is another superhero whose deafness is compensated for by enhanced abilities. She is a Hispanic teenager showcased in a DC mini-series in 2000. Natalie is an accomplished archer who competes at Olympic level. She also displays an unnaturally superb skill in reading lips. This ability ultimately saves a friend's mother from wrongful conviction.[22] Despite the exaggeration of a deaf attribute, and the consequent accusation of Natalie being a stereotypical supercrip, there are some realistic elements of deaf experience. For instance, Natalie collides into people when she cannot hear them. Her speech is slurred and indistinct, causing problems for her hearing colleagues, a common feature for many who lose their hearing at an early age.

An aspirational role model that encourages the wearing of hearing aids is seen in *Batman Beyond: Hear No Evil* (2002). This is a small comic book intended for younger readers.[23] Tommy, a young deaf boy, encounters Shriek, a villain who lost his hearing in an experiment that went wrong. Shriek is very angry and destroys buildings with sound waves. He can only understand people by reading their lips. When Tommy is rescued by Batman, Tommy tells him that the vibrations remind him of the sensation of sound he has lost. After inadvertently putting Tommy at risk again, Shriek rescues him, but Tommy cannot read Shriek's lips because of his costume. Shriek is caught by Batman and sent to prison, where he uses his engineering skills to build a hearing aid for Tommy. The character of Tommy recounts common experiences of recently developed deafness. Hearing aids are shown to be very effective, a laudable goal when the book may be read by a child who needs encouragement to wear them. Tommy is shown using signing handshapes, but the value of signing is diminished. The boy is shown to have an unrealistically high level of competence in signing and reading lips after learning the skills for just one year. Children may also be intimidated by Shriek's frightening example of living with deafness. Like Allegro, Shriek is shown to be in pain, angry, and upset. There is an implication that Tommy can only be truly happy by being able to hear with his new devices. A child may become disappointed if their aids do not work as well as they are portrayed or if their deafness is severe enough to prevent them from being prescribed.

---

[22] Peter David and Eric Battle, Young Justice League 1 #24 (New York: DC Comics Inc, 2000).

[23] Scott Petersen, John Delaney, Mike DeCarlo and David Tanguay, Batman Beyond: Hear No Evil (New York: Random House, 2002).

The use of ASL on the cover of *Supergirl* #65 (2002) was a landmark in the representation of deaf characters.[24] Deaf children are shown spelling out the name "Supergirl" in hand shapes from the ASL alphabet. Appropriately entitled "Louder Than Words", the issue begins with Supergirl rescuing a deaf boy, Bradley, from the path of a lorry he neither sees nor hears. There are no speech bubbles for several pages until Bradley is asked whether he is deaf. Supergirl visits Bradley's specialist school where his fellow pupils are depicted communicating by reading lips and signing. None of the children are shown to wear hearing aids. Supergirl's companion Buzz is fluent in ASL. Buzz deliberately mistranslates a conversation between Supergirl and Bradley to cause himself amusement. Bradley is disturbed by this, and becomes upset again when he tries to read lips at a distance and misunderstands the conversation. Supergirl discovers that an unscrupulous developer intends to buy and bulldoze the institution. His chemical plant is already known to pollute the local water supply which has been blamed for causing the "defects" that have made the children deaf. Supergirl thwarts the developer by mobilising public opinion against him and gains the support of the hearing community. There are many positive features of this issue with the cover making a major symbolic statement that highlights sign language and promotes deaf identity. The spelling of Supergirl's name should be recognisable to anyone with a basic knowledge of ASL, although three of the characters are not so clear. The back page helpfully contains pictures of the signed alphabet along with a brief history of ASL, making this graphic statement accessible to a non-signing audience. There are problems in trying to portray signing, a language that takes place in three dimensions, in a two-dimensional medium. The absence of speech bubbles highlights Bradley's experience of silence outside the school, especially among hearing people. Lip reading is included not as a super power but as a skill that has limitations. Deaf children are likely to recognise the poorly developed verbal speech shown by some of the characters, and the difficulties caused when hearing characters turn away while speaking. The lack of hearing aids shown in a deaf school, which would be very unusual, emphasises the fact that children are communicating through sign language. Stress is placed on the need for specialised education and preconceptions of the hearing are superficially explored. Bradley is seen to be very much at home within a deaf community. This issue makes a positive contribution with its inclusion of ASL, but there are three problems, two of which are stereotypes. Buzz deliberately mistranslates Supergirl when speaking to a

---

[24] Peter David, Leonard Kirk, and Robin Riggs. Supergirl #65 (New York: DC Comics Inc, 2002).

child. In some circumstances, deaf people rely on translations from spoken languages and must trust those interpreting for them in order to retain confidence. The role of the ethical and accurate translator has already been explored in the previous chapter when examining the Paige Northwood novels. Second, the notion that children are deaf because of pollution is unfounded and suggests that the writers intended to make an ecological point by showing the recklessness of the developer. The last is that once again deafness is described as a "defect", implying the frequently held belief that deafness is an inferior state needing correction.

It is technology rather than treatment that is shown to restore perfect hearing in the adult sci-fi thriller *Avatar: A Look into the Abyss* (2003).[25] This addition to the genre has Spanish authorship but is written in English. The main character Lt Manuel Gomez of the Cyber Crime Division, is a "deaf-mute" detective who can speak and hear only when he wears special glasses. The ability to read lips superbly well is a common trope of the crime genre, but Gomez is not a lip-reader. This is a striking, gritty story that has well-designed and vividly illustrated graphics. The plot involves Gomez investigating a series of apparent suicides that are found to have occurred when the victims enter a virtual reality world by using specially made spectacles. Presumably this plot device is paralleled by Gomez's use of glasses, underlining a profound change of state experienced by the victims and in a different way, by Gomez. It is the technology that is crucial, not the deafness. The story perpetuates two myths. First, that technology will inevitably restore absent hearing. Second, that people who do not experience sound are without speech, and are incapable of any form of communication. The technology employed makes the fact that Gomez is deaf largely irrelevant, and therefore the presence of a deaf character, in the main, superfluous.

Maya then returned as the main character in her second and last story arc, the five-part series *Vision Quest* (2003-4).[26] In the first issue she is the only character. Her identity, memories and origins are explored in depth. Images of her father appear alongside pictures of Maya as a child in interlocking and overlapping panels, with ASL and Plains Indian signed handshapes in the background. Maya remembers her father as a storyteller and decides to speak in pictures through painting. She remembers being called "deaf" and "retarded", and wondering what different sounds were like. Maya discovered unheard words could take the form of shapes, memories and emotions. These are presented graphically as an interlocking

[25] Juan Miguel Aguilera and Rafael Fonteriz, Avatar: A Look into the Abyss (Celje, Slovenia: SAF Comics, 2003).
[26] David Mack, Daredevil #51-55 (New York: Marvel Worldwide Inc, 2003-4).

framework of childlike pictures, signing hand shapes, and scenes from the present. Maya's Cherokee father related traditional stories with shadow puppets, and told her

> "God uses sign language. I am his sign language to you, and you are his sign language to me."[27]

Maya visits The Chief who taught her father to sign. He proposes a vision quest, during which Maya encounters Wolverine and becomes sensitive to the "sign language of God". Maya decides to follow her father's path as a storyteller, and performs to deaf and hearing children with signs, dance, music, and shadow puppets. Daredevil learns that Maya has become a shaman to a tribe without boundaries of race or speech. She acts as an intermediary between the seen and unseen to communicate stories in various languages to any child who will watch or listen. Maya is no longer defined by her superhero persona. The last page indicates Maya's acceptance of her identity and calling by stating in ASL hand shapes the significant phrase "That silence is where you will find me".

Mack says he taught in deaf schools abroad.[28] The artist explained that *Vision Quest* was about the power of story-telling. He believes that storytellers are the shamans of our world and Echo continued in this tradition.[29] Mack was inspired by his Native American uncle to research Plains Indian sign language. The inclusion of two different signed languages is emblematic of Maya being more than just a superhero. She is a strong well-defined character with a rich heritage, and is able to explore on our behalf, the meanings of sensation, the power of memory, tradition, storytelling, and the search for purpose. Maya's vision quest demonstrates the sort of mythic notions often seen in comics such as "Entering the Otherworld".[30] The evolution of Echo's character throughout the story arc exemplifies common superhero comic themes such as transformation, identity, and difference,[31] as well as the grand theme of redemption, a feature strongly evident in the genre.[32] There is an emotional and spiritual

[27] David Mack, Daredevil #52 (New York: Marvel Worldwide Inc, 2003).

[28] David Mack, https:// davidamackarts.com.

[29] David Mack, In Sharon Pajka, "An interview with Creator (David Mack) of one of my favorite Deaf characters (Echo)".

[30] Valerie Estelle Frankel, Superheroines and the Epic Journey: Mythic themes in Comics, Film and Television (Jefferson: McFarland & Company Inc, 2017).

[31] Charles Hatfield, Jeet Heer and Kent Worcester (eds.), The Superhero Reader (Jackson: University Press of Mississippi, 2013), 3.

[32] Robert Jewett and John Shelton Lawrence, 2013. "Crowds of Superheroes." In The Superhero Reader, 80-83

depth to Echo in contrast to the typical one-dimensional way in which many deaf characters are written.[33] Although one deaf commentator states that Echo "isn't relatable, it's not the deaf experience",[34] deaf blogs are generally appreciative with one asking, "how often do we hear of a Native American, Latina, with a disability?".[35] Sharon Pajka, a deaf Professor at Gallaudet University with a particular interest in deaf characters appearing in adolescent literature writes,

> I originally liked Echo because she broke away from …typecasts of Deaf characters in literature. She wasn't a white male who was a victim of her own deafness. She wasn't isolated because she was unable to communicate with her peers. Echo is strong and confident…but that doesn't mean she is without flaws…the character goes through various levels of growth.[36]

The distinctive artwork for *Vision Quest* is described as a "kaleidoscope of words and images" that created "some of the most innovative comic-book sequences ever".[37] Echo's highly developed skills cast her as supercrip, but she has a strengthened identity rooted in silence and signing that makes her a role model for profoundly deaf young people. However, these major story arcs were not to last. For no apparent reason, following *Vision Quest*, the character was given greatly reduced roles.[38] [39] In her last appearance to date, Echo remains unaffected when Klaw uses sound to transform people into "zombies". Because she is deaf Echo is able to save Daredevil by covering his ears with headphones. Daredevil saves the day.[40] The beautifully

[33] "Deaf Comics/Graphic Novels", deafliterature, accessed April, 2016, https://deafliterature.wordpress.com/2016/04/10/deaf-comicsgraphic-novels/.

[34] Clint Nowicke, "Hawkeye, Blue Ear, why we need a deaf superhero and why I'm still waiting", Pop Mythology, accessed June 27, 2014, https://www.popmythology.com/hawkeye-blue-ear-why-we-need-a-deaf-superhero-and-why-im-still-waiting/.

[35] The Blerdgurl, "Echo – female, Native American, Latina, Deaf superhero", accessed March 30, 2016, https://theblerdgurl.com/comics/echo-female-native-american-latina-deaf-superhero/.

[36] Sharon Pajka, "An interview with Creator (David Mack) of one of my favorite Deaf characters (Echo)".

[37] Robert Schmidt, "Echo of the Cheyenne", accessed May 30, 2023, http://bluecorncomics.com/echo.htm.

[38] Brian Michael Bendis and David Finch, New Avengers 1 #11 (New York: Marvel Worldwide In, 2005).

[39] Brian Michael Bendis and Alex Maleev, Moon Knight 2 #8-12 (New York: Marvel Worldwide Inc, 2012).

[40] Charles Soule and Vanesa R Del Rey. Daredevil Annual #1 (New York: Marvel Worldwide In, 2016).

illustrated and well-defined role model has finished up like so many other deaf characters, as a plot prop.

Benjy, the baby of Peter Parker aka Spider-Man, is another minor plot device. He appears in a small number of issues of Spider-girl (2007). Benjy is born with superhuman powers because of his father's altered genetic code. Peter's family is attacked and a symbiote bonds with the baby. The ultrasound used to free Benjy causes bleeding from his ears and the baby no longer responds to sound.[41] His hearing parents are very frightened on being told their baby cannot hear. Benjy is offered surgery that eventually restores his hearing.[42] The deaf infant provides his older hearing sister with an innocent to rescue. Benjy also offers his parents a dilemma that needs to be solved. Medical intervention is deemed to be necessary, which is hardly surprising since the cause is unexpected and traumatic. What is surprising, perhaps, is the level of success achieved by the surgery.

In Chapter Three, I found that deaf characters and the silence they experience are often used as metaphors to emphasise estrangement and loneliness in novels. Silence and isolation are also prominent features of deaf characters in graphic literary forms. Helen Keller wrote long ago that "blindness separates people from things; deafness separates people from people".[43] The next example vividly conveys the profound distancing from others felt by a traumatised boy after he wakes to a silent world. *The Boy Who Made Silence* is a short graphic novel in which ten-year old Nestor falls from a bridge and into the river "that swallowed his hearing".[44] The images are stunning, bleak, and atmospheric, set in large panels using a sparse palate of colours with characters drawn in smudged details and indistinct outlines. The first five pages have no words and all the speech bubbles are empty. Nestor's mother visits the boy in hospital after his experience of nearly drowning. She is clearly estranged by his deafness and views him in the same way she would a suffering animal. After Nestor returns home, he questions the nature of what he is seeing. He has doubts and queries about the relationship with his mother, wondering whether she too has been traumatised early in her life. The boy witnesses his dog being

---

[41] Tom DeFalco and Ron Frenz, Amazing Spider-girl #12 (New York: Marvel Worldwide Inc, 2007).
[42] Tom DeFalco and Ron Frenz, Amazing Spider-girl # 18 (New York: Marvel Worldwide Inc, 2008).
[43] "Hearing sensitivity", Monash University, accessed n.d.,
https://ilearn.med.monash.edu.au/physiology/hearing/sensitivity.
[44] Joshua Hagler, The Boy Who Made Silence (Stevenage, UK: Markosia Enterprises Ltd, 2008).

killed by a wolf. Nestor is unable to communicate and runs away screaming, thinking to himself that,

> …in addition to your deafness and inability to speak clearly, you possess a scream from deep inside.

His mother finally shows empathy by holding Nestor as he cradles the dead dog. This is a powerful depiction of separation, fear, longing and emotional intensity, spoiled slightly by the unlikely cause of Nestor's deafness. However, the sweeping away of the boy's hearing by the flowing river acts as a powerful symbol of the uncontrollable and unconcerned progress of life and events swirling around him. It is a sombre depiction of pre-teenage angst that many deaf and hearing adolescents are likely to find relevant. There is a haunting quality of existential questioning that is inherent in one of the book's opening statements:

> Whether Esme, the twelve-year-old girl who brought him (Nestor) out of the river, saved his life or gave him a new one, remains a point of contention among those who discuss such notions.

The story depicts sudden deafness and its consequent silence as intense, frightening, and alienating, prompting searching questions without offering any answers. Some measure of hope is offered at the end of the story as Nestor and his mother are re-united in a close embrace. The use of "silent" pages that have illustrations without words and are filled with empty speech bubbles is an effective device often used by artists to represent deafness.

The Prophecy in Blue (2012) is a completely different type of graphic novel created by deaf artists. [45] It is a fantasy, available as an on-line publication, set in a dystopian parallel reality in which many people who are born deaf are gifted with a range of super powers. The Hearing Front wants to destroy the deaf community and outlaw sign language. A deaf underground opposition quickly emerges to protect the deaf community. The fact that deafness runs in the royal family is a closely guarded secret, and a newly born deaf royal baby is smuggled out of the palace to avoid capture. This is an interesting addition to the genre that includes BSL hand shapes in speech bubbles and illustrates some of the anxieties of signing communities. The story extols the need for strength within the deaf community and offers a high status of deafness through being carried in the royal genes and by being associated with inherited powers. In this imaginary

---

[45] Zamurrad Naqvi, CJ Hurtt, and Jr Jorge Correa, Signs and Voices Series 1– Prophecy in Blue, Episode 1 (On-line: Deaf Power Publishing House, 2012).

world, all deaf people are shown to be born into deaf families, experience profound deafness, and are fluent in signing. The deaf authors emphasise an ethnic and cultural identity of deafness by depicting a supposed homogeneity of deaf people exposed to extreme oppression by some hearing citizens. In reality, the overwhelming majority of deaf people are born into hearing families, most deaf people lose their hearing later in life, and many do not sign. The writers persist with the common stereotype of supra-normal abilities compensating deafness. There are problems in using this approach, but by doing so they state their characters are not limited by being deaf, and that they have an effective means of fighting back against the hearing opposition. By extension they are telling deaf young people they should not assume they will inevitably encounter limitations simply because they are deaf.

It is natural for children to want to fit in with their peers, including and perhaps especially deaf youngsters. This was the motivation behind the creation of a character expressly to encourage a young child to wear hearing aids. Blue Ear appeared in Marvel's *Iron Man: Sound Effects* (2012), in direct response to a mother's anxious request. Four-year old Anthony Smith, grandson of Senator D'Allesandro, refused to attend school wearing hearing aids, and referring to their colour, complained that "superheroes don't wear blue ears".[46] [47] In the resulting special story, Blue Ear's alter ego is a genius inventor working for Tony Stark aka Iron Man. Blue Ear manipulates sound and light energy and claims that "thanks to my listening device I hear someone in trouble!"[48] The strategy worked and Anthony was happy to identify with a superhero who wears hearing aids.[49]

It is not unusual for comics to re-invent characters. Hawkeye, who was created hearing, became deaf, and was then "retconned" once again into a hearing character in 2001.[50] Retcon is shorthand for "retroactive continuity", a device commonly used in comics, in which a previously

---

[46] Tim Stevens, "Iron Man introduces Blue Ear", Marvel, accessed October 31, 2014, https://www.marvel.com/articles/comics/iron-man-introduces-blue-ear.

[47] Annmarie Timmins, "Real-life Heroes", Concord Monitor, accessed May 20, 2012, https://www.concordmonitor.com/Archive/2012/05/999669239-999669240-1205-CM?page=0,0.

[48] Marc Sumerak and Karl Moline, Iron Man: Sound Effects (New York: Marvel Worldwide Inc, 2014).

[49] Paul Dakin, "'Super' heroes: Special powers in deaf characters", Hektoen International, Summer 2014. https://hekint.org/2017/01/31/super-heroes-special-powers-in-deaf-characters/.

[50] Kurt Busiek, Ian Churchill and Norm Rapmund, Avengers Annual #1 (New York: Marvel Worldwide Inc, 2001).

established narrative is changed. This revision, that could be described as the "causal jettisoning of a protagonist's disability",[51] threatened to snatch away from the deaf community one of the few examples of a major deaf superhero. However, this was not the last of Hawkeye's revisions, and in 2014 he reappeared as a deaf superhero once more.[52] In this issue, eagerly anticipated by a deaf blogger, [53] the name "Hawkeye" is spelt out on the first page in ASL hand shapes, twelve years after the historic cover of *Supergirl #65*. In contrast to "Louder Than Words" this comic is made deliberately inaccessible to non-signers by providing no English translation. The technique is designed to generate discomfort in hearing readers by allowing them to feel what it is like to be deaf in the absence of accessible communication. In what later came to be called "the silent issue",[54] we learn that the revised version of Clint Barton aka Hawkeye was rendered partially deaf as a child by physical abuse. We are shown Clint sitting separately from his parents in the doctor's office, unable to hear and understand what is happening. This is conveyed through indecipherable lines of dialogue, empty speech bubbles, and the positioning of a distant lonely figure, all evocative of the experience of a child isolated through lack of comprehension. There are pages of silence and misunderstanding. As an adult, Clint becomes angry, frustrated, finds it difficult to read lips, and is embarrassed to speak or sign. His communication problems are highlighted to hearing readers by the continued use of untranslated panels of ASL. There are some modest attempts to convey the idea of movement when certain signs are presented, either by showing two adjacent panels with the hand at the beginning and the end of making a sign, or an arrow suggesting movement. At some point in Clint's back story, he loses more hearing after being stabbed in the ears by the villain Clown. Clint neglects himself and develops an alcohol problem that causes fights with his brother Barney reminding him of their abusive childhood. Throughout, Barney who uses a wheelchair, encourages him to persevere and accept his deafness. Clint and Barney have become reluctantly interdependent. Barney helps Clint

---

[51] Jose Alaniz, Death, Disability and the Superhero: The Silver Age and Beyond (Jackson: University Press of Mississippi, 2014), 305.

[52] Matt Fraction and David Aja, Hawkeye #19 (New York: Marvel Worldwide Inc, 2014).

[53] Clint Nowicke, "A deaf comic geek's grateful review of 'Hawkeye #19,'" Pop Mythology, accessed August 4, 2014. https://www.popmythology.com/a-deaf-comic-geeks-grateful-review-of-hawkeye-19/.

[54] Kelsey McConnell, "Disability in Marvel Comics: The Necessity of Normalization," accessed May 9, 2017, https://comicsverse.com/disability-in-marvel-comics/.

communicate and Clint helps Barney mobilise. This symbiotic relationship represents a world in which disability is central but not solely as loss.[55] Eventually, Clint overcomes the painful memories and takes responsibility for his life. Clint pulls Barney's wheelchair to the roof where his neighbours have been asked to gather so that he can mobilise them against the gang that have terrorised the block. Barney translates Clint's signed speech starting with "I'm deaf and we need to talk," acknowledging that he can speak non-verbally. The deaf blogger who eagerly awaited the new incarnation of Hawkeye commented favourably about the silent issue:

> The doctor talks *about* Clint instead of *to* Clint which is a common experience for Deaf people, especially if we are with another person. Clint doesn't automatically know how to sign perfectly, which is a common deaf "trope" in movies and TV.

The writer continues by commenting on the way in which the two brothers sign to each other, consistent with their status as beginners:

> Their signs lack structure and follow English word order, and each sign is shown without an accompanying facial expression. This is common among "101 signers," who are often so intent on producing the sign that they ignore such aspects of the language as grammar (which is shown on the face). When Barney translates for Clint he does so one word at a time and *then* turns the phrase into a fluid sentence, which beginners often do as well

The visual device of demonstrating the lack of hearing also met with approval:

> The empty speech balloons floored me. They are the best representation of "not hearing" that I have ever seen in any medium, and make the lack of sound absolutely clear. *They make the issue purposefully difficult to read.* And until this point I have never been able to demonstrate what it's like to rely so heavily on lip-reading, but this issue made it perfectly clear in only a few panels.[56]

---

[55] Dale Jacobs, and Jay Dolmage, "Accessible Articulations: Comics and Disability Rhetorics in Hawkeye #19", The Journal of the Comics Studies Society, No. 3 (Fall 2018): 353-368.
[56] Nowicke, "A deaf comic geek's grateful review of 'Hawkeye #19'"

Favourable comments were also made by a Child of Deaf Adults (CODA), who maintained "this pop culture representation is affirming".[57] The Hawkeye #19 issue is viewed by some as unique and important for mainstream superhero comics.[58] However, as with Echo, this was not the end of the changes made to the character, and Hawkeye reappeared with a new artistic team just a year later in *All-New Hawkeye #1*.[59] The enthusiastic commentator who had eagerly awaited the deaf issue, was now angry that in the new version Hawkeye is shown wearing hearing aids that are almost invisible. The reviewer works in a deaf school and is familiar with children who do not want to wear hearing aids. They complain that wearing hearing aids makes them stand out from other children.

> My point is this: every time something like this happens, it teaches kids to be ashamed of their hearing aids. It teaches kids that they are not worthy of being represented, that they are somehow lesser because there is something obviously different about them and that this difference needs to be hidden.[60]

It seems a great pity that having produced an acclaimed issue, Marvel should then dilute Hawkeye's deafness to the point of irrelevance.

A book that largely succeeds in breaking the mould of stereotypes is *El Deafo* published in 2014.[61] This is the best-known example of a comic or graphic novel written by a deaf author that features a deaf character written for a mainstream readership. It is the autobiographical depiction of a young girl who develops meningitis and loses her hearing. The book, intended for older children, documents Cece's experience in hospital and school as she struggles to use hearing aids. She is frustrated by distortions of speech and sound. Set in the 1970s, Cece is sent first to a special school where "everyone is like me". She cannot readily understand conversations, and explains how reading lips is improved by predicting the correct word when people are talking to her. Cece is forced to switch to a mainstream school when she moves to a new area. The neighbourhood children are inquisitive

---

[57] Lydia Callis, "Superheroes who are deaf and the power of diversity", Huffpost, accessed September 16, 2014; Updated December 6, 2017.
https://www.huffpost.com/entry/deaf-superheroes-and-the-_b_5825054.
[58] Jacobs and Dolmage, "Accessible Articulations: Comics and Disability Rhetorics in *Hawkeye #19*", 353-368.
[59] Jeff Lemire and Ramon Perez, All-New Hawkeye #1(New York: Marvel Worldwide Inc, 2015).
[60] Clint Nowicke, "All-New Hawkeye, the 'Daredevil syndrome' and a step back for deaf readers" Pop Mythology, accessed March 6, 2015,
https://www.popmythology.com/all-new-hawkeye-daredevil-syndrome/.
[61] Cece Bell, El Deafo (New York: Amulet Books, 2014).

about her bulky hearing aids, and Cece finds it hard to explain why she cannot laugh at jokes they enjoy on the radio. Cece takes a special microphone to school that links with a Phonic Ear hearing aid helping her to understand the teachers. Sometimes she is amused to overhear people talking in other classrooms and the staff room, or when the teachers forget to turn it off and go to the bathroom. These experiences of illicit hearing allow Cece to fantasise that she can turn into a superhero called El Deafo who has the power of super hearing. This fantasy intensifies her feeling of isolation because

> Superheroes might be awesome, but they are also different. And being different feels a lot like being alone.[62]

Cece eventually uses the hearing aids to attract friends and grows in confidence. One of her classmates is domineering and manipulative, and another annoys Cece by speaking very loud and slow. She is patronised by a friend's mother at a sleepover. Cece wishes that she could tell her friends what she really thinks and wonders what would happen if El Deafo took control. She is embarrassed when people try to sign to her, especially when her mother takes her to a signing class. Eventually Cece establishes some good friendships. Her schoolmates think that Cece's ability to hear people at a distance thorough the microphone is amazing, and so she becomes more popular and confident until she is able to tell her best friend about El Deafo. *El Deafo* covers serious themes common to childhood and made more difficult by being deaf, such as hospital admission, starting school, moving home, and establishing relationships. Cece's silence and confusion is conveyed by absent or faded words in speech bubbles, and the clear expressions of puzzlement or emotion on the characters' faces. All the characters are drawn with exaggerated rabbit ears that denote the significance of hearing in the story. The rabbit ears also make Cece's hearing aids obvious. She is subject to medical intervention and can sign. Cece has attended a deaf school but otherwise there are few indications of a deaf community. As you would expect from a deaf author, there are good examples of deaf awareness. Bell is known to wear hearing aids, and instances of personal experience, such as Cece's unwillingness to learn sign language, inform each page, making the character accessible and inspiring to deaf young people. Professor Pajka, though generally appreciative of the book, was disappointed that Bell did not go further and allow El Deafo to

---

[62] Bell, El Deafo, 46

stand up for Cece by saying "I am different and awesome".[63] But in many ways, Cece was different and awesome. As Bell states in the epilogue "Our differences are our *superpowers*", a theme that we will see reiterated later in referring to the concept of Deaf Gain in the Afterword. Cece feels she has superpowers not because she is deaf, but because she wears hearing aids that partially correct her deafness. She tries to make her difficult life more comfortable by imagining that the hearing aids turn her into an alter ego endowed with superpowers. If Cece actually transformed into the superhero alter ego with heightened hearing, I would not hesitate to class the character as a stereotypical supercrip. The same accusation would apply if El Deafo became anything more than a comfortable figment of Cece's imagination, and appropriated El Deafo's attributes making her stand up for Cece. As it is I think Bell avoids this accusation, and as a result the character is more realistic and aspirational than most. Cece is not a plot device or a prop. She is the major character, and although her deafness and experience are crucial to the entire book, Cece is not defined simply by her deafness. She is portrayed as an ordinary girl who happens to be deaf, and despite the difficulties of school and friendships, she manages to achieve a modest measure of heroism through overcoming everyday problems.

In 2016 Marvel introduced another character intended to be overtly aspirational. Having designed Blue Ear to encourage a young boy to wear hearing aids, the same artists developed a four-part series in which Sapheara worked alongside Blue Ear.[64] Sapheara is the only comic superhero to have bilateral cochlear implants. She is a teenager who has the power to control the energy of light. Sapheara champions all deaf children by saying,

> It doesn't matter if we're struggling with hearing problems, bullying, or even super villains…what matters is that we don't give up.

Blue Ear and Sapheara can both be described as supercrips. They are the only superheroes created specifically to be aspirational role models. I wonder whether there is any significance in the name "Sap–*hear*-a", but perhaps I'm reading too much into it. Blue Ear is given bright blue prostheses and Sapheara has pink cochlear implants making them quite obvious. The intention is to encourage children to wear them. As far as I know, the artists are not deaf, and in order to produce this issue, Marvel

---

[63] Sharon Pajka, Review of *El Deafo* by Cece Bell, The Washington Post, September 23, 2014. https://www.washingtonpost.com/entertainment/books/review-el-deafo-by-cece-bell/2014/09/23/947aab00-402e-11e4-b0ea-8141703bbf6f_story.html.

[64] Marc Sumerak and Karl Moline, Blue Ear & Sapheara: Rooftop Rescue. (New York: Marvel Worldwide Inc, 2016).

collaborated with the Children's Hearing Institute. The Institute refers in its literature to deafness as "hearing loss", and its founder is a pioneer in the use of cochlear implants.[65] Although this might cause concern for some profoundly deaf signers, in the circumstances, I think it was quite appropriate for the creators to seek advice from an institution that exists to promote technological solutions. There are undoubtedly many children like Anthony who benefit from the provision of hearing aids and cochlear implants. It is up to the youngsters and their families to choose the best option, and since the majority of deaf children are born to hearing parents, I can understand why they may decide to pursue audiological intervention. Having said that, Blue Ear and Sapheara are unlikely to be aspirational for those young people who sign and live primarily within a deaf culture. This stresses the importance of deaf children being exposed to a variety of deaf characters that might provide hope and encouragement.

The final example is a relatively minor character who has attained more recent popularity due to the character's on-screen debut in the film *Eternals*. Makkari actually originated as a male hearing character in 1973, but as we have found, comics often re-invent characters and their abilities, and Makkari was retrospectively revised or ret-conned, as a deaf woman of colour in 2021.[66] In her brief re-introduction, Makkari loses her speech and hearing while trying to contact the dead Celestial. She can only communicate in ASL. What is notable about the issue are the attempts by the artists to convert what is a three-dimensional language onto a two-dimensional page. By its nature, signing is dynamic and fluid, with one sign morphing seamlessly into another. Hand movements are also accompanied by changes in facial expression and body posture that can emphasise or alter the meaning of a sign. Trying to express any of these elements in artwork is a challenge. However, these are significant improvements from the ground-breaking Supergirl issue that introduced static signing handshapes and the indications of movement presented in the Hawkeye silent issue. In some images, Makkari's artist reproduces the flowing movements of ASL quite effectively by drawing Makkari's hands in three different overlapping shapes and positions to signify the progression of a signed conversation.

---

[65] Children's Hearing Institute, Accessed n.d., https://www.childrenshearing.org/about-us/.
[66] Kieran Gillen and Kei Zama, Eternals: Celestial #1. (New York: Marvel Worldwide Inc, 2021).

Recurring themes in the portrayal of deaf characters

During the sixty years that deaf characters have appeared in comics and graphic novels, there has been a vague, general trend away from stereotypes readily identifiable to hearing readers, towards more sophisticated representations that are likely to reveal realistic aspects of deaf experience that in some cases, include deaf language and culture. This transition is by no means perfect or complete, and it is punctuated by examples of deaf characters that are no more than plot devices. I have described eighteen characters or groups of characters, one of whom, Jericho, was actually hearing. The deaf characters are evenly split between male and female, and nearly half are children: Shelley, Hope, Benjy, Nestor, Tommy, Bradley, and Cece. A greater proportion of the deaf characters found in comics are young when compared with those appearing in novels. This reflects the younger age of the readership, and the fact that two of the examples were designed specifically to be aspirational for children. Ten of the examples have superpowers. DC created three, and Marvel seven.

Most of the deaf characters identified are shown to use verbal speech to some extent, with the exception of Jericho who cannot speak because of his injury, the profoundly deaf inhabitants of *The Prophecy in Blue*, and Makkari. Nestor is only able to speak incomprehensibly and Benjy is too young. Most characters are shown to read lips with the exception of Professor Calculus, Allegro, and Nestor. Benjy is too young. Sign language is used by the main deaf characters in nine comics: Jericho, Shelley, Hope, Echo, Hawkeye, Bradley, Tommy, Cece, Makkari, and all the deaf characters featured in *Prophecy in Blue*. Despite this, there is surprisingly little acknowledgement of a signing community or even signing families outside the context of a deaf school. The exception is *Prophecy in Blue* in which all deaf people are shown to use BSL. The explanation may be that the main focus of a comic tends to be on a specific individual character, or team of characters, that usually represent a variety of skills and people from different backgrounds, rather than a group that share a single attribute.

Deaf education is mentioned in five of the examples. Following his injury, Jericho learns ASL at a deaf school. Hope, Maya, and Bradley all attend specialist schools. Cece is educated at both a deaf and mainstream school. Both Cece and Shelley feel isolated during their progress at a mainstream school. Natalie and Sapheara are shown to attend hearing senior schools. Sapheara is mocked and ridiculed by some of her fellow students. Compared with the descriptions given in novels, few details of the educational establishments are provided. All the deaf schools appear to teach and encourage signing, a position reflecting the teaching methods prevalent in the US at the end of the last century. Cece provides more information, especially about her mainstream school where the staff are keen to make themselves heard and understood.

Although the more recent portrayals suggest a shift away from perceiving deafness as a disability, some continue to show it as a type of loss that needs correction. Medical involvement therefore remains a common theme and appears in nine of the stories. In comics, the reader is often asked to mimic the role of the doctor when viewing the deaf character.[67] This is particularly true of *The Boy Who Made Silence*, *Hawkeye #19*, and *El Deafo*, in which we are invited to view the main characters when they are in hospital. We are told that five of the major characters are deaf because of trauma: Nestor, Allegro, Benjy, Makkari, and two versions of Hawkeye. As discussed in Chapter Three, trauma is a relatively uncommon cause of deafness but provides the writer with a useful plot device. Four characters are shown to have hearing aids-Hawkeye, Tommy, Blue Ear, and Cece. Sapheara has cochlear implants. All of these are provided by doctors and audiologists, although we see little of their involvement. Tommy, Blue Ear, the final incarnation of Hawkeye, and Sapheara, all appear to have successfully regained their hearing courtesy of their technological devices. Three of these characters were created specifically to encourage children and young people to wear their prostheses, and so we would expect their portrayal to be optimistic. However, many deaf young people actually struggle with hospital appointments and their devices and are more likely to identify with some of the experiences of Cece. People who wear hearing aids often report that background sound may be over-amplified, words remain indistinct, consonants are confused, and additional sounds such as feedback, distortion, and buzzing may swamp audible speech.[68] Those who embark on a cochlear implant procedure naturally hope they will be successful but the actual gain achieved by surgery may be partial and problematic.[69] Despite the best efforts of audiologists who use computer matching of auditory loss to boost sound in certain frequencies, deaf people are unlikely to enjoy a level of hearing that is more than adequate when using electronic aids.

---

[67]Jacobs and Dolmage, "Accessible Articulations: Comics and Disability Rhetorics in Hawkeye #19", 353-368.

[68] Fethullah Kenar and Mehmet Ali Babademez, "Problems encountered with hearing aids in adult population" Journal of Medical Updates 2015;5: Online Preprint Issue, doi:10.2399/jmu.201500100.

[69] L Masterson , S Kumar , J H K Kong , J Briggs ,N Donnelly , P R Axon and R F Gray. "Cochlear implant failures: lessons learned from a UK centre," The Journal of Laryngology & Otology , No. 1 (January 2012): 15–21.

All the deaf characters I have examined occupy major roles within their settings except Professor Calculus and Benjy. Deaf characters are much more likely to be central to the plot of a graphic text when compared to the positioning of their counterparts in novels. There are fewer characters depicted in comics, with considerably less written text and explanation and a limited number of illustrations. These conventional restrictions of the medium imply that a hearing artist must choose to invent a specific character more deliberately than may occur in the greater space of a novel with its panoply of players, and if the character is deaf, will be responsible for finding ways of effectively demonstrating their deafness. Although deaf characters are often shown at the heart of the plot with hearing characters revolving around them, many are still used as stereotypical props. The deafness of Calculus, Allegro, Jericho, Gomez, Benjy, Natalie, the earliest and latest versions of Hawkeye, and the final incarnation of Echo, does not develop the character but merely exists to advance the plot.

The only instance of a Granny character, a stereotype discussed in more detail in Chapter Two, is Professor Calculus. Such representations are unlikely to be of interest to a predominantly younger readership who will have limited experience of meeting older people who became deaf, and the majority of characters that appear in comics are much younger. Natalie is probably the only character in comics who could be categorised as Gifted as she is shown to have an amazing skill in reading lips. Echo is the only potential candidate for a Goldilocks stereotype. Although she experiences mistreatment and is rescued through Fisk's intervention, Echo's character is much better developed than most with an extensive back story full of complex emotions and nuanced behaviour. In contrast to what may happen in the plot of a novel, there are no examples that exemplify a trope of deaf innocence that is spoiled by being thrust into the hearing world. The absence of Goldilocks characters in comics suggests a desire to reject the trope in favour of major characters who are of more interest to young people.

Many artists try to convey a sense of the reality of what it is like to be deaf by using visual devices that have become standard conventions. These include a lack of written dialogue and empty speech bubbles to represent silence. Characters may be placed at a distance from one another and possibly facing in different directions to suggest isolation and estrangement. Plenty of images show deaf characters with faces that express confusion or sadness. Deaf people often appear to have difficulty understanding those who do not face them when they speak and cannot always read lips perfectly. More recently speech bubbles or narrative panels are likely to picture sign language hand shapes, with or without translation. Thoughtfully designed images are accessible to both deaf and hearing young people and help hearing people to be more aware of the communication issues and isolation experienced by those who are deaf.

Deaf commentators have expressed a range of opinions concerning the way in which deaf characters are portrayed in comics. In 2001 there were considered enough examples to prompt an evaluation for a deaf newspaper. The reviewer applauded the appearance of deaf characters in mainstream comics but criticised what he thought was the over-representation of females from ethnic minorities, many of whom came from a background of victimisation.[70] In fact, at the time when this article was written, I can find only two examples of females from ethnic minorities. It is possible that the writer knew of further examples that I have been unable to discover, but if not, his comments lead me to wonder whether they reflect the reviewer's own background when encountering such diversity. The comparatively low number of ethnic superheroes, whether deaf or not, led another commentator to observe twelve years later that the

> …lack of black superheroes has served as a source of concerned speculation and critique.[71]

By now, a greater, though not massive proportion of deaf characters in comics represent ethnic minorities: Hope, Echo, Natalie, and Makkari. All originate from a more recent era, from the late nineties onwards, since when the depiction of people with different ethnic origins has become more common. Each of the deaf characters I have studied, regardless of background, is shown to experience some form of misunderstanding and isolation. If the newspaper reviewer's main objection is to an over-representation of victimisation, rather than ethnic origin, I agree. The idea that deaf people are perceived inevitably as some sort of victim is seen in both comics and novels. That is why the emergence of deaf superheroes is so important. Superheroes, by their very nature, overcome obstacles and have an aspirational appeal. If they start out as a victim, they do not remain one. The same is true for deaf superheroes, perhaps even more so. They show that deaf characters, and by extension deaf people, need not be construed as victims, but can be powerful and able to break free from limitations imposed upon them. But representations of deaf superheroes are not without problems. Some portrayals, such as that of Allegro lend support

---

[70] John Lothridge, "Deaf comic book characters are diverse, sometimes inaccurate," Silent News, May 12, 2001, 15.
[71] Nama, Adilifu. "Color Them Black." In The Superhero Reader, ed. Charles Hatfield, Jeet Heer and Kent Worcester, (Jackson: University Press of Mississippi, 2013), 252-269.

to the view that disabled characters can be turned into freaks "stripped of normalizing contexts and engulfed by a single stigmatic trait",[72] but that is by no means true of all. A deaf reviewer posed an opposing view when he complained that

> Marvel has a bad habit of creating a character with a disability but doing *everything* to counteract that disability so that it seems non-existent.[73]

We are therefore faced with a dilemma fundamental to the portrayal of any deaf character–to what extent should the deafness be stressed? On the one hand, we have encountered examples of characters such as Benjy whose only attribute is deafness. On the other, characters such as Gomez, or two versions of Hawkeye, play down the fact that they are deaf at all, rendering their deafness irrelevant. More often there are instances, particularly from the superhero genre such as Marvel's Echo, in whom deafness is made very prominent, and the character is seen to possess exaggerated abilities precisely because she is perceived as "disabled". Are there then only two options available to an artist–reduce a superhero's deafness so far as to render it irrelevant or emphasise it so much to create a supercrip?

The supercrip

The supercrip could be considered as potentially the most significant stereotype of deaf characters seen in comics. According to the definition that I gave above, supercrips are disabled characters who possess exaggerated powers to compensate for a perceived loss of ability or sensation. It would seem then that any superhero perceived as disabled must be a supercrip including those that are deaf. Deaf superheroes manifest extraordinary gifts, with heightened senses, to compensate for their loss of hearing, or they exaggerate deaf skills such as lip-reading. I should point out that there is nothing wrong in wanting to see an individual rise above difficulties, whatever their physical attributes, but such narratives are thought to be overly moving and sentimentally aspirational. They are often viewed as patronising and oppressive by the individuals concerned.[74] But

---

[72] Rosemarie Garland Thomson, Extraordinary Bodies: Fighting Physical Disability in American Culture and Literature. (New York: Columbia University Press, 1997), 11.

[73] Nowicke, "All-New Hawkeye, the 'Daredevil syndrome' and a step back for deaf readers".

[74] Alaniz, Death, Disability, and the Superhero, 32

should deaf characters be viewed as supercrips? I believe there are important objections to this concept.

The idea that characters are compensated for being deaf and are granted additional powers is already well established in literature. Although deaf people may report that a lack of hearing can be compensated by enhanced natural sensations, particularly vision,[75] the extent of the improvement is not as great as the supra-normal powers suggested in fictional representations. The implication inherent in many graphic texts is that a deaf character is only of value when they are capable of extraordinary acts. One reason to reject the stereotype of supercrip is its lack of reality. For instance, giving deaf characters incredible lip-reading skills is unrealistic when a competent lip-reader without residual hearing can only understand thirty per cent of a conversation.[76] Such inaccurate portrayals encourage the hearing majority to have unrealistic expectations of deaf people.[77] They generate amazement at any ability deemed to be extraordinary and may be extended to more mundane activities, thus supporting a low expectation of what a disabled person is actually capable of achieving.[78] Hearing people may assume the deaf cannot communicate and are then surprised to observe the use of verbal speech and sign language, even though these are everyday activities taken for granted by deaf people. There seems to be an underlying assumption that disability and achievement, and more specifically, deafness and achievement, are somehow contradictory, and that any success, no matter how small, should be applauded. The concept of supercrip confirms that only unique individuals possessing the necessary perseverance and inner strength can achieve success, rather than considering the impact of the social context.[79] It is not surprising then that supercrips are considered to be oppressive by the people they portray, as they imply an exaggerated misrepresentation of an entire community.

The second reason to reject the supercrip stereotype is again specific to the portrayal of deaf characters. By definition, supercrips are perceived as

---

[75] Dye, Matthew. "Seeing the World through Deaf Eyes". In Deaf Gain: Raising the Stakes for Human Diversity, ed. H-Dirksen L. Bauman and Joseph J. Murray (Minneapolis: University of Minnesota Press, 2014), 193-2010.

[76] Neil Baumann, "Speechreading (Lip-Reading)", Center for Hearing Loss Help, accessed revised August 2020, http://hearinglosshelp.com/blog/speechreading-lip-reading/.

[77] Lothridge, "Deaf comic book characters are diverse, sometimes inaccurate," 15.

[78] Jeffrey J. Martin, Handbook of Disability Sport and Exercise (Oxford: Oxford Academic, 2017, p139-149.

[79] Ria Cheyne, Disability, Literature, Genre: Representation and Affect in Contemporary Fiction (Liverpool: Liverpool University Press, 2019), 63-64.

being disabled, and many deaf people, especially profoundly deaf signers, do not see themselves as disabled at all. They would therefore vehemently disagree with the idea that deaf superheroes should be labelled as supercrips. Disability identity theory speaks of themes such as communal attachment and self-worth, that are likely to be valued by any group, including deaf people.[80] The themes also include the affirmation of disability, and that is likely to be firmly rejected. The identity of deaf communities, and signing communities in particular, has evolved in recent years from a disability to a language model, so I wonder how many profoundly deaf people would subscribe to the notion of "disability identity" as applying to them? I suspect they would rather agree with Echo's attitude when she rejects Moon Knight's underlying perception of her "disability" when he states "You just don't *act* deaf". Echo immediately snaps back "Now what the hell does *that* mean?"[81] For those deaf people who see themselves as a linguistic minority, it would seem that the disability movement is complicit in perpetuating the construction that the deaf are disabled.[82] The supercrip narrative favoured in disability studies is in direct opposition to an ethnic model of deafness. It may work, perhaps, when applied to those deaf people who were deafened at a later age and continue to identify with the hearing majority. Some of the examples of deaf characters might be identified as falling into this group such as Hawkeye and possibly Natalie. But even so I would expect the larger group of deaf people that these characters represent to react against the idea of supercrip. It seems to me that the proponents of disability studies are lacking a proper and appropriate framework with which to engage specifically with deafness and deaf people, if indeed they should. I have been unable to find any evidence that the academic literature on superheroes and disability can differentiate between radically different types of deafness and therefore deal with the issue of deafness either thoroughly or adequately.

It is not only important to consider the way in which deaf characters are portrayed, but also the context. In a hearing world, deaf superheroes may be considered as supercrips, but in a deaf world they are simply superheroes. If an artist changes the context of a deaf character hearing readers may be able to perceive deaf characters in a different way. That is unlikely to happen as artists create characters that exist within a hearing framework for

---

[80] Dana S Dunn and Shane Burcow, "Thinking about Disability," Spotlight on disability Newsletter, American Psychological Association, November 2013.
[81] Brian Michael Bendis and Alex Maleev, Moon Knight 2 #8 (New York: Marvel Worldwide Inc, 2012).
[82] Chijioke Obasi, "Seeing the Deaf in 'Deafness'," Journal of Deaf Studies and Deaf Education, No. 4 (Fall 2008): 455-465.

mainstream consumption. The majority of authors and artists are hearing and few have little experience of deafness. The only example examined that even attempts to portray deaf characters in a different context is *The Prophecy in Blue* written by deaf authors.

Role models

There is, I think, a better way of understanding the representation of deaf characters in a genre in which many possess superpowers. It is possible to counteract or modify some of the features of a deaf character that might otherwise prompt the accusation of supercrip. Echo has a history of extreme victimhood as well as a complex and emotional back story. She has certainly been granted amazing gifts that are exaggerated by loss, but she is also a multi-faceted character whose psychological struggle demonstrates many features likely to resonate with both deaf and hearing young people. The great depth of Echo's depiction is similar in many ways to that of Daredevil, whose character is founded on the character's internal conflicts, and treats his blindness and heightened senses as "opportunities for development instead of mere plot devices".[83] As a result Daredevil "succeeds not in spite of but because of his disability /superpowers".[84] It does not matter if a character like Echo is in danger of categorisation as a supercrip just because she is deaf and has superpowers. All superheroes, even deaf ones, have extraordinary abilities. The issue is whether in spite of these she can be thought to have a relatable depth that overshadows the stereotype. Characters exhibiting unusual powers may be aspirational but by their very nature are distanced from reality. They may encourage deaf people to overcome obstacles but do not represent the typical existence of being deaf. It is this balance between portraying the relatable normality of a deaf character, alongside the awesome power of their superhero alter ego, that is the key to avoiding supercrip. I believe we see this in the representation of Echo, a view supported by two widely differing on-line comments that imply the balance is probably about right. A CODA wrote that Echo's "supposed 'disability' works to her advantage" making her "a great representation of deafness",[85] whereas a deaf commentator complained Echo

---

[83] Young, Frank Miller's Daredevil and the ends of heroism, 35
[84] Alaniz, Death, Disability, and the Superhero, 305
[85] Callis, "Superheroes who are deaf and the power of diversity"

"...could copy anything she saw and practically lipread through a concrete building. This isn't relatable, it's not the deaf experience".[86]

These considerations are not simply academic and may be of prime importance when designing portrayals for young people, as some fictional characters have been shown to be admired or identified with.[87] This is especially true in the superhero genre, [88] and superheroes may provide role models for adolescents.[89] (Melnick 2002). This includes deaf youngsters:

> Since the early days of comic books, superheroes have been a source of inspiration and hope for people around the world. They give us someone to look up to, someone to aspire to be like. They teach us that no matter who we are, we have the potential to be great. For people who are deaf, superheroes can be especially important. They provide representation of a group that is often underrepresented in mainstream media. They also give **deaf people** the opportunity to see themselves as powerful and capable, which can be empowering.[90]

However, since it is the depiction of realistic deaf characters that is found to be beneficial to deaf adolescents,[91] we should offer young people not only examples of well-developed superhero characters such as Echo, but also those characters that do not appear in the superhero genre. In this study there are four: Calculus, Shelley, Nestor, and Cece. Calculus is not intended to be anything more than a humorous plot device, but the other three show elements of realism, especially Shelley and Cece. These elements include practicalities such as getting hearing characters to face the deaf character, incomplete understanding, fiddling with hearing aids and batteries, partial success with lip-reading, and the emotional aspects of coping with deafness, such as feelings of loneliness among hearing people. In comics that are not

---

[86] Nowicke, "A deaf comic geek's grateful review of 'Hawkeye #19'"

[87] Rollin, Roger B. "The Epic Hero and Pop Culture." In The Superhero Reader, 53-61.

[88] J.H. McCrary, "Children's heroes and heroines: Developing values manifested artwork", Paper presented at the annual meeting of the Mid-South Educational Association, Point Clear, AL, 17-19 November, 1999. http://eric.ed.gov.

[89] Samantha Melnick, "A Student's Perspective: Fictional Characters in Books as Positive Role Models for Adolescent Females," Gifted Child Today, No. 2 (April 2002): 44-45.

[90] Samantha J. "The Most Notable Deaf Characters in Marvel Comics", ICPHS2019, accessed November 30, 2022, https://www.icphs2019.org/the-most-notable-deaf-characters-in-marvel-comics.

[91] Sharon Pajka-West, "Representations of Deafness and Deaf People in Young Adult Fiction". M/C Journal, Vol.13 No.3 (2010). https://doi.org/10.5204/mcj.261

of the superhero genre, it is vital that the representations are shown to be realistic. There is nothing wrong with using deaf characters to exemplify silence and isolation–that is the reality for many young people. The way in which this is done however, is crucial. Shelley and Cece provide good examples of ordinary youngsters who tackle everyday problems and experience the added difficulties of communicating with hearing people, especially in communal hearing settings such as schools. Their example demonstrates that "super powers are not necessary for a girl to become a superheroine".[92] I would imagine that deaf young people would find their experience relatable and perhaps aspirational. I suspect Shelley's author researched deafness, and Cece is of course based on the writer's own experience of being deaf. The only other deaf authors were those who created *The Prophecy in Blue*, which is intended to be a fantasy in an imaginary world.

Looking forward, I would suggest that artists are careful when contemplating adding deaf characters to their stories. I hope that hearing artists will copy Mack's example and conduct more research into deaf life, allowing even minor characters to avoid the pitfalls of stereotypes. The only credible example created by a deaf author, *El Deafo*, is distinguished largely because of the detailed authenticity given to the main character and the narrative. Apart from the depiction of the "rabbit ears" there is nothing visually to mark it as fundamentally different from the creations of hearing writers. Although there are hints of a wider cohesive context, most deaf characters are shown as living in a cultural and personal vacuum, dominated by silent loneliness and having contact only with hearing characters. This of course is not true for all deaf people, but the depictions could be explored and expanded much further. For instance, it would be helpful and more realistic to show deaf characters, especially those who sign, as belonging to a wider community and enjoying aspects of deaf culture. In addition, there are artistic features that could be taken into consideration. If characters are shown to be signing and space permits, it would be more accurate to use the dynamic forms of representing sign language as seen in the Hawkeye silent issue and used with Makkari. Although some look forward to a greater number of deaf characters who only use only sign language,[93] this would not be representative of the deaf population as a whole. The profoundly deaf often feel misunderstood and marginalised so it is reasonable for them to look for aspirational role models who sign to inspire their young. Children who wear hearing aids or cochlear implants also want to see characters that

---

[92] Robbins, Trina. 2013. "The great women superheroes." In The Superhero Reader, 53-61.

[93] Lothridge, "Deaf comic book characters are diverse, sometimes inaccurate," 15

reflect a different set of issues such as problems with the prostheses. The majority of deaf people, including many who can sign, choose not to identify with the signing subculture, and are able to vocalise. They may also read lips and wear hearing aids, and are more likely to identify with the hearing majority into which they were born. Hearing readers can relate to the problems posed by schools and friendships, and deaf children can relate to those as well as the issues of communication. There is therefore a wide range of potential characteristics to be considered when creating a deaf character. A more representative portrayal of deaf characters in comics generally would lead to a greater number depicted and a much wider variety of examples drawn from real-life deaf experience, in particular, older deaf characters shown to wear hearing aids. I would also make a final plea that if an artist has created a well-developed deaf character, it should not be allowed to fade like Echo, or be ret-conned into a hearing character like Hawkeye.

CHAPTER FIVE

VERSE AND VIDEO –
DEAF CHARACTERS IN POETRY

There are two fundamental differences between the portrayal of deaf characters in poetry compared with those that appear in most other forms of literature. The first is that the proportion of poets who include deaf characters in their poems for a mainstream readership and are deaf, is much greater than the proportion of deaf authors who invent similar imaginary creations in their novels. The nature of poetry allows deaf people to write candidly and persuasively from a personal perspective, and they may often choose to position themselves in the poem as the main character. Poetry is capable of eliciting an immediate, then a longer lasting reaction from the reader, arguably more intense and provoking than the response elicited by other literary forms. The emotional undercurrents disturbed by a poem may be less obvious and extend far beyond the level of conscious appreciation of the words themselves. Because deaf people find poetry to be a powerful medium through which to express their pain, anger, anxiety and hopes, they are more likely to want to use this medium to communicate with a mainstream audience, and will therefore constitute a greater proportion of the poets who include a deaf character. The appeal to hearing writers however, may not appear so obvious when considering the structure of this literary form.

The second difference is the type of medium chosen for the poem. Traditional poetry consists of carefully chosen arrangements of words that build a pattern dependent on rhythm and stresses, that may not be fully expressed when read silently, and are only fully appreciated when spoken and heard. The sequences of words, some of which may be repeated and may be designed to rhyme, are intended to be lingered over, savoured, and enjoyed, allowing layers of meaning to engage both our conscious thoughts and emotions. The form uses the language of the hearing majority making poetry generally accessible, if not totally comprehensible, to all literate members of both communities. This type of metrical poetry would have been standard, particularly in the eighteenth and nineteenth centuries, making it difficult for a contemporary deaf person to read a poem adequately, and just as hard if they so desired, to write one. The emergence of freer forms in the twentieth century eventually allowed deaf poets a greater freedom and scope to write about deafness and deaf characters that broke open the traditional conventions of written poetry.

During the last fifty years however, an alternative form of visual poetry has been created by profoundly deaf poets and is performed in sign language. Many, though not all, of these works use readily recognisable iconic signs that are likely to be understood by hearing people with no specific training in signing, making the performances accessible to both the deaf and the hearing. This form of signed poetry may be translated into words and written in books, but it is also recorded and disseminated by video, film, and the internet. Although it has been my intention throughout this book to explore fictional characters depicted in mainstream works, the quantity and quality of the autobiographical products of deaf poets in both written and visual forms, some of which but not all, have entered mainstream poetry, means that I feel compelled to include them. The themes apparent in these autobiographical works also link very well with those already described and discussed in previous chapters. They provide evidence of a continuity of historical and cultural development that remains broadly consistent across various forms of literature. I begin with a review of the relatively small number of poems that are written about deaf characters, and then discuss some of the emerging themes.

Perhaps the earliest example of a deaf character to be found in a poem is that of the Wife of Bath who complains about being assaulted by her fifth husband.

> He stopped my gadding round, my hide-and-seek.
> By God, he smote me once upon the cheek
> Because I tore a page out of his book,
> And that's the reason why I'm deaf. [1]

From *The Canterbury Tales*,
Geoffrey Chaucer 1340–1400.

The blow from the Wife of Bath's husband causes traumatic deafness. The fact that she is deaf, adds to the character's own description of her age and infirmity. The incident provides information about her hearing

---

[1] Geoffrey Chaucer, The Canterbury Tales ed. by E.V Rieu, translated into Modern English by Nevill Coghill (Harmondsworth: Penguin Books, 1952), 299.

husband's nature, and gives the man another reason for him to ask her forgiveness.

Deaf characters in eighteenth century poetry

In 1717 Pope created a deaf character that was based on a real person, the Countess of Suffolk, the mistress of George II.

> I know the thing that's most uncommon;
> (Envy be silent and attend!)
> I know a Reasonable Woman,
> Handsome and witty, yet a Friend.
>
> Not warp'd by Passion, aw'd by Rumour,
> Not grave thro' Pride, or gay thro' Folly,
> An equal Mixture of good Humour,
> And sensible soft Melancholy.
>
> 'Has she no Faults then (Envy says) sir?'
> Yes she has one, I must aver:
> When all the world conspires to praise her,
> The Woman's Deaf, and does not hear [2]

> *On a Certain Lady at Court*,
> Alexander Pope (1688-1744).

Deafness it would seem, has rendered the lady impassive to the endless gossip and intrigue taking place around her at Court. Because the Countess is deaf, she is able to resist the temptations of passion, rumour, pride, and folly, adding to her appearance of virtue and complacency. There is an element of guileless humour too that is present in the next example. Alexander Pope was great friends with the satirist Swift. They enjoyed spending a lot of time together, but during their encounters the pair experienced difficulties in communicating freely due to the fact that Swift was deaf and Pope had a very soft voice. In 1727 Pope wrote a poem about the two of them trying to exchange ideas in which this verse appears:

> Pope has the talent well to speak,
> But not to reach the ear;
> His loudest voice is low and weak,

---

[2] Alexander Pope, Pope: Poems (Harmondsworth: Penguin, 1985), 103.

The Dean too deaf to hear.[3]

> *From Dr Swift to Mr Pope, while he was writing the'Dunciad',*
> Alexander Pope (1688-1744).

In this verse Swift is of course the Dean. He points out the problems that exist when the two are trying to converse together with some measure of amusement. Swift wrote several poems about being deaf, often with a sense of humour directed at his own situation. In keeping with his time, he regarded being deaf as a physical complaint that had finally set him free from being bothered by undesirable sounds.[4] In 1734 Swift offers what is perhaps the first poem written by a deaf person with himself as the main character.

> Deaf, giddy, helpless, left alone,
> To all my Friends a Burthen grown,
> No more I hear my Church's Bell,
> Than if it rang out to my Knell:
> At Thunder now no more I start
> Than at the Rumbling of a cart;
> Nay, what's incredible, alack!
> I hardly hear a Woman's Clack. [5]

> From *On his own deafness,*
> Jonathan Swift (1667-1745)

In this poem Swift does not write with his usual style of amusement. He records a sense of loneliness, and believes he is burden to other people. He is unable to hear dangerous sounds, and implies that he feels as if his life is over. Swift is thought to have suffered from Meniere's disease that started at the age of twenty-three. He experienced episodes of tinnitus, giddiness and nausea that were sometimes quite disabling. This was accompanied by progressive deafness and he eventually died with the features of dementia.[6]

---

[3] "Dr. Swift to Mr. Pope", The Literature Network, www.online-literature.com/swift/poems-of-swift/63/.

[4] John Lee Clark, "Jonathan Swift's Deaf Poems", Wordgathering, A Journal of Disability, Poetry and Literature No. 2, (June 2014), https://wordgathering.com/past_issues/issue30/.

[5] Jonathan Swift, Poems (London: Faber and Faber, 2011), 103.

[6] JMS Pearce, "The legacy and maladies of Jonathan Swift", Hektoen International, Fall 2019.

Recent research has shown that if a deaf person becomes isolated, they have an increased risk of developing dementia.[7]

As we have seen with Pope, and on occasions Swift, both hearing and deaf authors may use deafness to add to the humour of a character or situation. This is a commonly described trope in novels.[8] In 1774, Oliver Goldsmith employed this literary device when describing the artist Sir Joshua Reynolds.

> To coxcombs averse, yet most civilly steering,
> When they judged without skill he was still hard of hearing;
> When they talked of their Raphaels, Corregios and stuff,
> He shifted his trumpet and only took snuff. [9]

> From *Retaliation: A Poem. Including Epitaphs*
> *on the Most Distinguished Wits of this Metropolis,*
> Oliver Goldsmith (1730-1774)

Reynolds was deaf following an infection as a young man. He is observed to switch the hearing trumpet to his deaf ear in order to avoid the ignorant comments of his fellow art enthusiasts.

Deaf characters in nineteenth century poetry

In Chapters Two and Three, it was noted that during Victorian times deafness was seen not only as a physical impairment, but one that should be borne with patient endurance. It was commonly believed that any difficulties experienced by disabled people should be overcome with an uncomplaining perseverance that led to a greater purity of soul. This belief applied to those who were deaf, and appears to be expressed in contemporary poetry.

The auditory silence experienced by deaf people was imbued with a notion of protection from the noise and strife that accompanied the busy, fractious lives of the commonplace world of the hearing. This was particularly true for those deaf people who were imagined as living harmoniously in idyllic bucolic settings, far from industrial areas that were filled with smoke and disease. They were often considered to be romantic "primitives" rather like

---

[7] "Hearing loss and dementia: how are they linked", RNID, accessed March 1, 2023, https://rnid.org.uk/hearing-research/hearing-loss-and-dementia-how-are-they-linked/.

[8] See Chapter Two.

[9] Oliver Goldsmith, Retaliation: A Poem. Including Epitaphs on the Most Distinguished wits of this Metropolis. (London: JM Dent & Sons Ltd, 1944), 41.

Psyche in the novel *In Silence*, whose lives were unspoiled, not only by escaping urban commotion, but also left untouched by education, inane conversation and the worries of mundane domesticity. This theme is evident in Wordsworth's 1814 depiction of the solitary Dalesman.

> Almost at the root
> Of that tall pine, the shadow of whose bare
> And slender stem, while here I sit at eve,
> Oft stretches toward me, like a long straight path
> Traced faintly in the greensward; there, beneath
> A plain blue stone, a gentle Dalesman lies,
> From whom, in early childhood, was withdrawn
> The precious gift of hearing. He grew up
> From year to year in loneliness of soul;
> And this deep mountain-valley was to him
> Soundless, with all its streams. The bird of dawn
> Did never rouse this cottager from sleep
> With startling summons; not for his delight
> The vernal cuckoo shouted; not for him
> Murmured the labouring bee. When stormy winds
> Were working the broad bosom of the lake
> Into a thousand, thousand sparkling waves,
> Rocking the trees, or driving cloud on cloud
> Along the sharp edge of yon lofty crags,
> The agitated scene before his eye
> Was as a picture: evermore
> Were all things silent, wheresoe'er he moved; [10]

From *The Excursion*,
William Wordsworth (1770-1850)

The poet expresses regret that the deaf Dalesman has missed so much beauty inherent in natural sounds, but also relief that his silent contentment had been spared the agitation of the storm. His patience and calm were indicative of a higher moral state. Admirable and virtuous qualities were often believed to be gifted to the deaf as a form of divine compensation as we saw clearly demonstrated in the early novel *Duncan Campbell*. However, despite the virtues conferred upon it by romantic hearing observers, deafness was nonetheless viewed as an inferior and unwelcome state, that needed correcting by medical intervention, education, and above all, the ability to speak. This belief is reflected, though not necessarily

---

[10] William Wordsworth, The Excursion (Ithaca: Cornell University Press, 2007), 240-241.

espoused, in the works of Lydia Sigourney, a hearing American author who championed marginalised groups, including deaf people. In 1827 she wrote *Opinions of the uneducated deaf and dumb,* in which deafness is the cause of shame and embarrassment to an unschooled deaf girl.

> The ear in durance bound,
> The lip divorced from sound,
> Seem'd to thy innocent mind, a cause of blame,
> A strange, peculiar, deprecated shame;
> Nature's unkindness, thou didst meekly deem
> Thy *blemish* and thy *crime*, which marr'd thy peaceful dream.

Even though an unkind Nature had inflicted what the girl perceives to be an injury, and even an affront to others, Sigourney goes on to speak of the natural innocence of the deaf child who muses over the nature of God and takes delight in creation.

> Though from thy guarded portal press
> No word of gratitude or tenderness,
> In the starting tear, the glowing cheek
> With tuneful tongue the soul can speak,
> Her tone is in the sigh,
> Her language in the eye,
> Her voice of harmony, a life of praise,
> Well understood by *Him* who notes our secret ways [11]

> From *Opinions of the uneducated deaf and dumb,*
> Lydia Sigourney (1791-1865)

The poem ends with a declaration that even though she is unable to speak, the girl is able to worship her Creator in a form understood by Him. Sigourney rejects the idea that speech is the ultimate goal of the deaf. If it is not necessary to speak in order to worship, and deaf people are counted as valuable and accepted by God, then why is deafness perceived as abhorrent by contemporary hearing society? The inability to use vocal speech seemed to many hearing people to be more fearful than any lack of hearing. Because many deaf people had no clear and comprehensible voice, they were seen as somehow lesser than the hearing.[12] Those who at a later date were to argue in favour of oral education at the Milan conference, would maintain that the ability to use audible words should be regarded as

---

[11] "Poems Sigourney 1827", Wikisource, https://en.wikisource.org/wiki/Poems_ Sigourney_1827/Opinions_of_the_Uneducated_Deaf_and_Dumb.
[12] John Lee Clark, "Melodies Unheard", Poetry Magazine, May 2005, 165-170.

a sign of obvious intelligence, with verbal speech lifting humanity to a level above that of "savages" and brute animals.[13] In 1834, nearly fifty years before Milan, Sigourney wrote about a deaf wedding she had witnessed, at which love was clearly displayed without the use of any vocal speech.

> So ye voiceless pair,
> Pass on in hope. For ye may build as firm
> Your silent altar in each other's hearts,
> And catch the sunshine through the clouds of time
> As cheerily as though the pomp of speech
> Did herald forth the deed. And when ye dwell
>
> Where flower fades not, and death no treasured link
> Hath power to sever more, ye need not mourn
> The ear sequestrate and the tuneless tongue,
> For there the eternal dialect of love
> Is the free breath of every happy soul.[14]

From *Marriage of the Deaf and Dumb*,
Lydia Sigourney (1791-1865)

Mrs Sigourney lived in Hartford, Connecticut, close to where the American Asylum of the Deaf and Dumb was situated at the time. The institution that had recently been established is referred to in the same section of the 1845 book from which this verse is taken.

> When yon mute train who meekly bow
> Beneath affliction's rod,
> Whose lip no utterance hath for man,
> Pour forth the soul to god.
>
> They have no garment for the thought
> That springs to meet its Sire,
> No tone to flush the glowing cheek,
> Or fan Devotion's fire;[15]

From *Prayers of the Deaf and Dumb*,
Lydia H Sigourney (1791-1865)

---

[13] See Chapter One.

[14] Lydia Huntley afterwards Sigourney, Illustrated Poems (Philadelphia: Carey and Hart, 1849), 257.

[15] Mrs Lydia H Sigourney, Scenes in my native land (Boston: J. Munroe & Co 1845), 219.

Although the ideas of "meekness" and "affliction" would seem alien and appear rather patronising to many deaf people today, the author recognises that the deaf person portrayed is capable of communicating with God in ways other than verbal speech. This would have been highly unusual at a time when many hearing people attributed idiocy to those who were deaf and unable to speak vocally.

In Chapter Three, I considered the different experiences of people who are blind compared with people who are deaf. John Burnet, another deaf American poet, expresses his views in a poem written in 1834, that he presented at a charity fair held at the New York City Hotel for the benefit of the blind. The poem consisting of fifteen verses, speaks movingly of the suffering he conceives blind people to experience when not being able to see the many beauties of nature. In the sixth verse however, he declares that being deaf is even worse than living as a blind person.

> Yet we were more unfortunate,
> Than ever were the blind!
> Your darkness is but of the eye,
> But ours was of the mind.

Burnet conveys the commonly held belief that the deaf were ignorant because they were unable to hear, and were incapable of speaking knowledge and truth. This appears to contradict the essence of the views put forward by his contemporary Sigourney. However, the poet states in the tenth verse that education, provided by philanthropic agencies, had brought many deaf people to a much better position, and Burnet offers the same hope of improvement to his blind compatriots.

> As others pitied *us*, 'tis ours
> In turn to pity *you*
> We who have learn'd to read God's Word
> Wish *you* to read it too.[16]

> From *Address of the Deaf and Dumb to the Blind*,
> John R Burnet (1808-1874)

Burnet believes that although blind people can hear and speak religious truth, they will only properly benefit when they are able to read it. This may seem fanciful, but the poet offers the prospect of charitably funded education as a means to allow the blind to read the Bible. He relies on the

---

[16] John R Burnet, Tales of the deaf and dumb: with miscellaneous poems (Newark, NJ: B. Olds, 1835), 221-222.

pity of the hearing and seeing majority to provide the money required. This view shared the perspective of many who thought that the "disabled" should elicit pity and be considered as objects of charity. It was a social and religious obligation for wealthy devout people of the era to pity those less fortunate than themselves and try to make their lives more manageable. This may seem to be unwarranted and patronising from our historical viewpoint nearly two hundred years later, but it should be remembered that work was in short supply, and living from the generosity of other people might be one of the few means available that permitted a deaf or blind person to survive. It is evident from their poems that both Sigourney and Burnet anticipated the successful outcome of specialist education as the deaf and blind being able to learn about God and become active in worship. This seemed to be the desirable endpoint of teaching the deaf to speak verbally and finding ways to help the blind to read. The same volume includes a great deal of interesting history about deaf education and anecdotes about deaf people that would encourage the well-intended interest of hearing benefactors. A few years later in 1847, another American deaf poet shows how much the prevalent view of the deaf being pitiable could be internalised by deaf people.

> I move – a silent exile on this earth;
> As in his dreary cell one doomed for life
> My tongue is mute, and closed ear heedeth not;
> No gleam of hope this darken'd mind assures
> That the blest power of speech shall e'er be known.
> Murmuring gaily o'er their pebbly beds
> The limpid streamlets, as they onward flow
> Through verdant meadows and responding woodlands,
> Vocal with merry tones – *I hear them not.*

This bleak first-person description of deafness speaks of loneliness, silence and loss, and the inability to vocalise. It appears in the first issue of the oldest and most widely read professional journal concerned with deaf education. As such it appears from our position in the twenty-first century to be utterly incongruous, but from its context, the poem should be assumed to convey the views of contemporary deaf people and deaf education. Typically for the era Carlin writes romantically of the natural world, using a wonderful array of auditory descriptive words such as "murmuring" that I can only presume meant little to him as an auditory phenomenon. The nineteenth century was a difficult time for a deaf poet, as the use of metrical verse was standard, the rhythms of which may not have been easy to comprehend or compose. During the course of the poem, he includes the stanza "I hear them not" four times, emphasising his grief at being unable to hear. This provides a strong and deliberate contrast to the final verse which is a proclamation of faith.

> My ears shall be unsealed, and I shall hear;
> My tongue shall be unbound, and I shall speak,
> And happy with the angels sing forever! [17]

From *The Mute's Lament*
John Carlin (1813-1891)

Carlin looks forward to the time when his situation will be different in heaven. He will be able to hear, and more importantly, and in stark contrast to the title he chose for the poem, he looks forward to being able to speak. Many deaf people today might find this a difficult statement of identity and aspiration. They would choose to celebrate their deafness, and see no reason to live with the hope of change in the next world. Indeed, the self-denigrating title of the piece is shocking to read. But Carlin is simply expressing the general expectation of an age in which so many people suffered and died when young, and in which there were many obvious causes of infirmity and injustice. He shares the belief that deafness and lack of vocal speech were limiting factors both in society and in worship. The day would finally come when everything would be well. Although the poem was accepted for publication in the inaugural issue of the American Annals of the Deaf and Dumb, the editor who was hearing, was obviously surprised that a man, totally deaf from birth, was capable of writing poetry. In a preface to Carlin's work, he offers the following opinion:

> How shall he who has not now, and who never has had the sense of hearing; who
> is totally without what the musicians call an "ear;" succeed in preserving all the niceties of accent, measure and rhythm? We should almost as soon expect a man born blind to become a landscape painter, as one born deaf to produce poetry of even tolerable merit.[18]

It seems an extraordinary comment on both the poem and the poet. The editor appears to be in awe of the idea of a deaf man producing a poem, and at the same time, astonished that such a thing is actually possible. Perhaps

---

[17] John Carlin, "The Mute's Lament", American Annals of the Deaf and Dumb, No. 1, (October 1847); 15-16.
[18] Luzerne Ray, "The Poetry of the Deaf and Dumb", American Annals of the Deaf and Dumb, No.1, (October 1847), 14.

he shared the notion that deaf people could be given unusual abilities to compensate for their lack of hearing? This is an idea that has been encountered several times in both the preceding chapters. Nonetheless the nature of deafness perceived as a disability appealed to Victorian creatives. The deaf could be thought of as suffering nobly in silence, making them the deserving objects of their pity. They did not have a disfiguring condition, allowing them to retain the natural beauty that befitted their attainment of a higher moral state because of their suffering. This idea is expressed by Browning in his poetic description of a sculpture that immortalises a deaf and dumb brother and sister.

> Only the prism's obstruction shows aright
> The secret of a sunbeam, breaks its light
> Into the jewelled bow from blankest white;
> So may a glory from defect arise:
> Only by Deafness may the vexed Love wreak
> Its unsuppressive sense on brow and cheek,
> Only by Dumbness adequately speak
> As favoured mouth could never, through the eyes.[19]

Deaf and Dumb. A group by Woolner.
Robert Browning (1812-1889)

The poet was asked by the pre-Raphaelite sculptor Thomas Woolner to write a short piece as a catalogue entry for the Great International Exhibition of 1862. He was exhibiting a sculpture of Constance and Arthur, that had been commissioned by their father Sir Thomas Fairbairn, an industrialist and art patron. This poignant verse was in fact designed to attract public attention to the work.[20] There is nothing in the artwork to distinguish the children as being deaf. The children are positioned sitting closely together and appear beautifully formed. They are not shown, as far as we can tell, straining to hear, attempting to speak vocally, or sign. The features of the children themselves are expected to be angelic enough to convey an innocent silence and infirm nobility. Browning implies that the "defect" of deafness has produced an unperturbed purity. It is because of the "flaw" that true beauty becomes visible. This is reminiscent of the Goldilocks characters found in novels that were discussed in Chapter Two. As adults,

---

[19] Robert Browning, Dramatis personae; and dramatic romances and lyrics (1864; Philadelphia: JB Lippincott, 1969), 105.
[20] Sophie Ratcliffe, "The trouble with feeling now: Thomas Woolner, Robert Browning, and the touching case of Constance and Arthur", Interdisciplinary Studies in the Long Nineteenth Century, (December 2016), DOI:10.16995/ntn.766.

the subjects of the sculpture, Sir Arthur Fairbairn and his sister Constance, were active in championing deaf people, and promoted finger-spelling at the time when oralist theories were gaining ground in deaf education.

Figure 4-1: A sculpture by Thomas Woolner of a brother and sister, entitled "Constance and Arthur", on show at the International Exhibition, South Kensington, London 1862. Photograph by William England. London Stereoscopic Company/ Hulton Archive via Getty Images.

Deaf characters in twentieth century poetry

By the beginning of the twentieth century, the romanticized perception of deafness as a damaged state, revealing nobility and beauty, and redeemable through education, was gradually being superseded or at least amended. The metrical structure of the form however, was retained into the early and middle parts of the century, and continued to be used by many poets, both deaf and hearing. The theme of contentment, enjoyed by the deaf and observed affectionately by the hearing, partially mitigates the continued narratives of loss and imperfection that dominated the previous hundred years. As a result, deaf characters often elicit kindliness from hearing authors. This is seen in Betjeman's touching accounts of happily spending time with his deaf father. For instance, he recounts the comfortable rambles they took together in the countryside:

> He took me on long silent walks
> In country lanes when young
> He knew the names of ev'ry bird
> But not the song it sung. [21]

From *On a Portrait of a Deaf Man*
Sir John Betjeman (1906-1984)

There is a poignancy and wistfulness as Betjeman reports that his father could identify each bird that he saw but "not the song it sung." The poet's characteristically gentle approach enlightens a second poem written in 1960. In it, Betjeman apportions a quiet dignity to his elderly parent as he converses with a shopkeeper.

> We'd stand in dark antique shops while he talked,
> Holding his deaf appliance to his ear,
> Lifting the ugly mouthpiece with a smile
> Towards the flattered shopman. [22]

From *Summoned By Bells*
Sir John Betjeman (1906-1984)

---

[21] Sir John Betjeman, "On a Portrait of a Deaf Man", The Quiet Ear, Deafness in Literature, ed. Brian Grant (London: Andre Deutsch, 1987), 225.
[22] Sir John Betjeman, Summoned by Bells (London: John Murray, 1960), 11.

It is interesting to note the use of the "deaf appliance" with one end held to his father's ear and the "ugly mouthpiece" catching the words of the shopkeeper.

Although evidence of medical intervention in the lives of deaf people is frequently seen in novels from the twentieth century, it is not demonstrated nearly so strongly in the few examples of deaf characters drawn from contemporary poetry. For instance, Betjeman alludes only in passing to the difficulties his father experiences when using his hearing trumpet. The poet concentrates rather, on discreet observations of his father, linking them with his feelings regarding their relationship. Deaf writers may of course write about deaf characters in very different ways from hearing authors, particularly if the character they depict is themselves. Robert Panara, a deaf American poet, writes movingly of how words can recall particular sounds, long unheard, that inspire his imagination and emotions with great intensity.

My ears are deaf, and yet I seem to hear
Sweet Nature's music and the songs of Man,
For I have learned from Fancy's artisan
How written words can thrill the inner ear
Just as they move the heart, and so for me
They also seem to ring out loud and free.

In silent study, I have learned to tell
Each silent shade of meaning and to hear
A magic harmony, at once sincere,
That somehow notes the tinkle of a bell,
The cooing of a dove, the swish of leaves,
The rain-drop's pitter-patter on the eaves,
The lover's sigh, the thrumming of a guitar
And, if I choose, the rustle of a star![23]

On his deafness,
Robert Panara (1920–2014)

In the preface to Panara's book of poems *On his deafness and other melodies unheard*, he wrote about how he valued the deafness that had given him a new insight into the world. Panara became deaf after developing spinal meningitis at the age of ten.

---

[23] Robert Panara, In Deaf American Poetry: an anthology, ed. John Lee Clark (Washington, DC: Gallaudet University Press, 2009), 141.

> I learned to count the blessing of deafness in still another way. This came
> with the discovery of Poetry and the realization that, at last, I had found that
> elusive nymph whose magic seemed to transcend that of her sister muse of
> song. Under her spell, the inner noises experienced a fine "sea change/Into
> something rich and strange" [24]

Panara was highly regarded as a deaf educator and as a pioneer in studies
on deaf culture and in deaf theatre. As is evident from Panara's work, poetry
tends to be more personal and intimate than other forms of writing. It will
often record autobiographical experiences or observations that have struck
the writer as profound or intriguing. It is only the necessity of deaf education
that has been mentioned in poems, rather than any specific details of
schooling. Also, the existence of any form of deaf community is omitted,
despite these themes weaving consistently through many novels containing
deaf characters that were written in the twentieth century.

The next poem however, is an exception, in that it records information
concerning both a deaf school and its deaf community. The verses are based
on a note made when the author visited a deaf school in Paris, while working
with the dramatist Peter Brooks, in the early 1970s. Hughes' visits to the
school were the result of Brooks' search for a universal form of drama, one
that would allow dramatisation without vocal speech. As part of their
activities in the school, Hughes and Brooks invented improvised plays with
the deaf children.[25] Hughes describes the children signing:

> The deaf children were monkey-nimble, fish-tremulous and sudden.
> Their faces were alert and simple

He observes their rapid hand movements:

> What they spoke with was a machine,
> A manipulation of fingers, a control-panel of gestures

There is an implication that they employ a mechanistic means of
communication that appears devoid of feeling and self-awareness:

---

[24] Robert Panara, On his deafness and other melodies unheard (Rochester NY: Deaf
Life Press, 1997).
[25] The Quiet Ear, Deafness in Literature, 233

Their bodies were like their hands
Nimbler than bodies, like the hammers of a piano,
A puppet agility, a simple mechanical action [26]

From *Deaf School*,
Ted Hughes (1930-1998)

In the letter referred to above, Hughes expresses a high opinion of the children by describing them as "incredibly quick and subtle" and "wonderfully resourceful". However, the poem compares the deaf children to "little animals" saying that they "lacked a dimension", and describes their faces as being "in darkness" and "unaware". He also uses the word "simple" four times, and appears to revive some of the ideas expressed in poetry a hundred or more years ago. Hughes was no doubt impressed by the intense visual concentration of the children as they observed the teacher, but deaf children who sign, certainly in the UK and US, employ a full range of body language and facial expressions. Their faces are animated not "unused". Perhaps the poet was so absorbed by the "manipulation of fingers" that he remained unaware of the students' faces. Hughes appears to try and capture the deftness and fluidity of rapid hand shapes, but still speaks of "lack" and "darkness", implying the need for education and speech. The choice of words and their implications were heavily criticised fifty years later by the deaf poet Raymond Antrobus, as we shall see below.

Towards the end of the twentieth century, American hearing writer Miller Williams highlights the awkwardness of trying to communicate by using a more detailed description of a deaf character confronted by the misunderstandings and impatience of hearing people.

No matter how she tilts her head to hear
she sees the irritation in their eyes.
She knows how they can read a small rejection,
a little judgment, in every *What did you say?* [27]

From *Going Deaf*,
Miller Williams (1930-2015)

---

[26] Ted Hughes, Moortown (New York: Harper Colophone Books, 1979), 104-105.
[27] Miller Williams, "Going Deaf", Poetry Foundation, accessed n/d, https://www.poetryfoundation.org/poems/52373/going-deaf. Reprinted from "Points of Departure: Poems by Miller Williams," by Miller Williams, University of Illinois Press, 1995.

Despite being written by a hearing poet, many deaf people will recognise the accuracy of these observations as the deaf lady becomes increasingly distressed and aware of the annoyance and rejection of the hearing people around her. Problems in communicating are particularly devastating when a child is distanced from his parents. The refusal to acknowledge the deafness of a child, unwillingness to communicate effectively, or apathy, may result in a parent not wanting to find an appropriate means of conversing. Bellitz, another American poet, describes his own experience with haunting regret.

> I never cared much about the sound
> of radios and bands.
> What hurts me is I never heard
> My parents signing hands.[28]

From *Thoughts of a deaf child,*
Stephen J Bellitz

As the twentieth century progressed, there was an increasing trend for deaf characters in poems to be depicted more realistically and often autobiographically. There is a move away from deafness being used as a metaphor for alienation, and from displaying features of ideology and religion. The focus becomes much more personal, with descriptions of the problems of everyday life that include missed words, wrongly understood conversations, and the difficulties of communication. Painful emotions, triggered by these experiences, are expressed, such as frustration, anger, and disappointment.

Deaf characters in twenty-first century poetry

As poets passed the millennium, the examples given are of a freer form with written verse, and increasingly abandon the written form entirely. Poems containing deaf characters are now exclusively autobiographical, often concentrating on the difficulties of schooling, growing up, and living within a hearing world. Many deaf people choose to wear hearing aids to alleviate communication difficulties, but as the following excerpts demonstrate they are not always free of problems.

---

[28]Steve Claridge, A poem called "Thoughts of a deaf child", accessed n/d, Stephen J. Bellitz, Reprinted from Senior News, July 1991, https://www.hearingaidknow.com/a-poem-called-thoughts-of-a-deaf-child.

So God said
Let there be volume control
let there be choice how loud life should be
and there came the power to fade
the voices, the annoyances, the noise
and that was mighty good for all the unnecessary drama

From *Ode to My Hearing aids*,
Camisha L Jones [29]

The American poet Camisha L. Jones alludes to the problems caused when hearing aids pick up an assortment of unwanted background noises, and interfere with the ability to concentrate on particular sounds of interest that the individual is trying to hear. This is a phenomenon to all who wear them. Although efforts are made by the audiologist to control the volume, and isolate frequencies, that cover verbal speech, this is not always successful. Jones speaks of the relief at finding the perfect balance. Hearing aids are also worn by the deaf British Jamaican poet, Raymond Antrobus, but in this piece, he recalls the difficulties of growing up deaf as a young boy before his deafness was recognised.

The day I clear out my dead father's flat,
I throw away boxes of moulding LPs:
Garvey, Malcolm X, Mandela, speeches on vinyl.

I find a TDK cassette tape on the shelf.
The smudged green label reads *Raymond Speaking*.
I play the tape in his vintage cassette player.

and hear my two-year-old voice chanting my name, *Antrob*
and Dad's laughter crackling in the background
not knowing I couldn't hear the word "bus"

and wouldn't until I got my hearing aids.
Now I sit here listening to the space of deafness —

Antrob Antrob Antrob [30]

Echo Pt 3,
Raymond Antrobus (1986-)

---

[29] Camisha L Jones, Flare (Georgetown: Finishing Line Press, 2017). Reprinted "Poems", poets.org, accessed n/d, https://poets.org/poem/ode-my-hearing-aids.
[30] Raymond Antrobus, The Perseverance (London: Penned in the Margins, 2018) 16.

Antrobus has rejected rhyme and created a much more open structure of verse to express his experience. The poignancy of discovering tapes of his own voice trying to speak his name when clearing out his late father's belongings is very powerful. His father clearly valued his boy's early attempts at speech. Antrobus is able to muse on his inability to hear, and mark the extent of his deafness before receiving hearing aids.

Jones also employs great written fluidity as she vividly expresses the intense frustration and embarrassment felt by not being able to hear questions and comments in everyday circumstances.

I'm-sorry-I'm-sorry-I'm-so-sorry-I'm-hard-for-the-hearing

The subject of the poem, presumably the poet herself, feels immense pressure to repeatedly excuse and explain her deafness in rooms full of strangers when making arrangements, attending appointments, and being in unfamiliar social settings. The reader can empathise with the sense of denigration as she feels obliged to apologise for being unable to hear and impels her to keep asking people to repeat what they have said. The character feels so deeply ashamed and utterly belittled that she finally reaches the point when she says sorry for just being there.

Dear (again)
I regret to inform you

I   am

Here

From *Disclosure*,
Camisha L Jones [31]

This awful and demeaning experience will be familiar to all who are deaf and have verbal speech. Hearing people can only imagine the fear that may be generated when deaf people find themselves dealing with unexpected difficulties or the anxiety provoked when anticipating the likely problems related to straightforward arrangements. This is likely to cause a significant loss of confidence and low self-esteem when presented with situations that most hearing people can negotiate with ease.

---

[31] Camisha L Jones, "Poems", poets.org, accessed n/d, https://poets.org/poem/disclosure-0. Originally published in Poem-a-day on January 3, 2020, by the Academy of American Poets.

Issues of identity are frequently explored by modern deaf poets, often with more certainty and self-acceptance. This burgeoning confidence means that many modern deaf poets are more likely to object to inadequate descriptions or misplaced assumptions made by their hearing counterparts. Antrobus objected to some of the descriptive language used by Ted Hughes in his poem *Deaf School*, portions of which are reproduced earlier in the chapter. This is his response:

No one wise calls the river *unaware* or *simple pools*;
No one wise says it *lacks a dimension*; no one wise
Says its body is *removed from the vibration of air*.

The river is a quiet breath-taker, gargling mud.

Ted is *alert and simple*.
Ted *lacked a subtle wavering aura of sound
And responses to Sound*.

Ted lived through his eyes. But eye the colossal
currents from the bridge. Eye riverboats
ghosting a geography of fog.

Mississippi means *Big River*, named by French colonisers.
The natives laughed at their arrogant maps,
Conquering wind and marking mist.

The mouth of the river laughs, a man in a wetsuit emerges,
pulls misty goggles over his head. *Couldn't see a thing.*
He breathes heavily. *My face was in darkness.*

No one heard him; the river drowned him out. [32]

After Reading 'Deaf School' by the Mississippi River,
Raymond Antrobus (1986-)

In *The Perseverance*, a collection of poems By Antrobus, Hughes' *Deaf School* is made unreadable by printing black lines across the stanzas, entirely redacting the content. The poet's riposte then appears on the next two pages. As well as using Hughes' own descriptions from *Deaf School* against him, Antrobus implies that Hughes was writing about something grand and powerful that he did not fully understand. His observations were made from the point of view of an outsider, very much as the colonisers

---

[32] Raymond Antrobus, The Perseverance, 41-42.

looked down on the mighty river. In an article from 2021, Antrobus talked about how much he had loved Hughes' work when he was at school. However, he describes reading *Deaf School* for the first time, and how the impact of the words was a "violent offence to me". Antrobus concluded that Hughes had been "ignorant" of deaf people.[33] Although Antrobus was very grateful that he had won the Ted Hughes prize for poetry, he could see the irony considering the opinions he expressed about Hughes' work. Another reviewer aware of Antrobus' response, thought that Hughes had written his observations on the Parisian deaf children from a position of highly detached observation. He also understood why comparing the children to animals, even with no malicious intention, could be misinterpreted.[34] Antrobus, who signs and wears hearing aids, believes that it is not only the choice of certain words that is of great importance, but also the language they have chosen to use. He asserts that this is particularly true in deaf education. This next work was short-listed for the Griffin Prize in Poetry in 2019:

I have left Earth in search of sounder orbits,
a solar system where the space between
a star and a planet isn't empty. I have left
a white beard of noise in my place and many
of you won't know the difference. We are
indeed the same volume, all of us eventually fade.
I have left Earth in search of an audible God.
I do not trust the sound of yours.
You wouldn't recognise my grandmother's *Hallelujah*
if she had to sign it, you would have made her sit
on her hands and put a ruler in her mouth
as if measuring her distance from holy.
Take your God back, though his songs
Are beautiful, they are not loud enough.

I want the fate of Lazarus for every deaf school
you've closed, every deaf child whose confidence
has gone to a silent grave, every BSL user
who has seen the annihilation of their language,
I want these ghosts to haunt your tongue-tied hands.

[33] Ryan Asmussen, "The Hierarchy of Language in 'The Perseverance'". Chicago Review of Books, March 29, 2021. https://chireviewofbooks.com/2021/03/29/the-hierarchy-of-language-in-the-perseverance/.

[34] Matthew Clegg, "Second glance at 'Deaf School'", Longbarrow, accessed September 15, 2020, https://longbarrowblog.wordpress.com/2020/09/15/second-glance-at-deaf-school-matthew-clegg/.

I have left Earth, I am equal parts sick of your
oh, I'm hard of hearing too, just because
you've been on an airplane or suffered head colds.
Your voice has always been the loudest sound in a room.

I call you out for refusing to acknowledge
sign language in classrooms, for assessing
deaf students on what they can't say
instead of what they can, we did not ask to be a part
of the hearing world, I can't hear my joints crack
but I can feel them. I am sick of sounding out your rules –
you tell me I breathe too loud and it's rude to make noise
when I eat, sent me to speech therapists, said I was speaking

a language of holes, I was pronouncing what I heard
but your judgment made my syllables disappear,
your magic master trick hearing world - drowning out the quiet,
bursting all speech bubbles in my graphic childhood,
you are glad to benefit from audio supremacy,
I tried, hearing people, I tried to love you, but you laughed
at my deaf grammar, I used commas not full stops
because everything I said kept running away,
I mulled over long paragraphs because I didn't know
what a *natural break* sounded like, ~~you erased~~
~~what could always have been poetry~~

You erased what could have always been poetry.
You taught me I was inferior to standard English expression –
I was a broken speaker, you were never a broken interpreter –
taught me my speech was dry for someone who should sound
like they're underwater. It took years to talk with a straight spine
and mute red marks on the coursework you assigned.

Deaf voices go missing like sound in space
and I have left Earth to find them.[35]

Dear Hearing World (after Danez Smith),
Raymond Antrobus (1986-)

It is possible to watch the video of Antrobus reading this polemic poem
at the Griffin Prize event.[36] In his speech, the poet states that he wrote *Dear*

---

[35] Raymond Antrobus, The Perseverance, 36-38.
[36] Poet Raymond Antrobus reads from The Perseverance, https://www.youtube.com/watch?v=yJuIxbSspYM.

Hearing World after he had decided to return to deaf schools and teach. The poem is filled with anger, disgust, and despair, at the closure of some specialist schools in the UK, with an increasing number of deaf children educated in units within a mainstream framework. This has diminished the role of BSL in deaf education. A similar theme is expressed in Sara Novic's novel *True Biz*.[37] How astonishing it is to see the reverberations of the Milan declaration impacting deaf education over a hundred and forty years later. Antrobus upbraids a schooling system that erodes the confidence of deaf children and leaves them feeling inadequate as "broken speakers". The content of Deaf Hearing World contrasts dramatically with the work of nineteenth century deaf poets who applauded the value of teaching deaf children to use vocal speech. Their God was described as a hearing God, whereas Antrobus would agree with his American predecessor Sigourney, that it is possible to engage with the divine through sign language.

Not all poetry that contains deaf characters is observational or autobiographical. Ilya Kaminsky's *Deaf Republic* is a parable set in an unidentified country that is invaded by soldiers. The fictional town of Valenka is occupied by the army. The deaf boy Petya is killed, and the gunshot that killed him is the last sound that the local population hear. All the townspeople have taken the decision to become deaf. This is a sign of solidarity, and also provides a means of evading orders given by the occupiers. Dissent is coordinated and encouraged by signing.

Deafness, an Insurgency, Begins

Our country woke up next morning and refused to hear soldiers.[38]

As the protest spreads, a mother holds up a placard that reads "THE PEOPLE ARE DEAF".[39] In response to the spreading disobedience, the soldiers announce that "DEAFNESS IS A CONTAGIOUS DISEASE".[40] They declare the town to be "infected" and begin to remove the most troublesome protestors into "quarantine" at an unknown location. The remaining inhabitants continue to sign as they believe deafness to be "our only barricade".[41] Civil disobedience against the invading forces becomes widespread.

---

[37] See Chapter Two.
[38] Ilya Kaminsky, Deaf Republic (London: Faber & Faber, 2019), 14.
[39] Kaminsky, Deaf Republic, 17
[40] Kaminsky, Deaf Republic, 22
[41] Kaminsky, Deaf Republic, 22

Deafness is suspended above blue tin roofs
And copper eaves; deafness
Feeds on birches, light posts, hospital roofs, bells;
Deafness rests in our men's chests.[42]

This is a haunting, bleak story, that is arranged in episodic stanzas revealing deafness as a symbol of dissent against the hearing soldiers, and signing to be the language of protest. There are very few ways in which to successfully oppose the powerful occupying forces, but the refusal to use verbal speech, and to hear them, makes total domination impossible. This renders the invaders' orders meaningless, and allows the townspeople to communicate in a form that the soldiers cannot understand. The hearts and minds of the townspeople remain free. In the notes at the back of the book, Kaminsky writes that

The deaf don't believe in silence. Silence is the invention of the hearing.

This is a concept that is encountered in the discussion of deaf characters in novels, and has been expressed in the works of other deaf poets, but only in *Deaf Republic,* is verbal silence construed as a political act, and a form of not so passive resistance. The book is also a potent, and in these days, a pertinent, reminder that it is morally impossible to remain "silent" in the face of tyranny. Any of the townspeople who remain aloof are inexorably drawn in to make a personal and communal response. Throughout the book, there are a few illustrations of signed handshapes. Some of these shapes originate from a variety of sign languages, while others are invented. Their presence emphasises that vocal speech is not necessary in order to disseminate ideas. The story filled with deaf characters is strange, but the book makes a powerful and defiant statement. Kaminsky became deaf at the age of four following infection with mumps and wears hearing aids. He has lived in the United States from the age of sixteen, having escaped with his family, from anti-Semitic persecution in Soviet Ukraine.

Sign language poetry

It is important to take note of a development created by deaf poets during the last fifty years that has largely dispensed with the written and spoken word. Dorothy Miles, a British deaf activist, writer, and poet, is generally credited with the birth of signed poetry. This is quite distinct from translating works written in English into BSL. In the late sixties Miles

---

[42] Kaminsky, Deaf Republic, 39

travelled to the United States, and joined the National Theatre of the Deaf. The company were working on performances of poetry in which spoken English was combined with ASL. Following this experience, in the early seventies Miles took these advances further by creating poems that were presented only in sign language with no accompanying speech. In these performances, she employed a repeating rhythm of similar handshapes that was a parallel to verbal rhyming. In the groundbreaking *Gestures–Poetry in Sign Language*, she uses a very flowing and elegant form of BSL, that is extremely expressive, with exaggerated changes in body posture. This work originally created in 1976, consisted of BSL poetry captured on a video cassette and accompanied by a package of written poems, lyrics, and music.[43] The best-known sign language poem that Miles produced is probably *Language for the Eye*. It is available to watch in several forms on the internet.[44] Miles beautifully employs very dramatic signs that reference people and nature, with careful attention given to motion, symmetry, and space, so that one sign morphs seamlessly into another. It is also possible to see a version in spoken words and ASL in which a signed phrase is interpreted:

> The word becomes the picture in this language for the eye
> The word becomes the action in this language of the heart.[45]

In an interview, Miles said she originally created the poem so that hearing children could discover what fun could be had with sign language.[46]

Miles pioneered the use of the whole body to present powerful three-dimensional images directly to the eye rather than using one-dimensional words to generate images in the mind.[47] This type of visual poetry was designed to be accessible through the use of simple straightforward iconic visual signs, likely to be understood by both hearing and deaf audiences. Some of the poems involve BSL or ASL handshapes that require prior specialist knowledge. As with any medium of communication, there are

---

[43] Dorothy Miles, Gestures – Poetry in Sign Language (Northridge, California: Joyce Motion Picture Co., 1976).

[44] Language for the Eye by Dorothy Miles, https://www.youtube.com/watch?v=VPbVc0nLB54.

[45] Road signs: Poem of "Language for the Eye", https://www.youtube.com/watch?v=EVsPVXT5qpU.

[46] Rachel Sutton-Spence, Analysing Sign Language Poetry (Basingstoke: Palgrave MacMillan, 2005), 19.

[47] Sutton-Spence, Rachel. "Deaf Gain and creativity in signed literature". In Deaf Gain, ed. H-Dirksen L. Baumann and Joseph J. Murray (Minneapolis: University of Minnesota Press, 2014), 457-475.

certain conventions that are commonly used, such as the repetition of signs to give a sense equivalent to "rhyming", blending signs, a symmetry of handshapes, adopting a persona, and the use of themes and metaphors. Sign language poetry permits the portrayal of characters such as Frankenstein in John Wilson's *The Fates*,[48] or Richard Carter's *Prince Looking for Love*.[49] The form also lends itself to depicting biographical tales of deaf characters, such as Carter's *Cochlear Implant*.[50] In this BSL poem, Carter signs the story of an individual who becomes deaf, has a cochlear implant fitted, and then throws it away, because the intensity of regained sounds is too painful. The content of sign language poems may be autobiographical such as Donna Williams' *Who am I?* [51]in which she reveals her search for identity when feeling caught between the hearing and deaf worlds. It comes as no surprise that sign language poets are described as being deeply concerned with visual representation,[52] and that the invention of videos is considered to be as significant for deaf signed poetry as that of the printing press was for the written word.[53] The importance of signed poetry to the profoundly deaf is emphasised by the recent appointment of the UK BSL Poet Laureate, Kabir Kapoor.[54]

Themes in the portrayal of deaf characters

Although the number of poems that include deaf characters is relatively small, I believe it is possible to determine certain trends inherent in their portrayal. The representation of deaf characters in poetry in many ways parallels that seen in the evolution of deaf characters in novels, although the shared themes are less pronounced. The earlier examples are provided mainly by hearing writers, who use them to amplify aspects of the hearing

---

[48] BSL poem "The Fates" by John Wilson, https://www.youtube.com/watch?v=2TS3q0vEh7A.
[49] BSL poem "Prince Looking for Love" by Richard Carter, https://www.youtube.com/watch?v=D4hPR6DCcDA.
[50] BSL poem "Cochlear Implant" by Richard Carter, https://www.youtube.com/watch?v=KskwGOyhLRQ.
[51] BSL poem "Who am I?" by Donna Williams, https://www.youtube.com/watch?v=npfpIQMHmxo.
[52] Christopher Krentz, "Book review: Sign Mind: Studies in American sign Language Poetics by Jim Cohn", Sign Language Studies, No. 3 (Spring 2001): (3) 2001, 316-323.
[53] Rachel Sutton-Spence, Analysing sign Language Poetry, 17.
[54] "UK BSL Poet Laureate", British Deaf Association, May 11, 2023, https://bda.org.uk/bsl-poet-laureate-kabir-kapoor/.

characters such as the Wife of Bath, or as devices to demonstrate specific themes, such as the humour of Pope's works.

In the nineteenth century, silence is used as a metaphor and is often associated with the notion of an undisturbed, romantic and bucolic contentment, as it is by Wordsworth and Browning. The virtues that resulted from a life of deaf silence were considered to be a form of compensation for the loss of a natural facility. Both deaf and hearing writers defined deafness as a state of loss, with hearing poets like Sigourney, and deaf poets, including Burnet, Carlin, and the earlier Swift, writing of themselves and others, as suffering an infirmity that they hoped could be corrected. There is a sense of regret and lack of self-confidence in the lines written by Carlin. Deaf people, especially children, were seen as objects of pity that elicited the generosity of wealthy benefactors. Poets mourned the lack of hearing, but especially the absence of verbal speech that is experienced by deaf people, partly because it separated them from other people, but mainly because it prevented any adequate level of learning. The importance of education, in order that they could read and especially speak, was stressed as the means of being able to worship their Creator. This appears to be the ultimate hope of deaf people as expressed in poetry, and the goal of specialist, and therefore oralist, education. Sigourney provides an important counter-balance, in that she applauds the deep love shown by the deaf couple getting married in the absence of verbal speech, and emphasises her belief that sign language alone was an adequate, and appropriate form of communication with an accepting God. Similar themes are expressed in contemporary novels, and reflect the sort of views prevalent in society and in education at the time.

In the twentieth century, hearing poets write about deaf people with fondness and understanding. They no more than hint at medical intervention unlike their novelist peers. It would appear that they have either known the deaf character portrayed such as Betjeman, or have observed or learned about problems associated with deafness like Williams. Their poetic accounts are more detailed and realistic than those provided by the descriptions of many deaf characters included in novels. At the end of the century, Bellitz's piece presages the type of poetry that is more commonly seen from deaf poets in the next. His poem is distinctly and painfully autobiographical, and laments a relationship with his parents ruined through the lack of signed communication.

In the twenty-first century, it is deaf poets who write more frequently about deafness and deaf characters, than their hearing colleagues. They write from their personal experience, recounting the difficulties of living in a hearing society, and express anger at being marginalised and misunderstood. They bemoan the lack of recognition of sign language. As poetry adapted into freer forms, deaf poets left behind the traditional metred verse, and instead explored a variety of written forms of poetry as well as recording visual forms of signed performance. Deaf education, the need to teach and converse in sign language, the use of hearing aids and cochlear implants, are all sources of powerful imagery and comment for deaf poets in both written and visual media. Jones and Antrobus reveal the benefits and limitations of prescribed prosthetics, and Antrobus makes a strident plea to protect signing. Kaminsky shows a new and profound way in which deafness can be used as a political metaphor. The emergence of signed poetry, rather than deaf poetry using written words translated into sign language, changed the narrative completely by employing a visual language so iconic it could be understood by non-signers. It has been suggested that comparing poetry in ASL and written English can "illuminate and enliven both".[55]

---

[55] Christopher Krentz, "Book review: Sign Mind: Studies in American sign Language Poetics by Jim Cohn", 316-323.

CHAPTER SIX

SOUND, SIGNING, AND SUBTITLES –
DEAF CHARACTERS IN DRAMA,
TELEVISION, AND FILM

Deaf Characters in Drama

Stage plays are not always easy for deaf people to access. Despite concessions and reserved places nearer the stage, they usually sit too far away to read the lips of the actors. If the person is wearing hearing aids, there are few reflective surfaces near their position in the audience to help bounce sounds. The theatre may be fitted with a loop, which I'm told is often either not switched on, or not turned up loud enough. Many theatres now offer at least one captioned or signed performance during the run of a play, but deaf customers don't always know about the dates far enough in advance to book. Of course, such considerations do not prevent a hearing playwright from including deaf characters in their work, but may prevent deaf people from watching a play and giving relevant feedback.

There is in fact, a long though not extensive history of portraying deaf characters in drama, much of it written before attention was given to the needs of a deaf audience. At least two examples provide plot devices in Shakespeare's plays. For instance, Julius Caesar advises Antony on which side he should speak to him, "Come on my right hand, for this ear is deaf",[1] perhaps hinting early on, that the imperial majesty is rather more human than divine. In *The Comedy of Errors*, Aegeon encounters a man he believes is his estranged son and says, "My dull deaf ears a little use to hear",[2] indicating that the effects of age have made the process of identification more difficult.

---

[1] William Shakespeare, Julius Caesar, Act I, Sc. ii, Shakespeare Volume III, The Tragedies (1599; London: JM Dent & Sons Ltd, n.d.) 369.
[2] William Shakespeare, The Comedy of Errors, Act V, Sc. i, Shakespeare Volume I, The Comedies (1594; London: JM Dent & Sons Ltd, n.d.) 275.

The American playwright Eugene O'Neill develops the plot of his one act play *Warnings*, written in 1913, around a recently deafened wireless operator on the ship SS Empress.[3] In the first scene, James Knapp is on leave from his maritime duties and thinks a cold has produced temporary hearing loss. He visits an ear specialist who tells him that he could become "stone deaf" at any time. Knapp and his wife are terrified that if he declares the situation, Knapp will lose his job at a time when they cannot afford for that to happen. The second scene shows Knapp at sea. The ship has struck a drifting vessel and is starting to sink. The captain runs into the radio room and asks Knapp whether any boats have responded to their signals for help. Knapp replies to every enquiry, "I haven't heard a thing yet, sir!" Eventually Knapp confesses that he is now "stone deaf", and although he sent out messages for urgent assistance, he hasn't been able to hear any replies. The captain sends for a replacement wireless operator who happens to be on board travelling home due to illness. Knapp's stand-in soon discovers that there are boats steaming rapidly to help. As the order is given to board the life rafts, Knapp is handed a copy of a message that was sent from another ship earlier, warning the Empress to avoid the derelict vessel and stating its position. Knapp realises that due to his failure to hear the message, it is his fault that the ship is sinking. In despair, he finds the captain's gun and shoots himself. The Titanic had been lost the year before the play was written making the subject of a ship at risk of sinking, topical and emotive. The tragic tale revolves around the plot point of Knapp's refusal to acknowledge his sudden and total deafness. Medical advice was sought, a diagnosis and prognosis given, but this was then kept secret. The play highlights a fear of poverty that impelled Knapp to disguise his deafness. Above all, Knapp depended on his hearing to do his job, but had he resigned from his position, it would not have been easy at that time for a deaf person to find alternative employment, as they were still considered to be "imbeciles".

Johnny Belinda from 1940 is a play written by another American, Elmer Blaney Harris.[4] It was apparently based on a real incident that occurred near the author's holiday home. The play has been adapted for film, radio, and television. The drama is set is an isolated fishing community in Nova Scotia at the end of the nineteenth century. Belinda MacDonald is a "deaf-mute" following an illness contracted when she was a one-year-old. She lives with her father and aunt. The father resents Belinda as her mother died giving birth to her. Belinda works in her father's shop, and understands a system

---

[3] Eugene O'Neill, "Warnings", Bookyards, accessed n/d,
https://www.bookyards.com/en/book/details/11638/Warnings.
[4] Elmer Harris, Johnny Belinda (New York: Samuel French Ltd, 1940).

of marks he writes in the ledger to identify each customer and their order. The villagers refer to the young woman as "The Dummy". Dr Richardson, the local doctor, is idealistic. He believes Belinda to be intelligent, and that she understands more than people think. He teaches her how to read lips more accurately, as well as the rudiments of sign language that he learned as a student working with deaf children. The doctor tells Belinda's father about a special school at McGill, but she cannot be spared. Belinda is raped by a local man, Locky, in the knowledge that she cannot speak against him. She gives birth to a son whom she names Johnny Belinda. Belinda asks the doctor whether her baby can hear. The local population assume that Dr Richardson has taken advantage of the young woman with whom he has spent so much time. Rumours spread, and both are shunned. Locky tries to take the baby away by force, and Belinda shoots him. At the subsequent trial Dr Richardson acts as Belinda's interpreter. The court assumes that Belinda is stupid until the circumstances of the shooting are revealed, and the facts are confirmed by Locky's wife. Belinda is released, she and Dr Richardson plan to marry, and their names are cleared. The play demonstrates themes that are well-established in novels. There is the common assumption, expressed even by Belinda's family, that equates deafness with idiocy, and a lack of vocal speech with the inability to communicate. Belinda is afraid that her child will be deaf. In some ways, she is a Goldilocks figure who is transformed in demeanour, appearance, and opportunity, by the dashing young hearing doctor. Belinda is changed, not through medical treatment, but by being taught alternative methods of communication. Her moral standing and innocence are taken away by contact with the hearing world. Belinda's inability to speak out her suffering and guilt is a metaphor for the silence of those who cannot accuse their aggressor. Belinda is shown to be vulnerable through her deafness and isolation, thus she is cast in the role of the victim, a fate shared with a number of deaf female characters that appear in novels.[5]

The Miracle Worker is a three-act play written in 1959 by William Gibson, in which the deaf character is neither threatened by sudden deafness or becomes a victim. In fact, the character is the young version of a towering historical figure. The drama is based on Helen Keller's autobiography *The Story of My Life* written in 1903, and adapted from his Playhouse 90 television script of the same name, produced two years earlier. The title of the play refers to Helen's teacher, Annie Sullivan, reportedly after a quotation from Helen's great friend Mark Twain, who said "Helen is a

---

[5] See Chapter Two.

miracle, and Miss Sullivan is the miracle worker".[6] The play begins in Alabama in the 1880's. Helen is deaf and blind after contracting a febrile illness as a baby. She is left to run free and unrestrained until, when she is aged five, a new teacher arrives in the household. Annie Sullivan was virtually blind as a child, but recovered some sight after an operation. Annie believes that she can control Helen's behaviour and teach her words and vocal speech. Helen is taught the deaf-blind alphabet,[7] and learns to spell words. Eventually Annie tells Helen's parents that she will accomplish more if she moves the child out of the house to continue their work without interruption. At the age of twelve, Helen returns to the house, and finger spells onto the hands of her astounded parents. When signing "water" she is able to speak the syllables of the word.[8] The portrayal of the deaf character in this play is of course based on a very famous true story. It shows Helen changing from an unruly feral child into a controlled and communicative adolescent. This was made possible by the patient and persistent use by her teacher, of oral methods, and the deaf-blind finger spelling alphabet, that reflected the educational mores of the time. The play recognises Annie Sullivan's unique contribution to the life of her young charge.

The dramas considered so far have been written by hearing authors. *Sign Me Alice* is a comedy based on Shaw's *Pygmalion,* written by the deaf playwright and American Sign Language (ASL) actor Gilbert Eastman in 1973. All the characters are deaf, and the play is performed mainly in ASL, with the addition of some invented signs. The work is unique in that it is intended to be performed exclusively to an audience that understands sign language. Alice works as a waitress in a hotel. Dr Zeno criticises the way in which Alice and other staff members sign. He offers to teach Alice his revolutionary invention, "Using Signed English", that promises the "rewards" enjoyed by hearing people. There is one condition, Alice must agree to become a "lady". Dr Yivisaker bets Dr Zeno that he can't turn Alice into a lady in time for the convention ball.[9] Alice succeeds and then wonders whether she belongs in the hearing or deaf worlds. She makes up her mind, and runs away with a handsome deaf man she bumped into earlier. Eastman's satirical work raises issues concerning the use of sign language, what it means to be deaf, and the interface between the deaf and hearing

---

[6] "The Miracle Worker", SuperSummary, accessed n/d, https://www.supersummary.com/the-miracle-worker/summary/.

[7] William Gibson, The Miracle Worker: (a play in three acts), (New York: Samuel French Inc, 1960), 31.

[8] Gibson, The Miracle Worker: (a play in three acts), 93.

[9] Gilbert C Eastman, Sign Me Alice & Laurent Clerc: a Profile (San Diego: DawnSignPress, 1997), 32-33.

worlds. Once again, we find a deaf character worrying about identity, reminiscent of some of the poignant poems examined in Chapter Five.

Mark Medoff's play *Children of a Lesser God* is perhaps better known as the film version. The play was first produced in 1979 and written specifically for the deaf actress Phyllis Frelich.[10] It is based partly on Frelich's relationship with her husband. The frontispiece quotes Tennyson's lines from *Idylls of the King*,

> For why is all around us here
> As if some lesser god had made the
> World,
> But had not force to shape it as he would.

The play takes place in the mind of James Leeds, an idealistic teacher, whose memories take shape and step onto the stage. He arrives at a deaf school to teach oral speech and reading lips. James soon encounters a former student, Sarah Norman, who now works in the school as a cleaner. Sarah has been deaf since birth and refuses to use vocal speech. Sarah reads lips and communicates in ASL throughout. At different points in the play, other characters translate her signs, otherwise James repeats what she has signed as a running commentary in spoken English. James engages with Sarah and they converse fluently in ASL. Sarah accuses James of wanting to make her "pass for hearing", whereas James argues that he just wants her to be able to function in the hearing world.[11] James wants Sarah to learn to speak so that she is not dependent upon anyone else.[12] Sarah insists she has "a language that's just as good as yours",[13] and disapproves of James' teaching methods that concentrate on vocal speech. The pair fall in love despite holding very different views as well as facing opposition from the faculty. They try to find an emotional space, and a means of conversing, that occupies neither the hearing or deaf world. This attempt is short-lived and they soon begin to argue with each other. Sarah rejects what she perceives as any sign of pity or patronising from James. Sarah moves out, even though they both acknowledge their love for one another. The play ends with the couple estranged, but with the hope of reconciliation. This is a powerful drama that explores the conflict between deaf and hearing worlds, issues of

---

[10] Cindi Calhoun, "Children of a Lesser God", StageAgent, accessed n/d, https://stageagent.com/shows/play/10884/children-of-a-lesser-god.

[11] Mark Medoff, Children of a Lesser God (New York: Dramatists Play Service: 1980), 13.

[12] Medoff, Children of a Lesser God, 67

[13] Medoff, Children of a Lesser God, 18

deaf education and consequent identity, and the search for a mutually acceptable form of communication. The title infers that the deaf characters exist in a state or setting that is somehow incomplete, at least, in the view of some people, perhaps including James. It is James, and his struggles in trying to impose his perspective upon Sarah, that provides the focus of the play, rather than on Sarah and her own experience of deafness. Sarah, and the other deaf characters, are portrayed as intelligent, forceful people, able to negotiate an educational process they don't wholly approve, making use of it to fulfil their own goals. Perhaps their state is not quite so imperfect after all. There is recognition of the need for the deaf characters to maintain strong personal identities, and a cohesive community. The mainstream press reviewed the play very well, but there are divided opinions within the deaf community that continue to be shared. Although most deaf people are pleased at any attempt to represent them within mainstream media, there is concern that James takes decisions on Sarah's behalf, and exerts pressure on her to use vocal speech even when it is clear that she has no wish to do so.[14]

Deaf Characters in Television

The first deaf actor to appear on mainstream television as a fictional character was Audree Norton in 1968. She played Jody Wellman in an episode of *Mannix* entitled *The Silent Cry*.[15] Her role is that of a stereotypical deaf person in a crime story. She "overhears", or more correctly "oversees", a plot involving kidnap and murder, by reading the lips of a criminal talking at a payphone. This is a convenient plot device beloved by crime writers, identifying Wellman as a Gifted character similar to those used in novels of the genre.[16] Ten years later, Norton auditioned for a part in *Mom and Dad Can't Hear Me*, a comedy drama about an adolescent girl embarrassed to introduce friends to her deaf parents. As is quite often the case, the casting director preferred to use a hearing actor, even though the character in the show was deaf. Norton complained publicly, protests followed, and she never acted again.[17]

---

[14] Christian Lewis, "Review: 'Children of a Lesser God' is as offensive as ever", Queer Voices, accessed April 12, 2018, https://clewisreviews.medium.com/review-children-of-a-lesser-god-is-as-offensive-as-ever-436b44b26a20.

[15] "The Silent Cry", Mannix, Series 2 Episode 1. CBS, First broadcast September 28, 1968.

[16] See Chapter Two.

[17] "Audree Norton", The Scotsman, https://www.pressreader.com/uk/the-scotsman/20150516/282273843943891.

The recurring trope of a deaf person reading lips with uncanny skill, and risking the accusation of becoming a supercrip,[18] was continued in the extremely successful series *Sue Thomas F.B. Eye*. This was broadcast between 2002 and 2005, with Deanne Bray playing the lead role in fifty-six episodes. Bray was the first deaf actor to be the star of a television programme. At the time, it was one of the two highest rated shows on PAX Network. The character is a surveillance agent for an elite team of the FBI, whose role is to read lips at a distance or on video footage. She also plays "the good cop" during interrogations. Thomas has a hearing dog, and one of her colleagues can interpret for her by using ASL. The show's original title *Lip Service* stresses the importance of reading lips and vocal speech, both for the character and the plots. Ironically, for a series with a central deaf character, there appear to be no captions provided for deaf viewers. The premise is based on a real person, the first deaf individual to be employed by the FBI as an undercover lip-reading specialist from 1979 to 1983.[19] Throughout the series, there are glimpses of the main character's experience of deafness. She is given an appropriate back story, and the pilot episode included scenes that had really happened in Bray's life.[20] The importance of deaf awareness, and the ability to communicate in ways other than verbal speech, are stressed through the interactions between Thomas and her team.

The Silence is another crime drama, this time from the BBC, that follows the story of Amelia, a deaf teenager who witnesses the murder of a police officer. It was filmed in 2010 as a mini-series with four episodes, and unlike most productions in this genre, the main character's ability to read lips exists only as a minor plot device. Amelia is recovering from a cochlear implant, a procedure desired mainly by her mother, and is staying with her uncle to recuperate. She witnesses the violent killing of a woman, later identified as a police officer. Coincidentally her uncle is the senior detective appointed to investigate the death of his colleague, and a second murder, that is apparently unrelated. The episodes show Amelia using imperfect vocal speech, and the soundtrack is muffled when she takes out her implant, giving the viewers an impression of what she hears. Amelia is shown in

---

[18] See Chapter Four.

[19] Debbie Clason, "As an FBI lip-reader, Sue Thomas broke new ground in Deaf community", Healthy Hearing, accessed July 4, 2022, https://www.healthyhearing.com/report/52636-Sue-thomas-breaking-barriers-with-faith-perseverance-and-a-sense-of-humor.

[20] Jamie Berke, "An interview with first deaf television star Deanne Bray-Kotsur", verywellhealth, April 10, 2020, https://www.verywellhealth.com/deanne-bray-kotsur-sue-thomas-1048660.

post-operative rehabilitation with a speech therapist. She is told not to sign so that she can concentrate on improving her speech. Amelia's parents are hearing and have never signed. Her mother talks about Amelia and states, "She's not shy, she's just stubborn." When arguing with her mother, Amelia pulls out the implant so that she can no longer hear what her mother is saying. Amelia attends a deaf youth club and identifies with the deaf community. When she is shown signing, captions in written English are provided. The screenplay almost steers clear of the lip-reading trope, in that Amelia actually witnesses the crucial event, rather than "oversees" the criminals talking about it. However, she does read their lips on security camera footage, providing her uncle with the evidence that links the two killings. Amelia recognises one of the murderers as a police officer, and subsequently unravels a web of corruption. There is good mention of aspects of the deaf community, and the tension between Amelia and her hearing parents is exposed and explored. Amelia's character is not patronised by the script. Although Amelia's mother blames the deafness for her behaviour, similar to the pejorative view expressed by Sarah's father in the novel *Manservant and Maidservant*, Amelia is certainly no Goldilocks character. She is wilful, headstrong, and difficult. Her ability to read lips is perhaps a little exaggerated, but the battles with the new cochlear implant are described effectively. It is the character, who is well-developed, that is shown to deserve our interest, rather than the technological intervention. Surprisingly this mini-series was filmed only five years after the end of *Sue Thomas F.B. Eye*, and its depiction of deafness is much more down to earth and realistic. The crimes themselves are also portrayed in a grittier style. There is quite a contrast between the American series and its approach as casual entertainment, and the darker style of *The Silence*. The series was well received by a deaf reviewer.[21] Amelia was played by Genevieve Barr, a deaf actor who grew up using oral speech. She learned British Sign Language (BSL) specifically for this role. In 2016, Barr appeared in a television advert for Maltesers, the first to be aired solely in BSL with English subtitles.[22]

Throughout the book, I have tried to avoid including contributions created specifically for children. However, I have to mention the Children's BBC production *Magic Hands*.[23] These short programmes feature poetry,

---

[21] Cathy Heffernan, "The Silence: a deaf writer's view of the BBC thriller", The Guardian, 13th July 2010, https://www.theguardian.com/tv-and-radio/tvandradioblog/2010/jul/13/the-silence-deaf-bbc-thriller.

[22] "Maltesers – The Light Side of Disability (Sign Language)", https://www.youtube.com/watch?v=0jJSsJiMhlY.

[23] "Magic Hands", BBC, https://www.bbc.co.uk/search?q=magic+hands.

Shakespeare, songs, and stories, expressed entirely in BSL by deaf presenters, and accompanied by vivid animation and graphics. They are intended for both deaf and hearing children, making culture accessible for the former, and introducing sign language to the latter. A total of twenty-three episodes were made in two series between 2013 and 2016.

The BBC seems to have acquired a significant track record in promoting deaf television performers. Rose Ayling-Ellis became the first long-term deaf character in a television soap opera when she joined the cast of BBC's *Eastenders* in 2020. She played the deaf character Frankie Lewis for two years. Her insights into creating a deaf character for television are revealing. When interviewed about the portrayal of deaf characters in television, Ayling-Ellis said,

> Deaf people always seem to get run over. I mean, we can *see* cars. We don't just stand around in the road waiting to get hit. It seemed that deaf characters are always victims.[24]

She continued, saying she was irritated by films,

> where the deaf person learns to sign or speak and everyone goes: oh amazing! Like *Children of a Lesser God.*

Ayling-Ellis, who was born into a hearing family, said people would ask her Mum if she'd seen the film and then tell her, "…your little girl will be alright, she'll be able to speak." The actress believes scripts by hearing writers are "frustrating", as the characters they create can follow everything spoken and read lips from an impossible distance "like I have a superpower", inferring this is the deaf experience. These comments tally with much that I have written about common stereotypes used by hearing writers. Ayling-Ellis wanted to make the Lewis character more realistic, and so a deaf scriptwriter was brought in to write her part. In 2021, she and her dance partner won *Strictly Come Dancing*. During the performance of Clean Bandit's *Symphony,* the music was cut for ten seconds while the pair continued to dance. The commonly used device of forced silence in television and film invite the audience to experience what it is like to be deaf. *Heat* magazine named it "the Unmissable TV Moment of the Year".[25]

---

[24] Helen Brown, "On TV, the deaf always get run over. We can see cars!", The Daily Telegraph Review, December 3, 2022, 8-9, https://www.telegraph.co.uk/theatre/what-to-see/strictlys-rose-ayling-ellis-tv-deaf-always-get-run-can-see-cars/.

[25] "Strictly's silent dance named TV moment of the year", The Irish News, December 7, 2021,

In a further BBC television production, deaf actor Rhiannon May joined the long-running forensic investigation drama *Silent Witness*. She has appeared as Cara Connelly, the niece of one of the main characters, from 2021 up to the present. Cara can read lips and only communicates by using BSL. When interviewed about the role on a deaf television magazine programme, May said the screenplays reflect real life by having the character use texts, gestures, writing and pointing when interacting with hearing characters.[26] The actress explained that some of the main characters in the series are learning BSL, and just as in a real-life, they are learning at different speeds and with varying levels of competency. A deaf BSL script consultant works on the show to translate lines of English. May hopes that at some point in the future, the character will be shown to use a BSL interpreter. The relationship between Cara and her uncle provides an important sub-plot within the series, and it is the emphasis on communication that remains the most important element of Cara's deafness. When she signs and hearing characters translate into English, or they explain out loud what they are signing, Cara acts as a ficelle or confidante, in the manner of Singer in *The Heart is a Lonely Hunter*.[27]

In 2021 Marvel Studios brought their comic character *Hawkeye* to the screen in a series of six episodes. As I stated in Chapter Four, characters from comics are often "ret-conned" or re-invented. In this television adaptation, the script owes some of its features to the Daredevil *Parts of a Hole* story arc,[28] though it differs in some very significant ways. The most notable is that Maya Lopez, pre-Echo, is pitched against Hawkeye rather than Daredevil. There are, therefore, two major deaf characters. In the first episode, we are immediately introduced to Clint Barton aka Hawkeye, who is experiencing muffled sounds through his hearing aids, that are made audible for the viewer. Clint and his son are later shown signing to each other, and Clint walks on one side of his prospective superhero partner Kate, so that he can hear her. In the third episode, we see a young Maya Lopez, long before she creates the persona of Echo, unable to hear at school and desperately struggling to read lips. At home, she makes handshapes and uses sign language with her father, as she does in the comics. Maya wants to go to deaf school, but her father tells her "You have to learn to jump between two worlds", inferring that she needs to learn how to watch people and read lips. Clint eventually meets the adult Maya, now a criminal working for the

---

https://www.irishnews.com/magazine/entertainment/2021/12/07/news/strictly-s-silent-dance-named-tv-moment-of-the-year-2528910/.

[26] See Hear, Season 42, episode 15, BBC, First broadcast 15th February 2023.
[27] See Chapter Two.
[28] See Chapter Four.

gang leader Fisk. She uses a sign language interpreter, a possibility not offered in the comics, as Clint's standard of signing is not very good. Maya also notices that Clint wears a hearing aid. Maya signs that Clint might be better without it. During a fight, Maya intentionally kicks the aid out of Clint's ear and stamps on it. Fisk tells Maya that Ronin killed her father, leaving a bloodied handprint on her face, which we know from the graphic stories is a foreshadowing of Echo's mask. Maya discovers that Clint had been Ronin. In a signed conversation with the interpreter that is captioned, Maya is shown to be emotionally repressed, unable to discuss the ongoing grief she feels about her father's death. When Clint and Maya fight again, he convinces her that although he had been Ronin, it was actually Fisk who killed her father. Maya confronts Fisk, shoots him, and leaves the city. This is the prelude to Marvel developing Maya into the Echo character for a forthcoming spin-off series due to be released in 2023. Maya is played by Alaqua Cox who has native American heritage and attended a deaf school. The series, with Hawkeye replacing Daredevil from the comic version, allows an interesting comparison between the two major types of deafness. Clint has become deaf later in life, and remains fully vocal. He struggles to hear with the help of a hearing aid. He cannot read lips and has moderate fluency in sign language. Clint remains immersed in the hearing world. His deafness is treated as a form of loss that needs correction. Problems arise when the technology fails. Maya has been profoundly deaf since early childhood and is fluent in sign language. She can read lips reasonably well, but sometimes requires the use of an interpreter when dealing with hearing people. Maya identifies primarily as a deaf person and lives on the fringes of both hearing and deaf communities. There is an interesting interplay between the characters, and in particular, concerning their differing modes of communication each time they meet. By stamping on Clint's hearing aid, Maya is declaring her allegiance to the signing world, and trying to force Clint to re-evaluate his identity. Both characters are well developed and shown to have an emotional and relational depth. The representation is largely praised by deaf reviewers for its authenticity, although there are considered to be some inconsistencies when compared with real life experiences of deafness.[29] [30]

---

[29] Alison Stine, 'What 'Hawkeye' gets right about deafness – and what it glosses over", Salon, December 6, 2021, https://www.salon.com/2021/12/06/hawkeye-echo-deaf-maya-lopez/.

[30] Sabrina Barr, "Hawkeye: deaf young people on what hearing loss representation in Marvel TV series means to them", Metro, May 5, 2021, https://metro.co.uk/2021/03/05/hawkeye-deaf-young-people-on-impact-of-hearing-loss-representation-14191141.

By comparison the character of Fenrick in *The Witcher: Blood Origin* (2022) is relatively minor and two-dimensional. In the Netflix mini-series, the role is played by deaf actor Amy Murray. Fenrick is the deaf assistant to Chief Druid Balor played by Sir Lenny Henry. They are shown signing together. No reason is given to explain why there is a deaf character in the plot. In some ways it is encouraging that Netflix chose to have a character who just happens to be deaf, rather than fixing her existence around a specific plot point.

This would have been unthinkable nearly sixty years ago when Audree Norton appeared in the ground-breaking episode of *Mannix*. Television has come a long way. But for some reason, the vast majority of deaf characters on television are female. Perhaps television producers still think that the viewing audience will only accept deaf characters who are physically appealing and potentially vulnerable, whatever skills and strengths they possess, and are not yet comfortable with the idea of deaf male characters on our screens. In the UK, deaf actors are more usually seen on television than on film, whereas the opposite is true in the US. In recent years, deaf people have been granted greater access to television programmes through closed captioning, although there is a remarkable disparity between channels as to their provision.

Deaf Characters in Film

Unlike drama and television, cinema hasn't always been an audible medium. Watching a silent film gave equality of access to hearing and deaf members of the audience. Many of the early film actors were in fact deaf, as directors appreciated the more natural movements that communicated emotion by florid gesture when acting, that arose from the ability to sign. Charlie Chaplin employed a number of deaf actors in his films and was close friends with Granville Redmond who taught Chaplin sign language.[31] Granville, who was also a famous landscape artist, appears as a dance-hall owner in *A Dog's Life* in 1918, the first film produced and directed by Chaplin, and in a further seven films made by Chaplin between 1918 and 1929. Chaplin collected Redmond's paintings and set up an art studio for him in the film production buildings. In his films, Chaplin uses gestures and expressions resembling those of deaf people. In 1919 Helen Keller met Chaplin during the filming of *Sunnyside*, and taught him some of the tactile

---

[31] Sarah Lawrence, "Charlie Chaplin – Film Industry Pioneer and Deaf Influenced?", Deaf Magazine, April 26, 2015, http://slfirst.co.uk/entertainment/film-cinema/charlie-chaplin-film-industry-pioneer-and-deaf-influenced.

sign language alphabet.[32] Following the release of the first full length all-talking feature film, Warner Bros' *Lights of New York* in 1928, deaf patrons found themselves with limited participation in a medium they had always been able to enjoy alongside their hearing peers. By the end of the following year, Hollywood was producing sound films exclusively, and opportunities disappeared for deaf actors who had previously been in so much demand. In opposition to this trend, Ernest Marshall, a deaf film director, continued making silent films with deaf actors for deaf people. The National Association of the Deaf had already funded films in ASL between 1913 and 1920, and then campaigned for the provision of captioning.[33]

A number of the stage plays considered above have been produced as films. *Johnny Belinda* was adapted for the cinema in 1948, with Jane Wyman starring as Belinda. It was also made into a tv movie in 1982. There are some differences between the scripts of the original play and the film. Belinda's father appears as a farmer in the film version, and much more is made of Locky's character. He is shown fighting with Belinda's father and pushing him over a cliff. Belinda starts the film as looking more obviously vulnerable. However, her appearance and clothing become cleaner, tidier, and more attractive in successive scenes, as her confidence and ability to sign improve. Belinda is shown to enjoy the movement and vibrations of music and dances with the doctor. Locky uses a violin he cannot play, as a lure to entice Belinda into the threatening situation that ends with her assault. The essential features concerning the portrayal of deafness are very similar in the play and the film. In the film version, there is the additional point of Dr Richardson taking a book to Belinda's father explaining that it contains signs used by L'Abee d'Epee, thus providing a historical link. Jane Wyman won the Best Actress Academy award, the first given to a non-speaking role since the end of the silent film era. Wyman's very sensitive portrayal of a naive and kindly young woman was based entirely on facial expressions and nonverbal communication.

Another film adaptation, *The Miracle Worker* from 1962, won eleven Oscars including those for Anne Bancroft who played Anne Sullivan, and Patty Duke who played Helen Keller. Although the role of the sign language teacher is paramount in both films, the characters of the deaf people being educated are quite different. Belinda is a placid, well-intentioned adult, whereas Helen begins as an unruly, disruptive child who is blind as well as deaf.

---

[32] Helen Keller, Midstream (Garden City, New York: Doubleday, Doran & Co, 1929), 197.

[33] John S. Schuchman, "The Silent film Era: Silent films, NAD Films, and the Deaf community's Response", Sign Language Studies, No. 4 (Spring 2004): 231-238.

The 1986 film version of *Children of a Lesser God* from is broadly similar to the play, except that the introduction is longer and acted as real events, rather than as recollections from the memory of James Leeds. Marlee Matlin who played Sarah, won the Oscar for Best Actress for her role, and became the first deaf actor to receive this prestigious award, as well as the youngest, which remains true at the time of writing. As a result of Matlin's success, there was an increased demand for deaf actors in film and on television. Although the movie "changed the image of deaf people in popular culture",[34] it remains a love story rather than an account documenting how deaf people actually live. The story is intended to be shown entirely from the perspective of the hearing teacher, and so it is his interpretation of Sarah's life and experience that dominates. Nonetheless, there are interesting insights into the difficulties experienced by a non-verbal deaf signer, and the issue of language is brought to the attention of the hearing public in a way that had never been done so before.

See No Evil, Hear No Evil, a comedy produced in 1989, has an example of a typical Granny character,[35] as one of its two main protagonists. The plot revolves around Dave, a deaf man played by Gene Wilder, and Wally, a blind man played by Richard Pryor. Dave reads lips but does not sign. They both "witness" a murder by being present at the scene. Wally hears the gunshot, and Dave, who has his back turned when the gun is fired, sees the assassin running away. They become unlikely suspects and are chased by the Police and the villainous gang. The film has a number of amusing set pieces. The pair escape in a stolen car, with Wally driving, and Dave telling Wally how to turn the steering wheel. It is a simple plot with plenty of comic material. Typical tropes associated with deaf characters in literature transfer to the screenplay. Dave is continually shouted at, others think he is stupid, misunderstandings with words occur, and he is shown to read lips rather well. As is usual with the portrayal of Granny characters, Dave tells us little about the reality of being deaf. Gene Wilder a hearing actor who manages to look suitably unresponsive and confused for much of the film, apparently attended the New York League for the Hard of Hearing in order to prepare for the role.[36]

---

[34] Emmanuel Levy," Reel/Real Impact: Children of a Lesser God (1986)", Emmanuel Levy Cinema 24/7, February 20, 2006, https://emanuellevy.com/comment/children-of-a-lesser-god-1986-cultural-impact-4/.

[35] See Chapter Two.

[36] Emma Daly, "Revelations Gene Wilder: I thought, oh my God, Ms Webb is going to be some old busybody", The Independent, December 17, 1996, https://www.independent.co.uk/life-style/revelations-gene-wilder-i-thought-oh-my-god-ms-webb-is-going-to-be-some-old-busybody-1314910.html.

There is another comedy film that contains a deaf character whose role does not exist simply to convey humour. Released in 1994, *Four Weddings and A Funeral* includes Charlie's brother David, played by deaf actor David Bower. He and Charlie (played by Hugh Grant), are the only members of their tight group of friends to converse in BSL. It is used for comedic effect on occasion, for instance when David sees Charlie's new girlfriend for the first time, and Charlie mistranslates David's signs about her appearance. The value of David's ability to sign becomes a major plot point towards the end of the film. Charlie feels obliged to marry former girlfriend Duckface, when he is in fact in love with someone else. David interrupts the wedding ceremony and asks Charlie to translate his sign language statements. By doing so, he forces Charlie to express his doubts, and speak out the truth in front of the entire congregation. It is a good representation of a sign language conversation that lasts several minutes. The importance of BSL as a language in its own right, is shown by one of the group of friends, who learns to sign, because she likes David, and wants to get to know him better. Although David provides a plot device, the character is well developed and not a stereotype. The way in which the deaf character is treated in the film is considered by some reviewers to be a useful representation.[37]

Another common type of plot device is provided by the deaf character in the 1998 film *Break Up*. The main character, Jimmy, played by Bridget Fonda, is married to a cruel and abusive husband. He hits her head so hard that the blow causes traumatic deafness, a convenient sudden means of deafness much used by writers. After blacking out in a further domestic assault, Jimmy wakes up in hospital to discover that her husband has been killed in a car crash and that she is the prime suspect. Considering that she has only been deafened for a year, Jimmy reads lips extraordinarily well. Jimmy cannot respond to the detectives interviewing her unless they are within her line of sight. In fact, her husband has staged his own death and intends to terrorise Jimmy before killing her. Jimmy's deafness is used to heighten the character's fear and the tension of the viewers. For instance, she does not hear when he is breaking into the house or walking up behind her.

A similar use of a deaf character occurs in the 2016 film *Hush*. Maddie, a deaf writer, acted by Kate Siegel, lives alone in the woods. A childhood episode of meningitis caused complete deafness, and a temporary paralysis of the vocal cords which became permanent after surgery. Maddie is

---

[37] Lilit Marcus, "'Four Weddings' is still a pop culture starting point for sign language", bitchmedia, September 3, 2019, https://www.bitchmedia.org/article/four-weddings-and-a-funeral-1994-portrayal-deafness.

therefore deaf and cannot use speech. She can, however, read lips and sign. Maddie is stalked by a masked killer. He murders her friend outside the isolated house, and then proceeds to bait and provoke her. The film is mostly silent. There is a little dialogue and a soundtrack that is muted at times, so the audience can relate to Maddie's inability to hear the assailant. Maddie does not know whether he has entered the house, and if so, where, so that there is a great deal of psychological tension. He taunts her by suddenly appearing at a window or behind her in the house. Maddie is a strong character who has to invent strategies to survive. At one point, she triggers a smoke alarm for deaf people that uses flashing lights to disorientate him, rather like Echo in her fight against Daredevil in the Marvel story arc *Parts of a Hole*.[38] This home invasion slasher movie does not cast Maddie as a stereotypical deaf victim. It is her hearing friend who is killed at the beginning, and Maddie ultimately kills her hearing aggressor. The character is portrayed as a powerful and dangerous woman who employs skill and cunning to defeat her adversary.

The Silent Child, released in 2017, is a film with an overt message. The following year it won the Oscar for best live action short film. The main character is Libby played by Maisie Sly, a profoundly deaf six-year-old girl who lives in a busy hearing family. Libby is shown to be isolated and is left to watch television by herself until a social worker, Joanne played by Rachel Shenton, is hired as a specialist child-minder. Joanne realises that Libby is devoid of contact and starts to teach her BSL. Libby's mother wants her daughter to speak and is dismissive about attempts to use sign language. The relationship between Libby and Joanne grows closer because of the time they spend together, as well as the ability to communicate effectively. Libby's mother becomes jealous and insists on sending Libby to a mainstream school. At one point Libby signs to Joanne that "her ears are broken". Joanne is summarily dismissed and visits the school. She waits at the school gate and sees Libby standing in the playground alone and confused. Libby sees Joanne and signs "I love you". The screenplay was written by Shenton, and based on her experience as the child of a parent who became deaf. She learned BSL so that she could communicate with her father.[39] Libby's difficulties are very well demonstrated, as is the family's reluctance to learn a new language. The film "passionately drives home the

---

[38] See Chapter Four.
[39] "The Oscar winning short film: The Silent Child", accessed n/d, https://thesilentchildmovie.com/team.

need to break down communication barriers for deaf children",[40] and has a campaigning message. At the end of the film captions read:

> 90% of deaf children are born to hearing parents. 78% of deaf children attend school without specialist support. We hope this film contributes in the fight for sign language to be recognised in every school across the globe.

When Shenton accepted her Oscar, she signed her acceptance speech, fulfilling a promise made to Maisie Sly.[41]

Sign Gene was released in 2017, and written and directed by deaf actor Emilio Insolera. It is a striking sci-fi thriller, and the first film in which deaf people have superpowers.[42] Described as an "unlikely cult classic",[43] the premise of the film is that a specific genetic mutation has given rise to deafness accompanied by superpowers. The hands of deaf people can create shapes or signs representing objects and actions, and the object appears or the action happens. An assassin points at the intended target, and bullets appear at the ends of his fingers, then fly towards the victim. This ability can be seen in the illustration. Deaf "mutants" that possess such powers are closely monitored by a special squad consisting of deaf agents. They are asked to investigate a Japanese gangster who intends to purify the "sign gene" that confers these abilities, and inject it into hearing villains in order to create an army with superpowers. The name of the gangster's company is 1.8.8.0, a title that references the year of the Milan Congress. There are a number of other names and events well-known in deaf history that appear throughout the film. *Sign Gene* is a low budget production that lasts one hour. The film is based on a very interesting idea that transfers well to visual representation. The concept of a deaf gene producing superpowers is also seen in the graphic novel *The Prophecy in Blue*. In the same way, deaf characters with enhanced gifts can be accused of being the type of stereotype known as "supercrip".[44] Nevertheless, Insolera succeeds in his desire to portray deaf people as not being victims. He also prefers to use the phrase "visual speaking" rather than "deaf",[45] a concept that is amply

---

[40] Jonathan Blott, "The Silent Child", The Lancet Child & Adolescent Health, No. 6, June 2018, 394.

[41] "The Silent Child' wins Best Live Action Short Film", https://www.youtube.com/watch?v=QmQUWGuKxi4.

[42] Paul Dakin, "Sign Gene: The first deaf superhero film", Hektoen International, Winter 2019, https://hekint.org/2019/03/18/sign-gene-the-first-deaf-superhero-film/.

[43] "Sign Gene", IMDb, www.imdb.com/title/tt4715060/.

[44] See Chapter Four.

[45] Matthew Hernon, "'Sign Gene': Emilio Insolera on Creating the World's first Deaf Superhero Film", Tokyo Weekender, updated April 26, 2021,

demonstrated in the film, though a description that can only apply to those deaf people who use sign language.

Figure 5-1: Image of a poster advertising the film Sign Gene. With the permission of Pluin.

There are other films belonging to the sci-fi genre that have deaf characters. The post-apocalyptic horror thrillers *A Quiet Place* (2018), and its sequel A Quiet Place Part II (2021), star   Millicent Simmonds, a young deaf actor who plays Regan. The facts that she uses ASL and has a cochlear

https://www.tokyoweekender.com/art_and_culture/entertainment-art_and_culture/movies-tv/sign-gene-emilio-insolera-on-creating-the-worlds-first-deaf-superhero-film/.

implant are crucial to the plots of both films. The world has been invaded by blind monsters that possess extraordinarily acute hearing. The survivors including Regan's family, must move, live, and communicate, in complete silence in order to survive. The family has learned ASL from Regan who can also speak and read lips. When the audience sees events unfold from Regan's point of view, the sound is switched off, giving the idea of what it is like to be dependent entirely on vision. Regan has no idea whether certain objects or movements make a noise, and so she relies on watching how the members of her family behave. She remains completely unaware that a monster is close by, and since she is silent, the alien cannot detect her either. Regan's cochlear processor malfunctions, and by observing the monsters' behaviour, she infers that it creates painful noises loud enough to drive them away. Regan realises that if she can amplify the feedback by placing the processor near a microphone connected to a loudspeaker, the monsters become distressed and immobilised making them vulnerable to attack. I would imagine this is the only story in which a cochlear implant is transformed into a lethal weapon! These films show much of the reality of being deaf to a hearing audience without having to lecture or moralise.[46] A deaf reviewer doubted whether the cochlear processor could emit feedback in the way it was shown, and was critical of the fact that although the scenes in ASL were captioned for a hearing audience, the few sections of the film in which the actors used verbal speech were not captioned for the deaf.[47] Many deaf people have praised the film for its inclusion of deafness and ASL, but there are objections that silence is used in a negative way to unsettle the hearing audience,[48] and is depicted as "tragic" since the characters are shown as unable to fully express love or pain without verbal speech.[49] The advantages of being deaf that Gallaudet teaches through its emphasis on Deaf Gain are demonstrated in a stark and extreme form.[50] It is valuable and indeed crucial, for both deaf and hearing people to be able

---

[46] Lennard J. Davis, "Screening deafness", Los Angeles Review of Books, accessed September 19, 2021, https://lareviewofbooks.org/article/screening-deafness/.

[47] T. Frohock, "A Quiet Place: a review from the deaf perspective", April 23, 2018, https://www.tfrohock.com/blog/2018/4/23/a-quiet-place-a-review-from-the-deaf-perspective

[48] Anna Hewitt, "The representation of deafness in 'A Quiet Place'", patientworthy, May 17, 2018, https://patientworthy.com/2018/05/17/representation-of-deafness-in-a-quiet-place/.

[49] Pamela J. Kincheloe, "'A Quiet Place' falls into a tired trope about deafness", Huffpost, April 16, 2018, https://www.huffingtonpost.co.uk/entry/opinion-kincheloe-quiet-place-deaf-people_n_5ad10645e4b0edca2cb9acc6.

[50] H-Dirksen L. Baumann, and Joseph J. Murray, eds., Deaf Gain: Raising the Stakes for Human Diversity, (Minneapolis: University of Minnesota Press, 2014).

to sign. It is interesting to note that during the year that saw the release of a film in which being deaf proved to be an advantage, the film *Bird Box* also appeared. In this film being blind was shown to enhance survival.

Sound of Metal provides profound insights into the experience of becoming deaf and being deaf. It was produced by Amazon Studios in 2019. The main character Ruben, is a drummer in a heavy rock band. He is played by Riz Ahmed. We first see him when he is playing extremely loud music. The audience is offered a distorted soundtrack of ambient sounds and voices so that we can appreciate what Ruben is able to hear. One morning, Ruben wakes up with virtually no hearing. He and his girlfriend Lou, are distressed by the sudden change, and Ruben has an audiogram. The doctor tells Ruben how much hearing he has already lost, and that the provision of a cochlear implant may help. Ruben has a past history of drug use, and his sponsor refers him to a rural shelter for deaf addicts run by Joe. Ruben reads Joe's words that are picked by a microphone and displayed on a computer screen. Joe tells Ruben that he will need to learn how to read lips and use ASL. Ruben attends support meetings and goes to a local deaf school. As he watches people signing, no subtitles are provided for the audience, so they can share Ruben's confusion at watching conversations in an unknown language. This, of course, parallels the difficulties experienced by the profoundly deaf watching hearing people use verbal speech. Ruben becomes very angry when he realises that his life has changed forever. Lou returns to Paris to pursue her career. Ruben gradually settles, and encourages deaf children to drum by teaching them to watch his movements. Ruben takes a deaf boy onto a metal slide in the playground, and shows the boy how to feel the rhythmic vibrations on the metal as he drums a pattern with his hands. Ruben is shown typing words to connect to a deaf switchboard in order to contact Lou by phone. Ruben raises money for the cochlear implant, has the operation, and then finds that the post-operative sounds from the implant are very distorted. When Ruben returns to the shelter, Joe tells him he must now move out, as he believes Ruben's desperate quest to hear is the behaviour of an addict. Joe reminds Ruben that the shelter's ethos is built on the notion that "being deaf is not a handicap". Ruben travels to Paris to visit his girlfriend and reluctantly they acknowledge how much they have drifted apart. Ruben attends a party where he is bombarded with a cacophony of painful sounds received through the cochlear implant. The following day, he decides to return to the United States, and walks uncomfortably down a noisy street. As church bells clang overhead, Ruben removes his implants, and sits down on a bench in contented silence. Ahmed, a hearing actor, learned ASL for the film, and many of the cast come from the deaf community. The film won two Oscars.

It was well captioned. Although the movie shows there is nothing special about being able to hear, and silence becomes Ruben's solace, it has been criticised for creating a false dichotomy between cochlear implants and deaf culture by implying that the two cannot co-exist.[51] The decision to cast a hearing actor in the main role could have been more controversial, but since the character becomes deaf later in life and can already speak, it was thought to make sense.[52]

The 2020 teen movie *Feel the Beat* is an inspirational story about a team of unlikely dancers and their quest for success. April is a disgraced Broadway chorus girl who returns to her hometown and reluctantly agrees to coach a small group of pre-teenage girls. One of the group, Zuzu, is deaf. The regular dance class teacher and the other children sign all their conversations so she can understand what is going on. At first April is uncooperative and dismissive, but then discovers that if the class progresses to the finals of a dance competition, she will perform in front of a well-known Broadway impresario. April is strict, demanding, and officious, and cannot be bothered to remember the names of the girls in the class. She assigns them all nicknames, and calls Zuzu "Fingers" referencing her proficiency in ASL. As the team progresses through the stages of the competition, April softens her attitude, and she and the group of girls think of themselves as having become family. April has even started signing to Zuzu without realising. ASL is integrated into one of the final dance routines. The dance team comes second in the competition, and April continues to coach them after she has been offered the lead role in a Broadway show. Zuzu is not one of the major characters, but her role highlights the use of ASL. Although it would be remarkable for a group of hearing girls to all be able to sign, it seems natural that Zuzu's family and friends converse with her in ASL. The dramatic and elegant nature of sign language is demonstrated in one of the routines. Shaylee Mansfield, the deaf actress who plays Zuzu, was eleven at the time of filming. She is possibly the only deaf actor to be credited for a "sign over" performance in an animation. *Madagascar: A Little Wild*, is a 2020 Dreamworks series in which Dave, a deaf chimp, uses ASL with his sister Pickles. In one episode, a little deaf girl meets Dave. The girl was animated by using a video reference of Mansfield.

Makkari, the deaf superhero character, entered the Marvel cine-verse in *Eternals* (2021). Lauren Ridloff plays an immortal alien battling monsters for the fate of the world. She has helped to progress the world's

---

[51] Lennard J. Davis, "Screening deafness".

[52] Ahmed Khalifa, "'Sound of metal' review (from a deaf perspective)", Hear me Out, accessed May 13, 2021, https://hearmeoutcc.com/sound-of-metal-review/.

development, and introduces sign language to humanity. Makkari's main power is to be very fast. She is shown signing with the other Eternals, but very little is made of the character's deafness.

The same cannot be said about the deaf characters who appear in the AppleTV+ film *CODA* made in 2021. This is an English language remake of a 2014 French Belgian film *La Familie Belier*. Ruby, played by Emilia Jones, is the only hearing member of a Massachusetts fishing family. She dreams of becoming a singer. Ruby's parents and older brother are deaf, making Ruby the Child of Deaf Adults (CODA) of the title. Her father, Frank Rossi, acted by Troy Kotsur, and her brother Leo, struggle to make a success of their fishing business. Ruby is caught between the demands of the family to translate for them, in order to help grow the business, and the extra lessons she must take in order to prepare for music college. Frank and Leo have their fishing licence suspended after failing to respond to the Coastguard when they cannot hear the orders to stop their boat. The family blames Ruby, who should have been on board but was taking a singing lesson instead. Ruby tells the family that she can't always be there to hear and interpret for them, and says "I can't stay with you for the rest of my life". Ruby becomes angry and asks whether they are upset at losing their free interpreter. She tells her parents that their demands are exhausting. When her parents are discussing the situation, her mother Jackie, the actress Marlee Matlin, says she is afraid to lose her baby, but Ruby's father acknowledges that Ruby was "never a baby", inferring how much they have used her ability to speak and hear from a young age. Ruby asks her mother if she wishes that Ruby had been born deaf. Jackie admits that she prayed for a deaf baby, as she was afraid they would not connect if she was born hearing, in the same way that Jackie does not connect with her own hearing mother. Ruby helps her father and brother regain their licence, but there is a stipulation that they will always have a hearing person on board. Ruby offers to renounce her dream of going to music school in order to work full-time on the boat. The decision pleases her parents, but her brother objects, and signs that she has talent and should fulfil her potential. Ruby's family attend her choir concert even though they cannot hear. The soundtrack is switched off as Ruby's mother looks at the audience responding to the music she cannot hear. Her parents are impressed by the strength of the applause at the end of the show. When they go home, Frank asks Ruby to sing for him while he feels the vibrations of her vocal cords. Ruby's family attend her audition for music college. As Ruby sings *Both Sides Now*, she signs, so that her family will understand. There are some very amusing scenes. When Ruby goes with her parents to a doctor's appointment, her father causes her deliberate embarrassment with a vivid description of his genital problems.

Ruby retaliates by telling her parents that the doctor says they can never have sex again! Ruby's parents object to her listening to music at the table but are happy for her brother to look at Tinder profiles, because the whole family can join in as they are visual. Her boyfriend Miles meets Ruby's parents for the first time, and Frank embarrasses him with a very vivid visual description of putting on a condom. Ruby is accepted into the music college and discovers that hearing workers in the family fishing business have been learning how to sign, and will take her place on the boat. The film includes five deaf actors, including Marlee Matlin who plays Ruby's mother. The film won three Oscars, including one awarded to Troy Kotsur for his performance as Frank. Kotsur is married to Deanna Bray, star of *Sue Thomas F.B. Eye.* Marlee Matlin insisted that deaf actors should be cast in the deaf roles against the wishes of the film's financiers, and threatened to pull out if they did not concede.[53] Emilia Jones trained for nine months in ASL before filming began. The writer-director Sian Heder learned ASL, and forty per cent of the film script is in ASL.[54] She was assisted by two deaf collaborators. The film was generally well received by deaf reviewers who applauded the presence of deaf actors, but concern was expressed about continuing the trope that deaf people are unable to appreciate music,[55] and that Ruby was shown interpreting for her family in settings in which there is a legal obligation to provide professional interpreters.[56] The film covers many aspects of the reality of being deaf very well, and in particular, provides a detailed exploration of what it is like to be the hearing child of deaf parents. The choice of the song *Both Sides Now*, is very appropriate, given that Ruby knows what it is to live within a deaf and a hearing environment, and straddling both, strives to find her own position between the two. The considerable tensions felt between Ruby's wishes for her own independence and future, and the desire to continue helping her family, are made abundantly evident. Ruby's search to establish an identity separate

---

[53] Glenn Whipp, "Marlee Matlin on Sundance opener 'CODA': 'I hope it will create a tidal wave'", Los Angeles Times, January 28, 2021, https://www.latimes.com/entertainment-arts/movies/story/2021-01-28/marlee-matlin-coda-sundance-film-festival.

[54] Scott Iwasaki, "Sundance Film Festival 2021 opens with 'CODA'", Park Record, January 21, 2021. https://www.parkrecord.com/entertainment/sundance-film-festival-2021-opens-with-coda/.

[55] Davis, "Screening deafness".

[56] Amanda Morris, "Representation or Stereotype? Deaf Viewers Are Torn Over 'CODA'',' The New York Times, March 30, 2022, https://www.nytimes.com/2022/03/30/movies/deaf-viewers-coda.html.

from the deafness of her family is explored, and is reminiscent of the struggle Margaret experiences in the novel *In this Sign*.[57]

Review of themes

Hearing writers are largely responsible for the majority of screenplays in which deaf characters appear, so it is hardly surprising that many of the major stereotypes and tropes discovered in novels and comics are reiterated in films. Deafness is used as a metaphor for isolation (*Hush*), and deaf characters are positioned as plot devices for humour (*See No Evil, Hear No Evil*), to advance hearing characters (*Four Weddings and a Funeral*), and to increase the sense of threat (*Break Up*). Deafness may also be presented as advantageous (*A Quiet Place* and *Sign Gene*). Films may be used to campaign on behalf of deaf people (*The Silent Child*). As films often revolve around a central character, issues of identity are prominent (*Children of a Lesser God, Sound of Metal, CODA*).

The few examples of drama show a move away from deafness being perceived as a form of loss with the consequent medical intervention and oral education, towards an increased recognition of sign language as an alternate and equally valid form of expression. Television started its run of deaf characters with those that were more stereotypical, particularly regarding the ability to read lips, but continues to portray more realistic representations, with a variety of experiences of being deaf. Producers clearly want to depict deaf people signing, presumably because it is a visual and diverting way in which to establish deafness in a character. Deaf characters are becoming more prominent, and as such, are able to depict a more extensive back story that may include some elements of specialist education, medical intervention, and a wider deaf community. There is even an example of a deaf character who "happens to be deaf" rather than being further developed or proving to be a device to advance the plot. Scripts are benefitting from the use of deaf actors, but also from deaf writers and BSL advisers. Film, that was historically a favourite medium of deaf people, is becoming so again, thanks to the same reasons. It is true that some films employ deaf characters as plot devices, but the majority of more recent examples are more likely to represent the reality of deaf life and touch on quite complex issues such as the pros and cons of cochlear implants, and the pressures on a hearing person living within a deaf family. As deaf characters become more central, time is given to explain their histories of medical intervention and education. The majority are shown to sign, presumably for

---

[57] See Chapter Two.

the same reasons that have made them acceptable, and perhaps fashionable, in television. Sign language may even be construed as the "hero" of a film,[58] through transforming the deaf character as is seen in *Johnny Belinda*. The existence of a signing community is becoming more frequently acknowledged as we see in *Children of a Lesser God*, *Sound of Metal*, and *CODA*.

The acknowledgement of people who are deaf on stage and screen is to be commended. The fact that more deaf actors are appearing in productions is warmly appreciated. Deaf actors in the US are more likely to appear in films compared to their counterparts in the UK. This may be due to a larger film industry with greater opportunities or a more strident deaf community. Deaf people want to see themselves, their communities, their culture, and their various modes of communication regularly and accurately depicted on stage and screen. The greater representation of deaf people is to be applauded as is the willingness to highlight sign language. But is sign language always depicted from the best of motivations? Most deaf people who use sign language would be grateful for any attempt to bring BSL or ASL to the notice of the hearing population. However, there has been discussion within deaf communities about whether the commercialised use of sign language by hearing people is a form of cultural appropriation.[59][60] While encouraging the personal learning and use of signing by hearing individuals, it is feared that sign language, the fundamental basis of deaf culture and communities, may be copied, imperfectly taught, used as a form of virtue signalling by celebrities, or for financial gain in broadcast and social media without acknowledging its origin. As a result, deaf people can feel exploited and unrecognised,[61] possibly affecting how they view attempts, especially by hearing writers, to represent them within the mainstream media on stage and screen. There may be a reaction to this from within the deaf community, so that we may see the rise of more organisations like the Deaf Talent Collective,[62] who promote deaf actors,

---

[58] Miriam Nathan Lerner, "Narrative function of deafness and deaf characters in film", M/C Journal, 13 (3) 2010,
https://journal.media-culture.org.au/index.php/mcjournal/article/view/260.
[59] See Hear, BBC Television, Episode first broadcast on March 4, 2020.
[60] Joianta Lapiak, "Cultural appropriation. Deaf people's culture and signed languages", accessed January 13, 2021, https://www.handspeak.com/study/175/.
[61] Charlie Swinbourne, "We need to address cultural appropriation of deafness and BSL in the TV and film industry", The Limping Chicken, October 5, 2017, https://limpingchicken.com/2017/10/05/charlie-swinbourne-we-need-to-address-cultural-appropriation-of-deafness-and-bsl-in-the-tv-and-film-industry/.
[62] https://www.deaftalentcollective.com/.

film makers, and script consultants, and deaf social media influencers such as Jazzy Whipps.[63] In the meantime, hearing people are quite rightly, given access to the lives of fictional deaf families and communities through television and film. Hearing children and adults may be enthralled by watching signed dialogues, and might even be inspired to seek out sign language lessons. At the same time, it is important that deaf people share this equality of access by being able to visit theatres and cinemas that have adequate hearing loops and signed performances, and can watch television programmes with sign language interpretation and subtitles.

---

[63] https://www.youtube.com/c/JazzyWhipps.

AFTERWORD

I have examined examples of deaf characters from a variety of literary forms intended for a mainstream audience. In doing so, I hope to have redressed an historical imbalance by referring to both British and American works. I was particularly interested in trying to understand why a hearing author would create a deaf character. In the main they are included as plot devices, as props to demonstrate the actions and attitudes of more significant hearing characters, and as metaphors to express themes such as alienation, loneliness, misunderstanding, and redemption. Many deaf characters occupy a minor role that, although familiar to a hearing readership, tell the audience very little about the reality of being deaf.

Duncan Campbell demonstrates not only that deaf people can be educated and are able to communicate, they can also be granted divine compensation for what was regarded as an imperfect state. Though he is shown to sign, this particular ability of the deaf was to largely disappear from fictional literature for the next two hundred years. During the nineteenth century, the understanding of hearing authors shifted, and reflecting prevailing attitudes, they perceive deafness as an intellectual and moral deficit that could be rectified through appropriate education. Deaf poets, for there were no deaf authors, concur with these beliefs, writing of a shattered innocence, pitiable to the hearing, redeemable only by learning to speak, both with people and to God. The number of deaf characters devised increase rapidly during this era, with many minor portrayals typified by tropes and stereotypes. Hearing authors make assumptions and misunderstandings, through ignorance not malice. Many poor attempts to describe a deaf person are at least sympathetic, if not patronising. Words like "dumb" and "silent", that strike a modern reader as both offensive and inappropriate, are frequently applied to deaf characters, and copied by deaf poets and their advocates. Authors reflect the contemporary trends in specialist education with its increasingly oralist approach. Such a mode of verbal communication is deemed to be vital, as it proves to the hearing majority that the deaf are not imbeciles and could integrate with the hearing majority, and to the deaf themselves, that they are worthy of acceptance within a wider society.

By the beginning of the next century, the repercussions of the Milan congress had confirmed the superiority of oral education. From then onwards deaf characters, believed by now to be physically impaired, demonstrate how much medical involvement is sought to diagnose, treat, and if possible, eradicate, the real disease processes and supposed inadequacies revealed in deaf people. Deafness defined as an audiological loss is considered fixable. Any desire to sign rather than speak is classed as deviant behaviour. Authors and poets reflect contemporary beliefs of the innocent suffering of this reputedly once silent section of the population, and through a greater number of major deaf characters, testify in detail to the disappearance of sign language from many institutions and from the educational process. There are authors who are notable exceptions, and use their deaf characters as a means of campaigning for a more liberal educational environment and the necessity for deaf people to be allowed to sign.

In the latter half of the twentieth century however, writers begin to reflect a resurgent confidence in deaf people with characters who embrace sign language, determine their own identity, and demonstrate the existence of a thriving deaf subculture. Representations of deaf characters generally reflect the experience of the author. There is evidence throughout the book that where a writer has encountered deafness, deliberately sought out information, employs an advisor on a set, or is deaf themselves, the result is a much more life-like portrayal. There is also evidence, certainly in the past, that the way in which the deaf character is described by a hearing author reflects the attitudes of the society from which its creator originates. More accurate representations of deafness and deaf people are starting to be seen, especially in novels, comics, and poetry. This is because hearing authors are now making the effort to research their deaf characters more thoroughly, or because the writers are themselves deaf and include elements of their own experience. Autobiographical accounts illuminating deaf characters in poetry are becoming the norm.

This trend has persisted during the last twenty years, so that all forms of literature are likely to present deaf people as the main character of the piece, rather than as a caricature, stereotype, or stock character. This is seen particularly in the novels of Lodge, Pattison and Novic, the graphic works of Mack and Bell, the poetry of Jones and Antrobus, and a wide range of examples produced in television and film. Considerable detail is shown of modern liberal and inclusive educational methods. The existence of thriving deaf communities is made manifest in descriptions and depictions of a wide variety of clubs and societies. Sign language conversations are much more prominent, particularly in visual forms of fiction, such as television and film. Modern hearing authors are much better informed, and their characters, and those created by deaf writers, can in turn inform their readership. This is important, as deaf children and young people look for aspirational role models and find them in works of fiction.

Although the signing communities to which deaf characters are shown to belong signify the presence of a more ethnic and linguistic model of understanding deafness, recent representations of deaf people include the technological devices that enhance communication between the deaf and hearing worlds. These include hearing aids, cochlear implants, texting, and video calls. Of course, they may not always work well, or even be wanted by their users. There is also the growing acknowledgement by writers of the community's need for interpreters, including documenting the valuable but uncomfortable position of Children of Deaf Adults (CODAs). There is perhaps an increasing recognition that the helpful but polarised categorisation of deaf people, and consequently fictional characters, as either "wounded, deaf" speakers or "Warrior, Deaf" signers, may not be adequate. After all, there are people identifying with the profoundly deaf community who wear aids or implants, speak, and regularly use interpreters. Likewise, there are deaf vocal people who very much take their place in the hearing world, and have learned and often employ sign language. Writers cannot position all their characters in a "one size fits all" ethnic model of deafness that potentially excludes many deaf people, or within a framework that takes account of only two possible extremes. There is no longer, if ever there was, a simple dichotomy between audiological moderately deaf people and those who are profoundly deaf, with no variation in between. My expectation for the future is that this should be reflected in a spectrum of deaf characters, shown using a wide variety of means of communication, with or without technological help.

There is a greater desire than ever before for deaf and hearing writers and artists to reflect the reality of life as a deaf person. There are wonderful and accurate depictions, for example in Pattinson's novels, *True Biz*, *In This Sign*, *El Deafo*, and *Sound of Metal*. It would appear then that the age of tropes, and the stereotypes of Goldilocks, Granny and Gifted is over! However, hearing screenwriters in particular, continue to show evidence of misunderstandings about deafness. Certain tropes have established themselves historically as a short-hand to inform the reader or viewer that a character is deaf. For instance, silence is used in books, empty speech bubbles in comics, and switching off the soundtrack in audio-visual media. Stereotypes can still be found–the supercrip in comics, and Ruby's parents unappreciative of music in the film *CODA*. As I have reported in a previous chapter, research, deaf authorship, and the inclusion of sign language, does not always guarantee the avoidance of inaccurate portrayals, and in fact, I believe another stereotype may be developing. In the same way that we saw the emergence of supercrip in comics, I think there is the risk that the "super-signer" may evolve, especially in television and film. There has been quite naturally, a backlash against the domination of teaching verbal speech in deaf schools, and a desire to rejoice in the freedom to sign, as indicated in the poems of Raymond Antrobus. Writers have largely moved away from a simple auditory definition of deafness, and taken into account matters of language, identity, and culture. That is a good thing. There has also been a trend for screenwriters and producers to increasingly feature sign language to signal that a person is deaf. I can readily understand why. It is immediate, obvious, and visual. Signing is easily recognisable as a deaf attribute. While I, alongside many deaf people, am delighted to see BSL or ASL brought to the attention of the viewing public, there is a danger that again, this becomes just a stereotypical short-cut used by the media to indicate that a character is deaf. The presence of signing does not necessarily tell the viewer anything about what it is to be deaf, and it is important to indicate that learning to sign, like any language, takes time, practice and patience. Deaf people do not instantly and instinctively sign. There is an educational process, as indicated by Novic's novel and Antrobus' verse, that has resulted in the person being able to communicate in this way. Nor does it take into account the large number of deaf people who do not sign or sign moderately well. The "super-signer" character may replace the invariably accurate lip reader as a new stereotype, implying to the hearing public that all deaf people can sign inherently, instantly, and fluently. I hope this does not happen. I want to see sign language represented, but I also want to see accurate depictions of the lives of non-signing deaf people. Signing is an easy way in which to demonstrate that a character is deaf, and it has become increasingly acceptable, and dare I say, even fashionable, to include a signing character in fiction. I have no objection to this, far from it, but it is important to remember that the proportion of the deaf population that uses signing as a first language is 1-2%. The moderately deaf are consistently overlooked both by deaf ideologues and in deaf representations. They seem to have no place in an ethnic model of deafness, and it would appear that disability studies cannot provide an adequate framework to include them, so I look forward to the wider variety of deaf experience that is yet to be exhibited on our screens.

I also hope that there will be more deaf characters from different ethnic backgrounds appearing in books, programmes, and films. I would encourage writers to include deaf characters as "ordinary" people who do not necessarily need to be show-cased, and to remember the power of their characters to become role models. It would be interesting to see potentially divisive issues discussed, such as the provision of cochlear implants for deaf children. Although the philosophical debate about the pros and cons of being deaf continues,[1] there is perhaps, an additional model worthy of consideration by creatives, both hearing and deaf. Deaf Gain is a concept that originated at Gallaudet University with a series of presentations in 2009. It proposes that deafness can be seen as an evolutionary divergence carrying specific advantages for both deaf and hearing communities.[2] An understanding of this idea may help writers to create deaf characters that are even more meaningful for a mainstream audience.

Duncan Campbell brought the life of a deaf man to the notice of a hearing public who were amazed not only by his extraordinary powers, but also by his ability to communicate. In our day, it is a mark of progress that the lives of deaf people can be displayed as quite ordinary, and while they are not seen to possess supernatural abilities, nonetheless deaf people want their voices to be heard and their signing to be seen.

---

[1] Rachel Cooper, "Can it Be a Good Thing to Be Deaf?", Journal of Medicine and Philosophy, No. 6, (November 2007), 563-583, DOI: 10.1080/03605310701680940.
[2] H-Dirksen L. Bauman and Joseph J. Murray (eds.), Deaf Gain: Raising the Stakes for Human Diversity (Minneapolis: University of Minnesota Press, 2014).

SELECTED BIBLIOGRAPHY

Alaniz, Jose. 2014. Death, Disability, and the Superhero: The silver Age and Beyond. Jackson: University Press of Mississippi.

Antrobus, Raymond. 2018. The Perseverance. London: Penned in the Margins).

Austen, Jane. 1896. Emma. (1815). London: MacMillan and Co Ltd.

Barnes, FG. "The deaf in literature." Teacher of the Deaf, No.1 (1903): 42-45.

Batson, Trent and Bergman, Eugene (eds). 2002. Angels and Outcasts. Washington, DC: Gallaudet University Press.

Baumann, H-Dirksen L. and Murray, Joseph (eds). 2014. Deaf Gain: Raising the Stakes for Human Diversity. Minneapolis: University of Minnesota Press.

Bell, Cece. 2014. El Deafo. New York: Amulet Books.

Bergman, Eugene. "Literature, fictional characters". In Gallaudet Encyclopaedia of Deaf People and Deafness, Volume 2, ed. John V. Van Cleve, 172-175. (New York: McGraw Hill Book Company Inc, 1987).

Brien, David (ed). 1992. Dictionary of British Sign Language/English. London: Faber and Faber.

British Deaf History Society. "The History of the Life and Adventures of Mr. Duncan Campbell". Accessed n/d, http://www.bdhs.org.uk/timeline/the-history-of-the-life-and-adventures-of-mr-duncan-campbell-by-daniel-defoe/.

Burnet, John R. 1835. Tales of the Deaf and Dumb, with miscellaneous poems. Newark: B Olds.

Clark, John Lee (ed). 2009. Deaf American Poetry: an anthology. Washington, DC: Gallaudet University Press.

Clark, John Lee. "Melodies Unheard", Poetry Magazine, May 2005, 165-170.

Collins, Wilkie. 1861. Hide and Seek (1854). London: Sampson Low, Son & Co.

Dakin, Paul. "A Cut Too Far? Cochlear Implants and Division among the Deaf," No. 1 (February 2017):1023-5.

Dakin, Paul. "Goldilocks or Granny? Portrayals of deafness in the English novel", Journal of Medical Biography No. 4 (November 2015): 227-37.

Dakin, Paul. "Literary portrayals of deafness", Clinical Medicine, No. 3 (June 2009): 293-4.

Dakin, Paul. "Sign Gene: The first deaf superhero film", Hektoen International, Winter 2019, https://hekint.org/2019/03/18/sign-gene-the-first-deaf-superhero-film/.

Dakin, Paul. "Speech without Sound: Signing as 'Body Talk'". In Body Talk in the Medical Humanities, ed. Jennifer Patterson and Francia Kinchington 236-245. (Newcastle upon Tyne: Cambridge Scholars Publishing, 2019).

Dakin, Paul. "'Super' heroes – special powers in deaf characters" Hektoen International, Summer 2014, https://hekint.org/2017/01/31/super-heroes-special-powers-in-deaf-characters/.

David, Peter, Kirk, Leonard and Riggs, Robin. 2002. Supergirl #65 (New York: DC Comics Inc.

Davis, Lennard J. "Deafness and Insight: The Deafened Moment as a Critical Modality." College English, No. 8 (December 1995): 881-900.

Davis, Lennard J. "Screening deafness". Los Angeles Review of Books, accessed September 19, 2021, https://lareviewofbooks.org/article/screening-deafness/.

Defoe, Defoe. 1895. The History of the Life and Adventures of Mr. Duncan Campbell (1720). London: J.M. Dent & Co.

Denman, Ann. A Silent Handicap. 1927. (London: Edward Arnold & Co).

Dickens, Charles. 1911. Dr Marigold in Christmas Stories. Volume II (1863). London: Chapman & Hall Ltd.

Faulkner, William. 1962. The Mansion (1961. London: The Reprint Society.

Fletcher, Rev W. 1843. The Deaf and Dumb Boy. London: JW Parker.

Fraction, Matt and Aja, David. 2014. Hawkeye #19. New York: Marvel Worldwide Inc.

George, Elizabeth. 1992. For the Sake of Elena. London: Bantam Press.

Gibson, William. 1960. The Miracle Worker: (a play in three acts). New York: Samuel French Inc.,

Grant, Brian (ed). 1987. The Quiet Ear. London: Andre Deutsch Ltd.

Greenberg, Joanne. 1984. In This Sign (1970). New York: Henry Holt and Company.

Gregory, Susan and Hartley Gillian M (eds). 1991. Constructing Deafness. Milton Keynes: The Open University.

Gregory, Susan. "Deafness in fiction". In Constructing Deafness, edited by Susan Gregory and Gillian M. Hartley 294-300. (Milton Keynes: The Open University, 1991).

Guire, Oscar. "Deaf characters in literature." The Silent Worker, August 1961, 3-6.

Harman, Kristen. "On Deaf Literature," Bloomsbury Admin, January 18th 2019. Accessed January 18th, 2019. https://bloomsburyliterarystudiesblog.com/continuum-literary-studie/2019/01/on-deaf-literature.html.

Harris, Elmer. Johnny Belinda 1940. New York: Samuel French Ltd.

Hatfield, Charles, Heer, Jeet and Worcester, Kent (eds.). 2013. The Superhero Reader. Jackson: University Press of Mississippi.

Jackson, Peter W. 1990. Britain's Deaf Heritage. Edinburgh: Pentland Press.

Jacobs, Dale and Dolmage, Jay. "Accessible Articulations: Comics and Disability Rhetorics in Hawkeye #19". The Journal of the Comics Studies Society, No. 3 (Fall 2018): 353-368.

Jones, Lesley and Robin Bunton. "Wounded or Warrior? Stories of Being or Becoming Deaf". In Narrative Research in Health and Illness, eds. Brian Hurwitz, Trisha Greenhalgh and Vieda Skultans, 187-204. (Oxford: Blackwell Publishers Ltd, 2004).

Kaminsky, Ilya. 2019. Deaf Republic. London: Faber & Faber.

Kitto, JJ, D.D, "The lost senses. Part I. Deafness. The Land of Silence," Edinburgh Review, No. 207 (July 1855): 124-5.

Ladd, Paddy. 2003. Understanding deaf culture: in search of deafhood. Clevedon, England: Multilingual Matters.

Mack, David. "An interview with Creator (David Mack) of one of my favorite Deaf characters (Echo)" Interview by Sharon Pajka. Deaf Characters in Adolescent Literature, accessed September 15, 2007, http://pajka.blogspot.com/2007/09/interview-with-creator-david-mack-of.html.

Lothridge, John. "Deaf comic book characters are diverse, sometimes inaccurate," Silent News, May 12, 2001, 15.

Mack, David. 2003-4. Daredevil #51-55 (New York: Marvel Worldwide Inc.

Mack, David and Quesada, Joe. 1999. Daredevil #9-15. New York: Marvel Worldwide Inc.

McCuller, Carson. 1981. The Heart is a Lonely Hunter (1943). London: Penguin Books Ltd.

Medoff, Mark. Children of a Lesser God. 1980. New York: Dramatists Play Service.

Miles, Dorothy (ed). 1988. British Sign Language. London: BBC Books.

Miles, Dorothy. 1976. Gestures – Poetry in Sign Language. Northridge, California: Joyce Motion Picture Co.

Jonathan Miller, "The Rustle of a Star: An Annotated Bibliography of Deaf Characters in Fiction", Library Trends, No.1 (Summer 1992): 42-60.

Mirzoeff, Nicholas. "The Silent Mind: Learning from Deafness," History Today No. 7 (July 1992): 19-25.

Morcan, Lance and James. 2018. Silent Fear. Bay of Plenty NZ; Sterling Gate Books.

Nowicke, Clint. "A deaf comic geek's grateful review of 'Hawkeye #19,'" Pop Mythology, accessed August 4, 2014. https://www.popmythology.com/a-deaf-comic-geeks-grateful-review-of-hawkeye-19/.

Nowicke, Clint. "Hawkeye, Blue Ear, why we need a deaf superhero and why I'm still waiting", Pop Mythology, accessed June 27, 2014, https://www.popmythology.com/hawkeye-blue-ear-why-we-need-a-deaf-superhero-and-why-im-still-waiting/.

Novic, Sara. 2022. True Biz. London: Little, Brown.

Pajka, Sharon. "Deaf Characters in Adolescent Literature. Accessed April 25, 2021, https://pajka.blogspot.com./

Pajka-West, Sharon. "Representations of deafness and deaf people in young adult fiction", M/C Journal, 13 (3), 2010. https://doi.org/10.5204/mcj.261.

Panara, Robert. "Deaf characters in fiction and drama." The Deaf American, May 1972, 3-8.

Pattison, Nell. 2021. Hide. London: Avon; Harper Collins Publishers Ltd.

Pattison, Nell. 2020. Silent Night. London: Avon; Harper Collins Publishers Ltd.

Pattison, Nell. 2020. The Silent House. London: Avon; Harper Collins Publishers Ltd.

Pattison, Nell. 2021. The Silent Suspect. London: Avon; Harper Collins Publishers Ltd.

Payne, Arnold Hill. 1919. King Silence. London: Jarrolds.

Phelps, Elizabeth Stuart. 1871. The Silent Partner. Boston: JR Osgood and Company.

Ree, Jonathan. 1999. I See A Voice. London: Harper Collins Publishers.

Reynolds, Mrs Fred. 1906. In Silence. London: Hurst & Blackett.

Riddell, Riddell. 1934. Silent World. London: Geoffrey Bles.

Taylor, Gladys M. "Deaf characters in short stories," The Deaf American, May 1974, 6-8.

Thomson, Rosemarie Garland. 1997. Extraordinary Bodies: Fighting Physical Disability in American Culture and Literature. New York: Columbia University Press.

Yearsley, Macleod. "Deafness in Literature." The Lancet, April 14, 1925, 746-7.

Young, Paul. 2016. Frank Miller's Daredevil and the ends of heroism. New Brunswick: Rutgers University Press.

Zazove, Philip. Commentary on Lesley Jones and Robin Bunton, "Wounded or warrior? Stories of being or becoming deaf". In Narrative Research in Health and Illness, eds. Brian Hurwitz, Trisha Greenhalgh and Vieda Skultans, 203. (Oxford: Blackwell Publishers Ltd, 2002).

INDEX